W9-AAD-550

ADVANCE PRAISE FOR

Turning Point

"Bob Ehrlich stands out from the crowd. He's his own man, his own thinker, and his own voice. He is one of the most distinctive and refreshing politicians in America today. When he says something, I want to hear it (whether I agree with it or not). This volume gives you the authentic Ehrlichian voice—and a powerful critique of the Obama way."

—JAY NORDLINGER
Senior Editor, *National Review*

"Bob Ehrlich's new book embodies the thoughtful and principled leadership that Americans crave today. In Congress we fought side by side to balance the budget, cut taxes, and roll back unnecessary government regulations. This collection of essays and columns are Bob Ehrlich at his finest. They capture the same deep commitment to freedom he demonstrated as Governor of a deep blue state. In them Ehrlich offers a clear response to the Obama Administration's relentless attacks on traditional, pro-growth values."

—DAVID MCINTOSH
President
The Club for Growth

"Whether as state legislator, congressman, governor and now policy entrepreneur, Bob Ehrlich has always added an essential voice to conservatism: a practical—but also principled—call for fiscal sanity, a genuine concern for those less fortunate, and the need for an urban policy that works rather than panders. I hope these essays give his ideas the full attention they deserve."

—JOHN FUND
Columnist, *National Review*

"Bob Ehrlich writes what needs to be stated, whether opinion based on fact or analysis. Bob is insightful as he combines both his business and his governance experience. Reading his articles over the years is an ongoing exercise in critical thinking."

—DAVID WEBB
Talk Show Host, Fox News Contributor
The Hill Columnist, Breitbart Contributor
SiriusXM Satellite Radio

"Conservatives and responsible progressives consistently claim to yearn for the Republicans of the 1980s who would offer substantive and reasonable critiques of domestic and foreign policy issues from the right. Former Maryland Governor Robert L. Ehrlich is precisely that kind of conservative, and in this volume one finds the public policy analyses and recommendations that can turn America back to its core principles and renew her neglected economic and social greatness and her leadership position in the world."

—RICHARD E. VATZ, PHD
Professor of Political Communication
Towson Distinguished Professor
Towson University

"Bob Ehrlich's common sense conservatism is well reflected in this entertaining collection of columns. *Turning Point* is a one-stop-shop for anyone interested in a critique of the Obama era's relentless assault on traditional American values."

—THE HONORABLE RUDY GIULIANI

"A political leader who can both write and has important things to say is rare. And Bob Ehrlich is the only one I now. As an old *Baltimore Sun* reporter, I've been reading his pieces for years. He touches all bases from sage advice to his son to the danger of sanctuary cities. And there's always plenty of political wisdom. Anyone interested in politics—or life—will love this book."

—FRED BARNES
Executive Editor, *The Weekly Standard*

Also by Governor Bob Ehrlich

America: Hope for Change (2013)
Turn this Car Around (2011)

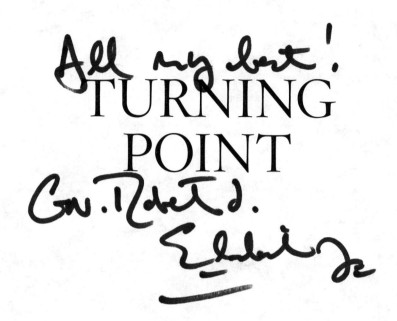

TURNING POINT

All my best!

Gov. Robert J.

Ehrlich Jr.

TURNING POINT

★ ★

Picking Up the Pieces After Eight Years of Failed Progressive Policies

★ ★

A Collection of Articles Indicting the Obama Era

Governor Bob Ehrlich

SelectBooks, Inc.
New York

Copyright © 2016 by Robert L. Ehrlich Jr.

All rights reserved. Published in the United States of America. No part of this book may be reproduced or transmitted in any form or by any means, graphic, electronic, or mechanical, including photocopying, recording, taping or by any information storage or retrieval system, without the permission in writing from the publisher.

This edition published by SelectBooks, Inc.
For information address SelectBooks, Inc., New York, New York.

First Edition

ISBN 978-1-59079-338-1

Cataloging-in-Publication Data
Ehrlich, Bob, 1957-
 Picking up the pieces after eight years of failed progressive policies : a collection of articles indicting the Obama era / Governor Bob Ehrlich.
    pages cm
 Summary: "Former Republican Governor of Maryland Robert Ehrlich presents his conservative political philosophy and indictment of the progressive policies of the Obama administration. Includes a collection of over one hundred new articles and previously published opinion pieces he wrote for The Baltimore Sun, The Washington Post, The Weekly Standard, and National Review"-- Provided by publisher.
 ISBN 978-1-59079-338-1 (hardbound book : alk. paper) 1. Obama, Barack. 2. Progressivism (United States politics) 3. United States--Politics and government--21st century. 4. United States--Social policy--21st century. 5. United States--Economic policy--21st century. 6. Conservatism--United States. I. Title.
 E907.E47 2016
 973.932092--dc23
                              2015029663

Book design by Janice Benight

Manufactured in the United States of America
10 9 8 7 6 5 4 3 2 1

To Mom, Dad, Kendel, Drew, and Josh

Acknowledgments

Acknowledgments are never easy, as so many people play a part in one's professional accomplishments. Such is especially true in the challenging world of book writing, marketing, and publishing.

Yet, the following individuals have been instrumental in this latest attempt to restore some sense of sanity to a world seemingly spun out of control.

Kendel Ehrlich: my wife, partner, advisor, and condition-less defender

Chris Massoni: my longtime assistant—for her tireless support and helpful observations over the many years

Professor Rick Vatz: my good friend and pro bono editor of all things Ehrlich

Greg Massoni: my long-term press aide and tireless defender of all things Ehrlich

Stephanie Krikorian: my wonderful editor, always willing to offer helpful suggestions the third time around

Ehrlich interns past and present: Jared Monteiro, Matt Zipp, Patrick Mulford, Curtis McRoy, and DiAndre Atwater

Kenzi Sugihara and SelectBooks for their faith in this latest tome

Contents

Part Four   191

The Disaster That Is *Obamacare*   193

Part Five   233
Abiding by Immigration Law   235

Part Six   249
A Weak Presidency Leads to a More Dangerous World   251

Part Seven   299

Cultural Divisions and Those Silly Lefties   301

Part Eight

Humor Made Oh-So-Easy by the Obama Era

Introduction

★ ★ ★

EIGHT YEARS AGO, SENATOR BARACK OBAMA audaciously promised to "fundamentally transform" America.

He delivered in ways large and small and to such an extent that the average American does not fully comprehend the profound and hugely negative changes inflicted on our culture and country. The more progressive among you may be reasonably happy with the Obama years. Indeed, there is reason for your enthusiasm given your hierarchy of values: The federal presence in our daily lives has never been more firmly entrenched. Tax rates are more progressive. Spending has skyrocketed. And political correctness pervades our public discourse. Conversely, those of us on the right are unhappy and downright embarrassed for the most part.

I've written about my discontent for the entire Obama presidency, sending up warning flares for the past eight years in a series of columns and opinion pieces illuminating (in no uncertain terms) the clear and present danger of the progressive agenda. This book is a collection of those pieces, assembled to remind you, as you listen to the 2016 debate circuit, the pundits, and the double-talk from the left, and then head to the polls in November: Do not make the same mistake again.

The majority of pieces chronicling Obama and the left's harmful deeds appeared as weekly Sunday columns in *The Baltimore Sun*—a paper once dedicated to my political demise. Alas, a new editorial board saw the wisdom in at least one dissenting voice in the Sunday op-eds.

A smattering of other columns ran in other newspapers (*The Washington Post, The Washington Times*) and certain periodicals (*National Review, The Weekly Standard*). One is unpublished, and a few have undergone minor edits. Most critique hyper-progressive maladies brought to our shores by the 44th President of the United States and his acolytes. They also seek to quantify the considerable damage inflicted on America, while offering some hope and ideas for restoring and advancing the reputation and operational power and influence of the most powerful nation in history.

Far-left liberals, progressives, and assorted lefties beware: *The critiques you are about to read do not take account of your feelings; some may constitute micro-aggressions; most, if not all, will likely cause extreme stress, anxiety, and a longing for November, 2008.*

In this regard, it is important to note that not so long ago, the arrival of a telegenic, articulate African American leader was accompanied by great fanfare. There was excitement in the air for citizens of all political stripes. A war-weary American public was engaged. Serious history was being made. The promise of better race relations was just around the corner. The mainstream press fell in love. (Most notably, as evidenced by MSNBC's Chris Matthews' infamous comment made on *Hardball* on February 12, 2008, "I felt this thrill going up my leg.") Even the vaunted Clinton machine could not compete—a stunning development for the former First Lady and President-in-waiting.

Remarkably, the general election saw some conservatives cast a Democratic vote for the first time in their lives; a few in protest of the Bush years, others captivated by the historical significance attached to the skin color of the freshman senator from Illinois.

The general campaign season of 2008 contained few surprises. A stacked deck was pretty obvious to even the most stalwart Republican activist. Arizona Senator John McCain may have been a genuine American war hero, but he was no match for a "hope and change" narrative that appealed to a wide cross section of the American public. Some pundits became unhinged to such an extent that talk of a "bipartisan" presidency began. How this could be achieved in a multi-party democracy was anybody's guess— but it sure sounded promising at the time.

This is where our story begins—at the outset of a unique chapter in American history. A time when the cynics fell silent and when the naysayers were forced to step back and recognize all the good that could come from the election of our first African American president. After all, 240,000 swooning admirers in Grant Park on November 4, 2008, couldn't all be wrong—or could they?

The answer is now painfully apparent. The arrival of Barack Obama as a unique leader has proven to be seriously oversold. The young guy turned out to be not much different from your run-of-the-mill, far-left progressive, albeit with a hip name and energetic appearance. Yet the political movement he created has been strong and enduring enough to impact just about every aspect of our culture.

In case you need reminding: Spending? A $1.2 trillion not quite "shovel ready" stimulus to nowhere broke the federal bank. Health care? The manmade disaster known as Obamacare has brought government intervention into the health care marketplace to historic levels. Immigration? The unilateral imposition of executive amnesty targeting millions of people is an unprecedented extension of presidential authority. Race relations? A preference for the race industry rather than racial harmony has turned the clock back in a most injurious way. Marriage? A flip and a flop on traditional marriage provided gay activists a huge boost in the culture wars. Entrepreneurism? Degrading "Joe the Plumber" and "You didn't build that" smacks of a countercultural push against the self-made man—now a fundamental element of American liberalism. Labor relations? The National Labor Relations Board has been transformed into a wholly owned subsidiary of the Democratic Party. Law enforcement? A stated preference for federal intrusion into your local police department (and an unwillingness to even see arsonists and looters and destroyers of legitimate businesses as "thugs") has the cops on their heels—and working at a slower and more deliberate pace. Voting rights? Sure, but don't you dare require showing that voter photo ID to the nice ladies at the voting booth (it's racist you know). American exceptionalism? Nope: no more exceptional than Greece, Greenland, or any other country you care to cite. (The president said so himself!) American might? Another nope: American strength embarrasses President Obama. You see it is the overly aggressive projection of American military strength that got so many countries (especially Muslim countries) to hate us. War on terror? Yet a third nope: "overseas contingency operations" and "workplace violence" are more socially acceptable descriptions (even of massacres) in this politically correct era. Supreme Court? Can you say Justice Kagan, Justice Sotomayor, and just one more liberal to *truly* transform this country for the long haul?

My bottom line is rather clear. America has reached a *turning point* in our unique journey. One option is to continue following Obama-ism to its logical conclusion: a Western European style social democracy specializing in confiscatory tax rates, intrusive bureaucracy, multiculturalism, and a retreating military. The other is a return to the qualities that (still) make America exceptional: individualism, pluralism, opportunity, and freedom. This collection of writings examines the considerable downside of the former and spectacular upside of the latter. Hope you enjoy the look back and that you will be properly energized to join the fight of your (and my) life that lies ahead.

Post-Partisan? Not Really.

January 22, 2009, *The Washington Post*

It is difficult to count the many positive messages about America that were broadcast to the world the moment Barack Obama placed his hand on the Lincoln Bible on Tuesday. America haters around the globe had a bad day (for a change). Regardless of one's political association, Obama's swearing-in was a joyous occasion for a country caught in the grip of an economic recession and facing a long, arduous war against terrorism.

Then came the much-anticipated inaugural address. The soaring oratory met, and in some quarters exceeded, expectations. Not surprisingly, the "usual suspects" really gushed—which is quite a bit of gushing.

It is also where I part company with so many caught up in the historic nature of the moment but blind to the substance of the speech.

To help divorce myself from the pageantry, I read the inaugural address rather than watch Obama deliver it. My goal was to discern whether the more moderate president-elect survived the transition to president.

The results were decidedly mixed.

A serious reading of the text makes clear that part of the moderate, post-partisan, post-ideological Obama did indeed come through:

"On this day, we come to proclaim an end to the petty grievances and false promises, the recriminations and worn-out dogmas, that for far too long have strangled our politics. . . . What the cynics fail to understand is that the ground has shifted beneath them— that the stale political arguments that have consumed us for so long no longer apply."

Such thoughts are meant to relegate old-fashioned philosophical battles to a harsh, partisan past—the change so many Americans say they want in their "new" politics.

But there was also the assurance that the federal government will "create new jobs" and "lay a new foundation for growth."

And this dangerous observation:

"The question we ask today is not whether our government is too big or too small, but whether it works." (As though Americans should not focus on whether their government is too big or not big enough.)

Then a nod to class-warfare rhetoric:

"The nation cannot prosper long when it favors only the prosperous."

And, finally, a full retreat to limited economic horizons and a collective national guilt trip:

To "those nations like ours that enjoy relative plenty, we say we can no longer afford indifference to the suffering outside our borders; nor can we consume the world's resources without regard to effect. For the world has changed, and we must change with it."

Toward the end of his speech, Obama referred to "the price and the promise of citizenship"—as though it were a patriotic duty to ante up more of your hard-earned dollars. His infamous exchange with "Joe the Plumber" was no accident; our new president was serious when he said he planned to share the wealth of producers and wage earners. That the top 1 percent of taxpayers shoulder 40 percent of the federal income tax burden no longer appears to be pertinent, or patriotic, enough.

Simply put, words matter. This is particularly true in an inaugural address. Words send signals about intentions. In this case, Obama's words reflect a stated desire to reconfigure the role of government and markets in our country. And not even casual observers can claim surprise.

The political talk shows have been full of debate as to how "red America" should react. Two baseline conclusions should be obvious:

First, all Americans should pray for the safety and success of the greatest democracy in the history of the world—and those prayers and good wishes must extend to the new president, his family, and the Administration. But when it comes to $825 billion in new deficit spending, increased taxes on producers, the elimination of secret ballots in union elections, protectionism, a "new" fairness doctrine, an end to moral clarity in the fight against terrorism, giving terrorists rights enjoyed by U.S. citizens, a future of limited horizons rather than growth and opportunity, and plain old divisive class-warfare rhetoric: count me (and millions of other Republicans, Democrats, and independents) among the loyal opposition.

The stakes are extraordinarily high—market capitalism, free speech, the war against terrorism, marginal tax burdens, workplace freedom. Let the great debate begin anew!

Bogus Bipartisanship

February 17, 2009, *The Weekly Standard*

A timely front page article in the February 4th *Washington Post* provided desperately needed insight into the most misunderstood term in Washington today. Of course, I refer to the term "bipartisan."

The media demands it. The political pundits love it. It polls extremely well—almost as high as "change." It is antithetical to its ugly twin—"partisan." And, the voters delivered a firm message they want more of it on November 4, 2008.

So, what does it mean?

The important take-away from the *Post* analysis was that an Obama-style bipartisanship is less about common ground and more about mutual respect and enhanced collegiality among Members of Congress. As a former House Member and assistant whip, I welcome this return to a more civil discourse in Washington, D.C. Hopefully, a more respectful environment means that nobody's idea, bill, program, or initiative should be shot down simply because it emanates from the other party. The vast majority of voters expect their leaders to maintain this even-handed approach regardless of partisan source.

My objection occurs when this common sense view morphs into an entirely different concept—where the loyal opposition is expected to roll over simply because his or her party lost an election. Not that President Obama was wrong in stating that he now gets to do things his way because he (and his party) won the election. To the winner goes the spoils—in this case, an issues agenda

Messrs. Obama, Reid, and Speaker Pelosi have advocated for years. It is an agenda of gigantic government, centralized authority, environmental extremism, and limited economic horizons. It is an agenda that has carried the day over the last two election cycles. It is also an agenda many Americans oppose.

So, what should have Republicans done (re: the stimulus)? Just gone along because of a charismatic president and his persuasive ways? Signed off after a few slices of pork are eliminated from the pig? Or, continued to fight in good faith for what you believe are the fundamentals of a true "rescue package": short-term safety net assistance, "shovel ready" infrastructure projects (don't forget upgrades to sewage treatment plants), tax relief for those who actually pay federal income tax, and no pork. Last time I looked, federal programs of all types and sizes could be debated and voted on as part of an annual congressional appropriations process still in place.

Further, a proposed spending binge leading to ever-widening deficits is the worst possible time to get in touch with one's bipartisan side. Here, getting out of the way to "prove" your bipartisan nature is misplaced emotion. It is also quite dangerous in light of the other serious items on the aggressively left-orientated agenda being pushed on Capitol Hill today.

Despite the results of November 4th, many Americans reject a bipartisan acquiescence to policies offensive to even centrist sensibilities: civil rights for terrorists, the elimination of enhanced (not torture) interrogation techniques on captured enemy combatants, a newly minted "Fairness Doctrine," the end of secret ballots in union organizing elections, a protectionist streak on trade, promises of activist judges, and trial lawyers gone wild. This is an agenda far out of step with (red and blue) mainstream America. And no media-induced redefinition of "bipartisan" can make such proposals acceptable.

Sometimes, a bipartisan resolution is not a sound resolution. Sometimes, walking away from a deal is better than a bad deal. Those of us in the loyal (and growing) opposition should not be afraid to say it, either.

Facts and Opinions in Election's Aftermath

Robert Ehrlich says gender gap and energized Democratic base made difference for Obama

November 11, 2012, *The Baltimore Sun*

Fact: The empathy factor was a big winner for President Barack Obama.

Opinion: It proved impossible for a wealthy CEO-type to compete in the "he cares about us" category. Mitt Romney's "47 percent" comment most certainly (further) strengthened this narrative. But it was the Obama campaign's relentless rhetoric against wealth and income disparity that carried the day with enough middle-class voters.

Fact: Democratic candidates successfully exploited the gender gap when nobody was looking.

Opinion: The Clintonian "It's the economy, stupid" strategy did not play out according to (Mr. Romney's) plan. In fact, most of the major media were preoccupied by the front-burner issue of the economy while the Obama campaign and down-ballot Democrats in swing states served up a steady dose of "war on women" rhetoric focused on contraception and abortion. A resulting gender gap of 36 percent with single women (11 percent with all women) reflects a successful strategy. Parenthetical note: The Obama Administration's aggressive attack on the conscience clause did not turn off a sufficient number of swing state Catholics to make a difference. In fact, the president won the Catholic vote outright.

Fact: Sandra Fluke was a featured speaker at the Democratic National Convention and an earnest campaigner for the president.

Opinion: Even in the pop culture age, it should take more than a stated desire for free birth control to make one a star attraction. Ms. Fluke's sex life is none of my business. I just don't want to foot the bill for her dalliances. My opinion, however, appears to be a minority view. Note to GOPers: It is now 50 years post-Pill, but too many female voters are buying into the "war" narrative. Perhaps a focus on the real war on women being fought by Islamic radicals across the globe or the real struggles of women-owned small businesses would be a more effective retort to how Democrats exploit the female gender gap every two and four years.

Fact: Governor Romney's "war on coal" theme was generally effective, but it was blunted by his stated opposition to pro-union project labor agreements.

Opinion: These controversial agreements may cost the tax-payers more money on large public construction contracts, but they remain the Holy Grail for many union voters in the Rust Belt. My pre-election, three-day weekend in north-central Pennsylvania only strengthened this perception. Otherwise, Mr. Romney carries even more union households dismayed by the Administration's anti-coal policies.

Fact: President Obama promised unemployment at 5.8 percent if Congress would pass his stimulus bill.

Opinion: Most economists find it difficult to predict with great accuracy future economic activity, so why do politicians believe they can do better? Reminder to all aspiring office-seekers: Voters may not remember much, but they tend to recall specific promises about their pocketbooks. While the president's far-too-optimistic prediction haunted him throughout the campaign, it was not the Election Day killer many had thought it would be.

Fact: President Obama was required to produce his photo identification as he participated in early voting at his home precinct in Chicago. (Such is a requirement under early voting procedures, per Illinois law.)

Opinion: The irony here is delicious. Where is Eric Holder when you need him? Where is all the incendiary outrage from the left? I wonder how a "racist" requirement could pass in such a Democratic stronghold?

Fact: "Hope" and "change" were effective Obama slogans four years ago; not so much in 2012.

Opinion: From the outset, the Obama Administration sought to define "change" in a more expansive way than voters at large. The Administration sought to "change" culture (government-run health care, income redistribution, Keynesian spending, gay marriage, Dream Act) while the people wanted to change Capitol Hill. But even a thumping in the 2010 midterm elections did not dissuade the Administration from its political focus on a left-leaning agenda of health care, education, and the environment. Tuesday, it appears that activists with strongly progressive views about these issues (teachers unions, greenies, government health-care advocates) came through for the president.

Fact: Sixty-nine percent of small business owners and manufacturers believe the president's regulatory policies are detrimental to their businesses.

Opinion: Progressives of all stripes may not wish to recognize this inconvenient fact. Nevertheless, numerous national surveys (and my many conversations with owners of medium and small businesses) tended to support this notion. More than a few offered that they would keep their employee count under Obamacare's threshold of 50 in order to escape its mandates. Talk about a job killer!

The Good, the Bad, and the Ugly about Obama's Administration

Despite some economic gains, this president's policies have had mostly negative results.

January 5, 2014, *The Baltimore Sun*

Clint Eastwood fans recall the popular shoot 'em up Western entitled *The Good, the Bad and the Ugly*. The moniker fits an Obama-led Washington, circa 2014. Don't believe me? Check it out:

The Good

Despite aggressive overselling of an economic recovery by Democrats, Republicans must recognize a number of positives on the economic front. Consumer spending has improved, and so have the markets. Unemployment has steadily (albeit too slowly) decreased to the "new normal"—around 7 percent. A natural gas revolution has produced thousands of new jobs and helped secure our energy future. Federal spending has slowed due in large part to the sequester imposed by the Budget Control Act of 2011—a spending discipline soon to be mitigated by the recently concluded bipartisan budget deal. Inflation has remained historically low as the economy continues to recover from a devastating economic downturn. Alas, the major question in today's Washington concerns when the Federal Reserve will curtail "QE3" (quantitative easing) and how the markets will react when the buying spigot is finally turned off.

17

The Bad

The redistribution-of-wealth initiative popularly known as "Obama-care" now applies to every American. Most of you have not heard much about the scope and variety of the new taxes contained within Obamacare's 11,000 pages, but you are about to receive a serious reminder. So serious, in fact, the National Bureau of Economic Research informs us that the 22 new and expanded taxes contained in the health bill will push marginal tax rates for medium income households to 50 percent—and almost exclusively targeted to those who work, produce, and employ. And now comes more bad news for Obamacare apologists: A bill that was originally projected to cost less than $1 trillion in 2009 is now projected to cost $1.8 trillion and increase the long-term federal deficit by $6.2 trillion, per the Government Accountability Office. And that promise of a $2,500 per family savings is nowhere to be found.

I will not (again) chronicle the myriad other deficiencies of the legislation that has brought the president's job approval and personal integrity numbers down to Nixonian levels. Suffice it to say the negligent overselling of a complex bill that has cost millions of Americans their doctors, hospitals, and health insurance plans culminated in the awarding of the "Lie of the Year" designation by PolitiFact.

On the foreign policy front, the "willing to negotiate with any rogue regime" Obama Administration has never overcome its inclination to subordinate the facts of recent history with its desire to strike a deal with the Iranians. Fortunately, this is one instance where the wishful thinking crowd may not prevail; there are plenty of U.S. senators (from both parties) intent on negotiating with the world's leading sponsor of terror and serial violator of arms control agreements from a position of strength. These leaders have not forgotten that bad guys (especially bad guys under pressure) regularly violate international agreements in order to buy time to achieve their nefarious goals. One thing we know:

Benjamin Netanyahu cannot afford to indulge the Administration's "trust first" approach—just too much downside for his embattled country.

In a related mess, the amateur hour known as American policy in Syria has strengthened the murderous regime of Bashar Assad and further degraded pro-Western elements of the rebel forces. At least for the next three years, U.S. "(red) lines in the sand" will be seen as unserious—a dangerous place for a superpower to find itself.

The Ugly

Contributing to the president's poor approval ratings is the notion that this lame duck White House tends to make it up as it goes along. And a weak staff appears unwilling (or unable) to tell the emperor when he has no clothes.

Politically motivated IRS investigations? Never heard of 'em. Justice investigation of a Fox News reporter? Ditto. Fast & Furious? Blame it on Bush. Phony cover story to explain Benghazi? "What does it matter?" (That one courtesy of the former secretary of state). Recess appointments while Congress is still in session? No problem. Waiving/extending statutory deadlines and granting waivers to politically favored groups? You betcha. Unilaterally changing immigration law prior to an election? But we needed the Hispanics on Election Day. Amending the Senate filibuster rule in order to secure activist judges on the nation's second most important appellate court? Priceless.

A rather unsettling bottom line: This Administration is willing to do just about anything for the good of the (progressive) cause. Pretty ugly, indeed.

Send a Message to D.C. on Election Day

October 26, 2014, *The Baltimore Sun*

For those of you inclined to send a message to Washington on Election Day, herewith a list of grievances that should get you plenty revved up:

Spending: A federal debt approaching $18 trillion. Interest on the debt cost taxpayers $221 billion last year alone. Yet the president seldom cares to discuss this national embarrassment.

Immigration: Border security is not a priority for the president. Accordingly, despite repeated warnings, the feds were woefully unprepared for last summer's mass influx of undocumented children. And this shoddy performance while a new iteration of terrorists threatens the homeland.

Obamacare: A careless act carried out under cover of darkness. Few Members understood its profound repercussions. Few of its promises have been met while many of its unintended consequences are now hitting home.

Dependency: Approximately 50 million on food stamps, a quadrupling of Social Security Disability Insurance benefits, and the regular rejection of welfare-to-work requirements by congressional Democrats speak volumes about today's culture.

Benghazi: Four American heroes dead and the best the Obama/Clinton team can come up with is a phony video story. A colossal failure of intelligence, preparation, and common sense. The extent of the cover-up remains unknown.

The I.R.S.: Political pressure applied to "slow-walk" administrative approvals of conservative non-profits during the president's re-election campaign. A formal investigation begins, after which the unit leader (Lois Lerner) has her Blackberry wiped clean. Then Ms. Lerner takes "the 5th." Not a happy chapter for First Amendment fans.

The NLRB: The arbiter of labor-management disputes is morphed into a wholly owned subsidiary of Big Labor. This unit means business—just not that kind of business. And it doesn't particularly care for those who create jobs for a living. After all, you didn't build that.

Voting rights: Updated voter rolls (deleting the deceased) and requiring photo identification in order to vote is now a racial indictment. I heard it from Eric Holder himself!

Foreign policy: An Administration inept at peace and uncomfortable at war. Hence, "status of forces agreements" are seen as nonessential, apologies are offered where none are required, and American exceptionalism is gratuitously degraded. Today, America is viewed as an unreliable ally, a non-threatening enemy and a declining superpower.

Employment: America's labor participation rate is at World War II levels, reflecting a severely depressed labor pool. Obamacare has converted many full-time employees to part-time status.

Energy policy: The president refuses to drill on federally owned land and remains undecided on the Keystone Pipeline. A domestic natural gas revolution awaits a president who will lead the nation toward energy independence.

Tax policy: Huge increases in the individual tax burden have failed to mitigate income inequality. On the corporate side, a respected rating agency places the U.S. 32nd out of 34 industrialized countries on tax competitiveness. Most economists believe high corporate rates lead to lower employee wages. Yet the president shows no interest in leading a long overdue rewrite of the tax code.

American culture: The man elected to help heal class and racial division has proven to be expert at both. But such damage was not enough. In coalition with Nancy Pelosi and Harry Reid, a newly energized "war on women" storyline has evolved alongside a narrative focused on the politics of personal destruction (see Koch brothers for context). No wonder the oceans haven't receded.

Fibs and worse: Finally, the president has been flat-out wrong about too many important issues: Bashar Assad faced no consequences for chemical weapons use in Syria, notwithstanding Mr. Obama's "red line"; Vladimir Putin rejected a "reset" in bilateral relations; Lois Lerner's IRS shenanigans amounted to far more than a "smidgen" of corruption; Obamacare failed to generate "$2,500 per family savings"; the stimulus did not produce "shovel ready jobs"; the Free Syrian Army was not merely "pharmacists and farmers"; ISIS was never the "JV"; six million Americans could not "keep their health plan and doctor"; al-Qaida was never "on the run"; the "tide of war" was far from "receding"; the White House did indeed rewrite Benghazi "talking points"; and Fort Hood was never about "workplace violence."

For my readers in Virginia, New Hampshire, North Carolina, Iowa, Kansas, Arkansas, Colorado, Georgia, West Virginia, South Dakota and Alaska—you know what you have to do. Now do it!

What Obama Should Have Said

November 9, 2014, *The Baltimore Sun*

H ere is what President Barack Obama should have said when he addressed the American people after his party's massive losses in Tuesday's election:

"The American people have spoken. I made this election a referendum on my policies, and now both houses of Congress are under Republican control. All of which leaves me with two options: (1) Continue to govern by the unilateral modus operandi I have followed for the last six years; or (2) Work with the Republicans to move the country forward, wherever and whenever possible.

"To be blunt, the former is far less viable now that Harry Reid can no longer do my blocking and tackling in the Senate. Harry was a wall of granite, but my extended losing streak in the Supreme Court was getting to be an embarrassment; even Justices Sonia Sotomayor and Elena Kagan were hammering me on executive pre-emption.

"Accordingly, I've decided to channel Bill Clinton circa 1995— you know, the one who morphed into a moderate after getting his lunch eaten in the 1994 midterms. That Bill Clinton could sign welfare reform and negotiate a federal balanced budget—even begin negotiations on Social Security reform—before the Lewinsky scandal shut down his bipartisan push.

"Truth be told, there *are* a number of substantial issues on which I could strike a deal with the GOP. Corporate tax reform (even a tax code overhaul) is a possibility here. Both parties want to cut America's job-killing, top corporate rate of 35 percent. I might even get some one-time revenues for infrastructure (a priority for my base) in exchange for 'revenue neutrality'—Washington-speak for no new taxes (a critical element for conservatives). In the process, a tax regime that allows more corporate profits to be kept at home might generate additional domestic jobs.

"On immigration, our unpreparedness for last summer's mass border crossings was a disgrace. But so is 12 million undocumented aliens hiding in the shadows. Betcha the Republicans will negotiate over legalization (if not citizenship) in exchange for serious border control.

"Another area ripe for compromise is trade. American manufacturers, farmers and consumers would benefit from pending trade deals with Europe and the Pacific Rim. Pro-trade Democrats would welcome such a move, although I would need to negotiate a few labor and trade assistance provisions to sweeten the pot. This would require horse trading with Members of Congress—not one of my strong suits—but I've decided to do it anyway. After all, I have the time—no more fundraisers for this lame duck, and golf season doesn't begin for another three months!

"Fatherlessness is another bipartisan issue. Everyone knows an epidemic of kids without fathers has led to generation(s) of (predominantly) men suffering from under/unemployment, addiction, and high rates of incarceration. I hosted a White House conference on this very issue this past summer. This critical cultural challenge will now be a priority issue for the remainder of my term. I know we can save many of our most vulnerable kids—but it will be a heavy lift. Count me 'all in' on this one.

"Of course, my most difficult challenge will be to become a war-time president. This not a natural role for me. I believed in my heart that Iraq was the 'wrong war'—and I was intent on ending our involvement there. Yet, I've seen the pitfalls of letting status of forces agreements slide. And I do understand that guerilla wars are only ultimately won with seasoned ground troops. For these reasons, I've decided to listen to my military chiefs—even if it means sending American special forces 'boots' on the ground to Iraq and Syria. I believe ISIS to be an existential threat in a famously unstable region. The defeat of such a barbaric enemy must be accomplished in uncompromising terms—with all necessary force.

"Alas, I know such militaristic talk will not go over well in the faculty lounges and campus coffee shops that are my political comfort zones. But being commander in chief is a lot more complicated than organizing against community banks and demonstrating against obscene corporate profits. Look, I know campus cops can be a rough lot—but have you seen how ISIS treats 'apostates'?

"Call it lessons learned the hard way. The world's sole superpower can't always lead from behind. Sometimes, good just needs to confront evil—whether that evil is a terrorist army murdering innocents in its path or a former KGB agent intent on recreating the Soviet Union. Repeated demonstrations of weakness in response to such miscreants is guaranteed to invite trouble. Such is a foundational lesson of history—one America must never forget.

"Now, for the really hard part . . . where *did* I put John Boehner's and Mitch McConnell's numbers?"

PART 1

Time for a Recalibrated Discussion on Race

IT IS THE ONE SHOWSTOPPER OF AN ISSUE guaranteed to quiet a room in an instant. And as the utensils are put down and the background noise dies away, all eyes turn to the speaker willing to engage such a delicate subject. What is he going to say? Which line is he going to cross? Why must he talk about this *now*—can't it wait for another time?

The answer is a resounding, "NO." Issues of race *need* to be addressed in the here and now. And, yes, such a dialogue will require many to recalibrate sensibilities. After all, it is never pleasant to be branded a *racist*, or in the immortal words of our former Attorney General, "cowards." But such is the language of the intolerant left, forever finding race in matters large and small, important and immaterial. So be it. "Unafraid" must be the new cultural mantra going forward—*if* real progress is to be achieved.

Americans are well familiar with the ugly, indefensible history of race in our country. Slavery remains the great stain on our grand experiment in freedom and democracy. A bloody civil war divided the land. Reconstruction was difficult, but ultimately successful. Jim Crow further denigrated the dream. Dr. King showed us the way. President Johnson promised a "Great Society." Urban riots demanded faster change. Affirmative Action aimed to narrow the divide. And our first African American president promised (another) "national conversation" on race.

Yet, the Obama years have failed to achieve progress, let alone deliver a healthy dialogue. The president's sole deliverable has been a continuing cultural indictment of racist America with a side order of identity politics: "beer summits" and lofty rhetoric aside. Left untouched has been the "deep poverty" of our inner cities—a status that has further regressed during Obama's tenure.

Of course it would be a mistake to place the entire blame for this regression on Barack Obama. Without doubt, unrealistic expectations (the logical result of an ill-defined—albeit highly effective and hypnotic—mantra of "hope" and "change") dogged our first black president. After all, the man is a politician, not a magician. But the opportunity for constructive engagement did present itself at the beginning of the Obama era—a rare opportunity to make us a better people. But this promising opportunity was missed. Let's do something about it now.

Blacks and Republicans:
An Overdue Debate

Robert L. Ehrlich Jr. says African Americans have reason to give the GOP a second look.

October 21, 2012, *The Baltimore Sun*

Quick quiz: What do LL Cool J, The Rock, 50 Cent, Karl Malone, Don King, Lynn Swann, Wilt Chamberlain, Eldridge Cleaver, Peter Boulware, Tony Dungy, and Alveda King, (niece of Martin Luther King Jr.) have in common?

If you guessed membership in the Republican Party, please go to the head of the class.

If you are unable to comprehend how any African American could make this political choice, please stay after school. You require remedial assistance. In fact, your intolerance is part of the problem—both for the Republican Party and the country at large.

For starters, it is this group of racial antagonists that regularly demonize prominent African American Republicans. For those of you with short-term memory issues, herewith, a sampling:

"[Y]ou got the privilege of living in the house if you served the master . . . Colin Powell's committed to come into the house of the master. When Colin Powell dares to suggest something other than what the master wants to hear, he will be turned back out to pasture."

—HARRY BELAFONTE
Radio interview on KFMB San Diego, October 8, 2002

"Republicans bring out Colin Powell and J.C. Watts because they have no program, no policy. They have no love and no joy. They'd rather take pictures with black children than feed them."

—DONNA BRAZILE

Interview with Bloomberg.com in Jan. 2000

when Al Gore's 2000 campaign manager

"A handkerchief-head, chicken-and-biscuit-eating Uncle Tom."

—SPIKE LEE

On Clarence Thomas, quoted in 1991 *U.S. News & World Report* article

The foregoing and so many others are able to offer such indictments with general immunity from their brothers and sisters on the left. That such statements carry so little consequence is not a healthy state of affairs. But it does offer interesting insight into the mindset of the modern progressive.

Not so long ago, the right was regularly charged with racial insensitivity, and far worse. The indictment was not groundless. Circa-1970s issues such as busing, affirmative action, and set-asides lent themselves to serious racial tension. In fact, many Republicans (myself included) believe these debates and the Nixonian "Southern strategy" remain the primary reasons for overwhelming African American support on behalf of Democratic candidates today.

This race-conscious era had another negative political impact for the GOP: It helped erase the memory of strident Southern Democratic opposition to the civil rights initiatives of the 1960s.

I was reminded of all this tortured history while reading about the death threats directed toward Stacey Dash, the African American actress who has come out for Mitt Romney in a very public way.

Hopefully, these death threats are limited to a very small group of unserious whack jobs. But it will be mainstream progressives that will criticize, even degrade, the successful actress.

As recited earlier, we have seen this movie before. The pattern is familiar: A famous African American supports a Republican, charges of "race-traitor" are made against the "offender," the press dutifully reports the ugly story, and the accusers . . . escape unscathed.

We have all witnessed the consequence-less vitriol directed at the likes of Michael Steele, J.C. Watts, Clarence Thomas, Thomas Sowell, Rep. Allen West, Herman Cain, and a laundry list of other conservative African-Americans. And God only knows what outright cruelty awaits congressional candidate Mia Love, the mayor of Saratoga Springs, Utah, who would be the first Republican African American congresswoman in U.S. history. Talk about breaking the glass ceiling!

I wish Mayor Love well. She is mightily impressive. She would be a welcome addition to the House Republican Conference. Her skin color, party affiliation, and intellect would make her a serious political newcomer. But she will not make history in another important sense.

You see, Ms. Love's district is more than 85 percent Caucasian. If she wins, it would be because of conservative white voters, and thereupon she would join a small but growing list of African American Republicans who have represented predominantly white districts.

Alas, we still await the day a conservative African American Republican will do what has never been done: win in a racially mixed district.

That accomplishment will mark the beginning of a new era—a time when it just may become more generally acceptable for a prominent African American to espouse Republican principles.

The momentous event will also begin an even more important discussion about what all this wholesale support for the Democratic Party has brought to the African American community. A quick glance at the state of urban education, black teenage unemployment, multigenerational poverty, and black family income would be a good place to begin this long-overdue debate.

Unconscionable Attacks on Blacks Who Don't Conform

Robert Ehrlich denounces suggestion that RGIII isn't black enough.

December 23, 2012, *The Baltimore Sun*

Author's note: This piece concerns racial healing in America. It is submitted as we continue to mourn the incomprehensible tragedy at Sandy Hook Elementary School in Newtown, Conn. May those families, that community, and the nation that grieves with them know the comfort that only faith can provide.

An open letter to Drew and Josh Ehrlich, from your parents:

Both of you have children of different races and ethnicities in your schools. They are your classmates, teammates, and friends. Some were born down the block, others on another continent. But it does not matter: You are taught to accept these diverse backgrounds in forming your friendships. More importantly, your mom and I want you to make friends and, yes, judge others according to the content of their character rather than their skin color. A famous man named Martin Luther King Jr. gave this same advice to a divided nation a long time ago. Unfortunately, too many adults continue to ignore his advice.

You are truly Ehrlich children; *SportsCenter* is the most popular television show in our house. But recently, you watched how one person's rejection of King's advice became a national news story and reminded us how far we (still) have to go before that character test truly defines how we interact with people who do not look like us.

The story began on an ESPN show entitled *First Take*, wherein a sportswriter named Rob Parker questioned Redskins' quarterback Robert Griffin III's racial credentials:

"My question, which is just a straight honest question: Is he a brother, or is he a cornball brother? . . . He's black, he kind of does his thing, but he's not really down with the cause, he's not one of us. . . . I want to find out about him. I don't know because I keep hearing these things. We all know he has a white fiancée. Then there was all this talk about he's a Republican, which there's no information at all . . ."

Mr. Parker's comments reflected a viewpoint that RGIII is not sufficiently black—his racial insufficiency stemming from the way he has gone about the business of being a professional athlete rather than a political activist. Apparently, he has also committed the racial-identity sin of getting engaged to a white woman, which, presumably, would be forgivable but for his other monumental (alleged) transgression: a Republican voting card.

If you find Mr. Parker's opinion confusing . . . we are proud of you.

Drew, you are studying the Civil War and the role that slavery played in that awful struggle. You are learning about the unconscionable brutality that accompanied the practice of buying and selling human beings. Later this year, you will learn how the vestiges of slavery lived on for many decades, marking a horrific chapter in American history—one that Martin Luther King sought to heal with his movement and teachings.

Unfortunately, that healing process is taking a lot longer than it should. Some people continue to harbor ill will toward black people. Others resent growing prosperity within the African American community. Fortunately, such racism has been on the decline for many years. Your generation's goal should be to eliminate it.

But there is another aspect to the issue that is difficult to comprehend. It's racial straitjacketing as practiced against African

Americans *by* African Americans who dare run against the grain. Which brings us back to Mr. Parker's unfortunate comment.

You see, some folks are so consumed by racial identity that they fail to understand how others with the same skin color can possess different opinions and values.

Your "Uncle" Mike (Steele) was also treated poorly by this crowd. He was degraded as a "token" and an "Uncle Tom." So was my friend, Congressman J.C. Watts. And Congressman Gary Franks. And Justice Clarence Thomas. And Secretary of State Condoleezza Rice. And columnist Gregory Kane. And Professor Walter Williams.

I could go on, but a smart 13-year-old gets the point: Racism knows no bounds. It comes in all colors and is never attractive. In fact, it's always ugly—and stupid. That's probably what King would have told your class if he had the opportunity.

As for RGIII, he graduated from Baylor in three years, won the Heisman Trophy, respects his parents, treats fans well, and is charismatic and articulate in dealing with the press. He might really be what we have taught you is the exception rather than the rule: a role model in professional sports.

With regard to Mr. Parker, he has issued an apology and been suspended by ESPN for 30 days. But is this really a suspend-able offense? The man spoke his mind about a major public figure. It is a point of view we should illuminate in order to take it down at every juncture, a goal made more difficult by the decision to shut him down.

Remember, value your friends for what they are, not who they are or what they look like.

We know you will.

Love,
Mom & Dad

From Pride to Disillusionment:
A Black Leader Sours on Obama

Robert Ehrlich on business advocate Harry Alford, who had high hopes for Obama but says the president is "hurting my members"

March 17, 2013, *The Baltimore Sun*

I can hear 'em now. "He's a good guy"; "He's a family man"; "He'll govern like a moderate"; "It will be so good for the country"; "He's post-partisan."

That the election of a mixed-race candidate for president sent positive messages about America around the world is without question; that the election occurred less than 50 years after the end of Jim Crow was stunning—and spoke volumes about how far we have progressed on race and politics.

Yet, the entire post-partisan narrative was quite a stretch (and silly to boot) in light of Barack Obama's reputation for aloofness and strongly ideological voting record in the Illinois legislature and U.S. Senate. But these and similar observations remained pervasive throughout Campaign 2008 (and, to a lesser extent, the recently concluded campaign of 2012).

The motivations behind such thoughts were (are) diverse, including activist progressives who saw an opportunity to elect one of their own, African American racial pride, white guilt, and weariness with Republicans who spent like drunken sailors and presided over two shooting wars. That Senator Obama was intelligent, handsome, athletic, and blessed with an equally attractive family did not hurt his cause one bit.

Such attributes led business leaders such as National Black Chamber of Commerce President and CEO Harry C. Alford to support the insurgent Obama campaign in 2008. It was an exciting time, as the neophyte junior senator from Illinois outdueled the preordained Democratic nominee, Hillary Clinton. And race trumped philosophy (albeit temporarily) in the eyes of the Harry Alfords of the world.

"I had hope because he was black. [But he's] hurting my members, my constituents. I had to back off. I had to represent my people."

Mr. Alford has witnessed five State of the Union addresses and as many congressional budget cycles. He has digested hundreds of presidential speeches and pronouncements. And he now sees how the Obama Administration's tax hikes and oppressive regulatory approach are negatively impacting his members' bottom lines.

To be blunt, Harry Alford is mad, and he's not going to take it anymore. He's concluded what many of us suspected all along: Barack Obama's hyper-progressivism is bad for black business (and all other colors as well).

Obamanomics did not cost the president his job last November. But life for Mr. Alford's members has mostly gotten worse. The indictment reads as follows:

- a $5.8 trillion deficit in four years, a number that exceeds the total accumulated under all presidents from George Washington through Bill Clinton (that's 53 total terms);

- an Obama-era debt equal to about $50,000 per U.S. household;

- a $1.2 trillion stimulus still in search of all those "shovel ready" projects Joe Biden was so enthusiastic about;

- a U.S. labor force participation rate at its lowest level since 1981;

- a black unemployment rate hovering around 14 percent (black unemployment hit a 28-year high in 2012) and a black teenage unemployment rate in excess of 37 percent (43 percent for black teenage males);

- an anti-business National Labor Relations Board wholly owned and operated by organized labor;

- two lock-step liberal appointments to the Supreme Court and 173 lower federal court appointments of similar philosophy;

- dozens of new taxes (many within Obamacare and targeted to small business owners) worth in excess of $3 trillion;

- demands that Congress increase the federal debt ceiling without any corresponding spending cuts;

- a Cabinet with few private-sector types but plenty of academics and public-sector careerists;

- a predictable parade of straw men ("the rich," "greedy bankers," "Fox News," "Wall Street," "private equity investors," "the NRA") regularly trotted out and in turn castigated in a continuous barrage of class envy/warfare speeches that would make George Soros blush.

As for Mr. Alford, it's all about lessons learned. His personal story is an up-by-the-bootstraps tale of hard work and taking advantage of opportunities provided, including: a football scholarship to the University of Wisconsin, company commander (Army Officer Candidate School), executive positions at Fortune 100 companies, award-winning opinion columns, and appointment as a Cultural Ambassador to the U.S. State Department. His growing organization remains dedicated to "economically empowering and sustaining African American communities through entrepreneurship and capitalist activity." It is, however, a charter made far more difficult in light of the president's instinctive distrust of markets and predisposition toward government regulation.

So, next time he hears of a politician vowing to grow the economy through public-sector job creation or discussing the virtues of government-enforced redistribution of wealth, he'll no longer ignore it. Skin color notwithstanding.

Court's Voting Rights Act Ruling Should Be a Cause for Celebration

Racism still exists, but it has been marginalized in the face of massive progress in access to the ballot box.

July 14, 2013, *The Baltimore Sun*

O K, the subject is race, so I'm going to ask the "haters" from both ends of the spectrum to step outside the chat room. You know who you are.

Some of you were upset when I asked Michael Steele to run on my gubernatorial ticket in 2002. A few of you told me so quietly—the way white racism usually plays out today. (Those who chose to engage on this issue received a none-too-polite response; few decided to press the matter.) You were also the ones with the disapproving stares at Kendel Ehrlich when she appeared in public with one of our black executive protection state troopers. Yes, even in this day and age.

On the other side are those who were equally upset by Michael's selection, but only because "he's not really black." Seems that unique combination of Republican, Catholic, and pro-life was just too much for you to handle. You certainly made your opinions known: "token" and "Uncle Tom" are just a few of the racial indictments thrown Michael's way by prominent Democrats. One of you even declared "party trumps race" when it came to the quite inconvenient Mr. Steele. And then there was all that ugliness (from a previous incarnation of *The Baltimore Sun's* editorial board) about how

Michael "brought nothing to [my] ticket but the color of his skin." There were no political consequences for such racist statements, as usual. Nothing new here; I observed similar epithets directed to other prominent black Republicans (J.C. Watts, Condoleezza Rice, Walter Williams, Thomas Sewell, Clarence Thomas) during my years in public office.

No, this news item is directed to the large majority of Americans who do not view every single issue or event through a racial lens; those who are able to appreciate real progress when they see it. And the news is truly historic: The U.S. Supreme Court has decided that civil (voting) rights have improved such that nine states (mostly in the South) plus a number of counties elsewhere will no longer be required to receive permission from the federal government in order to effectuate changes in their voting laws. (FYI: Even Judge Ruth Bader Ginsberg's dissenting opinion cites the "impressive" voting rights progress that has taken place in the impacted states.)

That such extraordinary federal intervention was required during much of the last 60 years is beyond question. Jim Crow-Era manipulation of the franchise (poll taxes, literary tests) was aimed at limiting minority-voting rights. Those and other deprivations spurred President Lyndon Johnson to overcome steep opposition from southern Democrats (who had successfully bottled up civil rights legislation for many years) to pass the historic Voting Rights Act of 1965. Henceforth, the feds would ensure that everyone who was qualified to vote was allowed to vote.

Now fast forward to 2013, where voter participation among blacks is higher than among whites in Mississippi, the passage of voter photo identification in Georgia has increased minority turnout on Election Day (so much for the "photo identification statutes are racist" argument), and ultra progressive Massachusetts suffers the greatest voting disparity between black and white turnout.

Nevertheless, the court's decision to recognize that the racial climate in the South has undergone substantial change over the past 60 years has leading Democrats and the breathless left-wing pundits on MSNBC (the Rev. Al Sharpton most especially) out there torching the Supreme Court and predicting the return of George Wallace and Bull Connor. (So much for the progressives' brief Obamacare-induced love affair with Chief Justice John Roberts, but I digress.)

Such overreaction might gin up TV ratings and raise money for certain left-wing groups, but it ignores the law of the land. Section 2 of the Act remains intact. That section bans discriminatory voting laws and practices. Does anyone truly believe today's Justice Department with its hundreds of career civil rights attorneys would turn a blind eye to any proposed change that negatively impacted the franchise?

The Voting Rights Act of 1965 was passed in the aftermath of Brown vs. Board of Education (1954), Rosa Parks (1955), Central High School in Little Rock (1957), Freedom Ride demonstrations (1961), Martin Luther King Jr.'s "I Have A Dream" speech (1963), and the Civil Rights Act of 1964.

Today, the Congressional Black Caucus counts 44 Members (including the former chairman of the powerful Ways and Means Committee), while legislative black caucus Members within the states of the former Confederacy now total over 280. And federal and state redistricting favoring the creation of additional minority seats will only increase these numbers.

Slavery represents a permanent stain on the moral fabric of our country. Desegregation took far too long. We are not a perfect people, nor a perfect country. But we have come an awful long way since 1965. Our African American president told me so . . .

An Open letter to the NAACP

The DOJ's claim that a school-voucher program impedes desegregation efforts in Louisiana demands intervention.

November 17, 2013, *The Baltimore Sun*

Those familiar with my life story understand my emotional approach to educational opportunity—particularly where the storyline ends in opportunity denied.

Simply put, I got lucky at a tender age. Enough athletic and academic prowess, in addition to scholarship aid, gave me the opportunity to attend excellent schools. These institutions set me on a successful path; each afforded me unlimited opportunities and important relationships that I have taken advantage of throughout my life. I remain forever grateful to everyone who took the time to invest in me.

This experience in turn has spurred me to support just about any initiative that removes kids from educational dysfunction—environments that are express tickets to under-achievement, under-advancement, and under-employment.

It's why my Administration fought so hard to pass the first public charter schools bill in Maryland. (Not surprisingly, over the vehement objection of the General Assembly's most progressive members and the state teachers union.) It's why I got so frustrated and dispirited with Baltimore City's determined (and ultimately successful) effort to stop then-state Superintendent Nancy Grasmick from throwing a life preserver to 11 of the country's most dysfunctional schools in 2006. (Seems the chance to rescue kids sentenced to educational dysfunction proved a bit too politically inconvenient for then-Mayor Martin O'Malley and the Baltimore City teachers union.) It's why I have been so critical of the president's repeated efforts to de-fund private-school vouchers for those mostly African American kids sentenced to the worst of D.C.'s public schools. (Recall that the president's daughters attend the prestigious, $40,000-plus per year Sidwell Friends School.) And it's why all of us should be up in arms regarding Attorney General Eric Holder and the U.S. Justice Department's latest attack on public school choice in Louisiana.

For those of your Members predisposed to support the Obama Administration in their selectively aggressive effort to transform civil rights in America, please try the following facts on for size:

In 2010, Louisiana's innovative Gov. Bobby Jindal and the Louisiana legislature enacted the "Student Scholarships for Educational Excellence" bill. Similar to other school choice programs around the country, the Louisiana initiative provides taxpayer-funded vouchers to poor children (families must be at or below 250 percent of the poverty level) who would otherwise be forced to attend an underperforming public school.

Unfortunately, Louisiana's Supreme Court struck down the law this spring. Seems the court found the program's funding stream to be constitutionally problematic. Yet the resourceful Mr. Jindal found a separate pool of dollars ($40-million worth) to pay for this year's vouchers.

Enter the Obama Justice Department with a novel spin: The voucher program violates pre-existing desegregation orders operating in 34 Louisiana school districts because use of the vouchers changes the racial composition of the failing public schools. In laymen's terms, providing 8,000 mostly African American school children private school vouchers "frustrates and impedes the desegregation process." FYI: DOJ's theory also puts at risk the future of Louisiana's public charter schools for similar reasons.

That this Justice Department is slow to recognize positive societal change is a matter of fact. (See my column of July 14 concerning the Obama Administration's dismissive reaction to the Supreme Court's striking down of federal pre-clearance voting changes in a number of southern states.)

But this one is a not a close call. In a response identical to Washington, D.C.'s experiment with vouchers, African American parents and grandparents of those fortunate enough to be chosen for the program are steadfast in their support; these families appreciate an opportunity when they see one. Also supportive are Governor Jindal, House Speaker John Boehner, and U.S. Sen. Tim Scott—a South Carolina Republican and an African American who knows a thing or two about real educational discrimination. They and others (mostly Republicans) have stepped forward on behalf of the kids. Good for them, but not enough to save the program from Eric Holder's Justice Department.

Which brings us to the purpose of this letter.

The NAACP has always been in the vanguard of the fight for equal economic and educational opportunity. But today, far too many poor black children are stuck in underperforming public schools—and far too many of these kids end up in our criminal justice system. Indeed, over-representation of black youth within our juvenile correctional system has been a top issue for you since the 1980s. Simply put, this vulnerable population is denied a chance to have their ticket into the middle class punched by a society (and economy) that demands educational literacy in an increasingly high tech world.

Paul Ryan Isn't a Racist, and the Democrats Know It

April 6, 2014, *The Baltimore Sun*

Rep. Paul Ryan, the Wisconsin Republican, recently pointed out that many anti-poverty programs create disincentives to work. Appearing on Bill Bennett's national radio show, the 2012 GOP nominee for vice president proceeded to bemoan a "tailspin of culture" where young men, many in our inner cities, fail to learn "the culture of work." He added a challenge for conservatives to help those who "fall through the cracks in America" to reach their potential. Mr. Ryan's remarks were immediately characterized as "racist" by the progressive blogosphere. Democratic Rep. Barbara Lee of California denounced the "thinly veiled racial attack."

The average person interprets this story as dog bites man; nothing new here. After all, conservative comments about the plight of the poor followed by race-based impeachments are familiar storylines. The only unique feather to this story is that the respective antagonists have worked together for years. Ms. Lee knows Mr. Ryan is not a racist. Yet, she felt free to drop the "R" bomb in this circumstance.

But why let fly the most venomous of personal insults? Answer: The race card is always the preferred option whenever a Republican dares to tread into the minefield of racial politics—especially where the criticism extends to the whys and wherefores of a seemingly permanent underclass. (The fact that poor whites outnumber poor blacks within the underclass always gets lost in this discussion.)

This reflexive use of the race card has another benefit: It keeps Republicans on defense. The calculus is easy to follow. Trot out a racial indictment whenever the shortcomings of the welfare state are at issue. Some (many) contestants will shy away rather than engage. After all, who enjoys having to defend charges of racism?

The narrative does not stop there. Once conservatives either back off or go silent, the left reminds its audience how much the right cares not about the plight of poor America. And there is nothing a liberal Democrat loves more than to dismiss critics on the right as selfish, uncaring 1 percent-ers. You can check out just about any 2012 Obama campaign ad for reference.

The strategy is a spectacular success. Today, Democratic candidates can expect between 85 percent and 90 percent of the African American vote. The numbers are most startling in blue-leaning states.

All of which has led to a cottage industry of GOP pundits eager to provide their two cents on the question of what to do about it.

My thoughts tend toward the realistic side of the ledger. The considerable damage (begun during the "Southern Strategy" era of Richard Millhouse Nixon) is now many decades old. And made all the more difficult to fix by the wildly successful demonization campaign against "tea party Republicans"—a narrative derived from the notion that a smaller federal government spells problems for a community grown fond of what government activism has done for it.

Another non-starter is for Republicans to place African Americans on political tickets in order to attract black votes. This strategy never works, as black Republicans continue to be subjected to the worst kinds of racial indictments from an intolerant progressive establishment. For context, recall the racial attacks against Mike Steele as a member of my ticket. And, no, I can assure you Mike was not invited onto the ticket with the expectation he would attract black votes—which he did not.

I'm not sure any Republican has come up with a successful approach to this racial divide. Nevertheless, personal experience leads to a few common sense steps.

First, showing up counts. Attending and participating in church-related events counts. Participation in job fairs and community outreach with established African American institutions counts as well. But, ultimately, it is the painstakingly slow process of making our case for more freedom and less government that will crack the present day monopoly.

Nobody said this task would be easy. Fifty years of dreadful voting patterns is not overcome in one or two election cycles. And the demonstrably effective labeling campaign from left wing Democrats will not cease. Why should it? It always works.

Serious Republicans (and conservatives) know a partisan majority will be impossible to sustain without some progress in the racial divide.

One caveat applies, however. When a respected leader such as Paul Ryan says what everyone knows to be true, and the Barbara Lees of the world nevertheless reply in usual form, an apology is *not* in order. We gotta start somewhere. Might as well be the truth.

A Permanent Family Crisis

The problem of fatherless children persists half a century after the Moynihan Report.

October 11, 2014, *National Review Online*

Hold your temper. Don't lose it with the kid. Take a deep breath . . .

That's me, reminding myself to refrain from screaming at the 11-year-old football player who seems oblivious to my instruction. And not only my instructions—everyone's instructions.

It's more than a youth-football coach's frustration with a recalcitrant player. You see, this youth coach has been a state legislator, congressman, and governor. As such, I have seen up close and personal the trials and tribulations of America's troubled youth—and the damage inflicted by successive fatherless generations within our most marginal communities. One good thing about politics: It makes you think about the world. Public life provides keen insight into how and why things turn out as they do . . . in real life.

I was intimately familiar with the "real life" of the young player in my crosshairs. He had some talent but little discipline. When things went bad in practice or in a game, he seemed to quit. I watched him dog drills and pretend to be hurt. If he didn't feel like practicing, he didn't.

Any other kid would have been cut from our sandlot team, but not this one. The coaches were intimately familiar with his daily challenges, the most significant being the lack of a male role model in his life. And so we, too, went along with the program—holding our tongues at behavior that would have been deemed unacceptable in (and probably never even thought of by) any of our other players.

It is only after practice, in the silent environment of my car, that I regain perspective. But I'm not calm. I'm angry—angry at a dysfunctional family that provides little opportunity for this young man to succeed and a culture grown accustomed to throwing money and programs at a problem that simply calls for the presence of a father.

How did we get to this cultural place where everybody knows the results of generational family breakdown, but nobody feels especially excited about fixing it?

A Historical Study

My liberal-arts education takes me back to the groundbreaking pronouncements of a then little-known government bureaucrat by the name of Daniel Patrick Moynihan, who nearly 50 years ago broke with liberal orthodoxy in cataloguing the considerable social ills inflicted by the federal nanny state. "The Negro Family: The Case for National Action" was authored by Moynihan in 1965, during his tenure as an assistant secretary at the U.S. Department of Labor. Rarely has a report issued by a little-known bureaucrat created such a national stir.

First and foremost among Moynihan's complaints was the increasing dysfunction of the black family unit (an enterprise that had held up remarkably well through the worst of Jim Crow), most especially the increasing number of poor, single, female-head-of-household families. This was big news at the time: a Democratic staffer taking on the abject failure of the welfare state, and during the days of Great Society activism yet. There was nothing subtle about Moynihan's report:

> [T]he deterioration of the Negro family [is the] fundamental source of the weakness of the Negro Community at the present time. . . . About a quarter of Negro families are headed by women. . . . The number of fatherless children keeps growing. And all these things keep getting worse, not better, over recent

years. . . . [The time has come for] a national effort towards the problems of Negro Americans. . . . directed towards the question of family structure.

Identifying a "tangle of pathology" around the deterioration of the black family and detailing the myriad social ills of poor blacks was not a costless proposition for the man who would become an iconoclastic senator. Indeed, Moynihan was subjected to a barrage of ugly indictments, including the always available moniker of "racist." Persistent attacks and continuing disapproval on the left did not, however, disabuse Moynihan from reasserting his thesis for the remainder of his public life. Yet even as mounds of supporting evidence continued to accumulate, Moynihan's calls for a "national effort" directed to the reconstruction of the black family went unheeded; destabilization and its attendant consequences proceeded apace.

Many pundits credit former Johnson-Administration spokesman and latter-day liberal pundit Bill Moyers with the ultimate rehabilitation of Moynihan and his report. Moyers's 1986 documentary "The Vanishing Black Family—Crisis in Black America" noted the senator's prescient observations about the impact of family dysfunction on multigenerational poverty among poor African Americans. And so it became socially acceptable in progressive circles to again cite Senator Daniel Patrick Moynihan.

Murphy in the Fast Lane

A few years later, it took a popular sitcom character to generate the next cultural (at least pop-cultural) examination of the rapidly changing American family. Yes, the liberated Murphy Brown (played by actress Candice Bergen) became the object of great cultural analysis when the show's writers made her an independent single mother, more than happy to go the single-parent route—a decision much celebrated on the show and in more liberal environs around the country. The storyline even became a chapter in the culture wars when Vice President Dan Quayle asked why a character who minimized the importance of fatherhood should be the object of so much adulation.

This well-reported questioning of a pop icon had progressive cannons turned on the VP in no time. And what a set-up it was, especially after the young conservative became the target of the media elite once again for misspelling "potato" at a campaign-stop spelling bee the following month. He was transformed into a convenient poster boy for culturally insensitive social conservatism. Conveniently lost in all of the hand-wringing was Quayle's point: that despite the heroic deeds of so many single moms, often against great odds, perhaps society should reconsider whether this family arrangement was optimal. But the VP never had a chance; the point was lost in the stampede to attach the latest "ics" and "isms" to his outdated, chauvinistic values.

(A rarely noted addendum to the story was a 2002 interview wherein Ms. Bergen expressed support for Quayle's view, calling it "a perfectly intelligent speech about fathers not being dispensable.") Alas, Murphy Brown and her child were white; this chapter of an important cultural debate (unlike past and future ones) would not get sidetracked on the issue of race.

Fast forward to the new millennium, and the specter of fatherless children and its fearsome consequences has spread far beyond a single community. An October 2004 report from the Howard Center for Family, Religion, and Society concluded that the plague of family disintegration had spread to white families at alarming speed:

> For the indices of disintegration that so disturbed Moynihan when he looked at the black family in the mid-Sixties—elevated rates for illegitimacy and divorce, low rates for marriage—are now just as high or higher among whites! . . . perhaps 2005—forty years later—is the time for "a national effort towards the problems of [white] Americans . . . directed towards the question of family structure."

There was to be no Moynihan Report regarding the spectacular unraveling of the white family unit, despite the senator's request (in 1985) that Congress "adopt a national policy aimed at saving the American family . . . without regard to racial distinctions."

A Presidential Lament

Now let's look at 2013, when President Obama bemoaned the absence of a father in his own life:

> I never really knew my father. I was raised by two wonderful grandparents. But I still wish that I had a dad who was not only around, but involved, another role model. . . . That's why I try to be, for Michelle and my girls, what my father was not for my mother and me.

And just a few weeks ago, the president hit the nail directly on the head:

> We've got to reconnect [young black men]. We've got to give more of these young men access to mentors. We've got to continue to encourage responsible fatherhood. We've got to provide more pathways to apply to college or find a job. . . . It's ultimately going to be up to these young men and all the young men who are out there to step up and seize responsibility for their own lives . . .

All wonderful words from President Obama; and the evidence supports the notion that the president puts his money where his mouth is. The busiest person in the world makes his wife and daughters a priority. Good for him and his family. But time is passing us by. Fifty years after a civil-rights revolution and the Great Society, and the empirical evidence is damning:

- 72 percent of black babies (compared with 24 percent when Moynihan published his report) and 29 percent of white babies are born out of wedlock.

- In 2012, 67 percent of black children (compared with about 25 percent when Moynihan published his report) and 25 percent of white children lived in single-parent households.

- Black children from fatherless households are twice as likely to commit crimes.

- 90 percent of all homeless and runaway children are from fatherless homes.

- 85 percent of all children who exhibit behavioral disorders come from fatherless homes.

- 75 percent of all adolescent patients in chemical-abuse centers come from fatherless homes.

- 71 percent of all high-school dropouts come from fatherless homes.

- 70 percent of juveniles in state-operated institutions come from fatherless homes.

- 63 percent of youth suicides are from fatherless homes.

These statistics are staggering. Not so long ago, they would have been intolerable. But no longer. Five decades of government-sponsored dependence has desensitized us to the enormity of the problem. Today, such devastation is the status quo, protected by a progressive intelligentsia intent on expanding the welfare state and a politically correct elite wholly engaged in explaining away the whys and wherefores of family disintegration rather than putting a stop to the damage. And because poor African-American families received so much attention in the aftermath of Moynihan, much of the progressive Left's attention is devoted to this subset of poor families. Indeed, their vehement denunciations of commentators from Moynihan forward begs a fundamental question: Do they or do they not believe the damage is real?

But It's Nobody's Fault

Rationalizations regarding the root causes of multigenerational poverty (particularly African American poverty) are all over the progressive literature. The same central thesis lies at the heart of many of the explanations: Those who criticize poor black families' disunity are unable (or unwilling) to understand the myriad deprivations imposed on the black underclass. Accordingly, it is not difficult to find reams of editorial reviews that indict conservatives (and other contrarians) for their unwillingness to recognize the complex challenges attendant to the plight of poor urban blacks.

The list of obstacles is long, but the primary offerings allow for how poor parents spend an inordinate amount of time making a living, and thus away from parenting; a dominant white hierarchy imposes class warfare on the most marginal minorities; an increasingly technological society leaves its lowest-skilled workers behind; a segregated educational system has failed generations of inner-city poor; and police targeting of minority youths leads to their over-incarceration in overcrowded jails and prisons.

This familiar litany contains both truth and hyperbole. But regardless of political ideology, there should be two primary responses to the narrative:

1. Recognition of "poverty reality." It's too easily dismissed on the right, and too often off-limits on the left. Americans should see it for what it is: a subculture wherein mostly African Americans continue to face substantial obstacles to punching their ticket into the American middle class. Dangerous neighborhoods and inadequate schools contribute to a disadvantaged run up the socioeconomic ladder. And although skin color is not nearly the burden it once was, it can nevertheless be a hurdle in achieving economic mobility.

2. The foregoing is not a stopping point. Yes, obstacles must be recognized, but life and expectations go on, and these expectations must be pointed skyward. It's 60 years since *Brown v. Board of Education*, 51 years since Dr. King's most famous dream, and 49 years since the Voting Rights Act. The most powerful person in the world is black, as is the world's most famous golfer (Tiger Woods), America's most noted cultural icon (Oprah Winfrey), and its most famous neurosurgeon (Dr. Ben Carson). The black middle class has expanded greatly, the economic playing field is flatter than it's ever been, and more black kids go to college than ever before.

All this represents real progress, not to be minimized because prejudice and economic inequality continue to exist in this imperfect world. It also means the larger culture has a right to expect more from the poor of all races—not least, the notion that maintenance of an intact family is the most effective way out of multigenerational poverty. The president's plea to "seize responsibility for [your] own life" is especially relevant here.

This central truth had been the glue that kept families of all races and ethnicities together during the worst of (economic) times—and there have been plenty of bad economic times for the nation's multicolored underclass.

But the welfare state is an equal-opportunity offender. Family dysfunction among the poor is now the national status quo, a state of affairs that eats away at the dreams and aspirations of those fully entitled to participate in the American dream.

Advocates from all sides of the political spectrum speak to the fight for economic mobility. But prescriptions from the left always call for more government: a larger entitlement state that invariably ends up feeding more dependence.

Context here is easy to find; just listen to the Occupy Wall Streeters or ACORNs of the world. The rhetoric is classic, but an observer will need to look long and hard to locate critical reviews of dysfunctional parenting and families. That same observer will have no problem finding all sorts of blameworthy evildoers allegedly intent on keeping the poor down, a list of miscreants that typically includes "big corporations," "the 1 percent," "the religious Right," and conservative media—convenient targets all for the cultural excuse-makers.

But the time has finally come for the common-sense majority of Americans to double down on truth—the objective kind that most people (still) recognize. This truth rejects the anti-intellectualism of the politically correct crowd; it does not particularly care that a person (or entire group of people) has its feelings hurt by the truth. Nor does it seek to create additional victims because some people are born with more money and/or more functional family circumstances than others.

The truth is that every child deserves a loving, nurturing family environment. Yet sometimes circumstances dictate that a single parent (usually the mom) runs the household. These single parents often achieve remarkable results in raising their children. But fathers are essential. They must be part of the family equation going forward. Anything less lowers the odds for ultimate success.

The statistics are in plain sight. They are easily understood. Failure means a vicious cycle of family dysfunction of the type we have grown accustomed to over the past 50 years. I (we) cannot afford more failure. My eleven-year-old football player deserves better . . .

* * *

A few days after completing the final draft of this essay, I found myself at the Clinton Library in Little Rock, Ark., on the next stop of my criminal-justice-reform campaign. As is my custom at such talks, I engaged in a critical analysis of our juvenile justice system, particularly with regard to the overrepresentation of minority youth within a resource-challenged system.

After a lively question-and-answer session, I was approached by a serious-looking lady who identified herself as a state employee in the office of parole and probation. In response to her familiar description of the problems attendant to an overcrowded, under-funded system in a poor state, I commented on the contribution of fatherlessness to her professional burden. Her disapproving response stopped me cold: "[Now] you just sound like another Republican."

Talk about a conversation stopper! It was a reminder of how far afield we have traveled. Here, dads in homes translated to partisan politics. Here, in one sentence, was the partisan stereotyping I have attempted to take down my entire public life—thrown back at me in a most direct manner.

Such incidents serve as a disquieting reminder that this cultural battle is far from won. But common sense should never lose out to partisan caricature. And a common-sense majority must not waver when confronted with devastating pathologies. There is simply too much at stake.

On Baltimore

May 28, 2015, *The Weekly Standard*

One unexplained death. So many negative images. So many pundits talking past real issues. So many obvious problems.

The storylines of Baltimore's latest riots are heavy fodder for observers from all sides of the political spectrum.

On the left, it's mostly about racism and bad cops and not enough social spending. The Ferguson-inspired slogan "Black Lives Matter" is renewed even though in the spate of highly publicized recent young black deaths there is no evidence that Michael Brown, who attacked a police officer, was deprived of any rights at all.

In Baltimore, the mayor turns to the feds in order to investigate her allegedly out-of-control police. A newly elected state's attorney promises to answer the angry mob's cries for justice. Yet, nobody asks the (indelicate) question of why the mayor and her chief prosecutor waited for Freddie Gray's death before asking for federal intervention. Another indelicate question: where was the street rage when 1/6 of the population of Baltimore was arrested in 2005?

On the right, it's a more complex debate, including the facts and circumstances of Mr. Gray's arrest and transport that fateful morning. Besides police process and procedure, I and so many others bemoan the considerable social ills that poison West Baltimore neighborhoods: too many pregnant teenagers, too many sick babies, too many fatherless children, too many single-income households, too many high school dropouts, too many welfare dependents, too few manufacturing jobs, too much drug culture, too little hope.

Our conclusion is familiar: Trillions of dollars directed into poor communities over the past 50 years has failed to produce better neighborhoods. Just too many left behind, with little hope. It seems a value-less culture trumps social welfare programs every time.

Going forward, it's not nearly good enough to ritualistically repeat the usual clichés regarding the importance of "healing" and "coming together." Here, we truly need to define our terms.

Healing is not about demanding your unique definition of justice or threatening to burn the place down if your demands are not met. Neither is it about a not-so-secret war on African Americans in a police department where the mayor, police commissioner, and nearly 50 percent of the force is black. Real healing is respecting the criminal justice system's search for truth and then working within the system for change if you disagree with the result. Kind of like Dr. King taught us to think and act.

Similarly, coming together is great if it means everybody working to bring about positive change. In this case, bringing the police closer to the community they are paid to protect and rooting out bad actors within the department along the way. There may be bad cops, but the Baltimore riots were not explained by a reaction to bad police work.

Most important, progress will only come if we are willing to think *really big and long term*. Such a new way of thinking about our inner cities would include parental demands for better schools; community leaders lobbying businesses to reinvest in their neighborhoods; political leaders willing to alleviate the dis-incentivizing impacts of high property taxes; a recognition that teenage pregnancy is a key predictor of cultural dysfunction; and a willingness to admit that young boys desperately need a strong male influence in their lives.

Leaders from both sides of the aisle will be willing to go "all in" if our leaders can shake off their Great Society blinders. Yes, big-time barriers will always be present—not the least of which is a newfound challenge to widespread acceptance of social welfarism—a central tenet of today's progressive thought. But the case against government subsidy and dependence grows day-by-day, month-by-month, year-by-year.

On the other side, the right must pursue reform of criminal sentencing laws and seek to better understand the rage—frustration—bitterness—that flashed across America's television screens two weeks ago. Such a task is far easier said than done as most conservatives live a life far removed from the realities of inner city life.

The bottom line: The issue in Baltimore is poverty far more than race. (After all, Baltimore has been a one-party town controlled by African Americans for decades.) People who grow up in stable families, attend functional schools, and are surrounded with examples of economic mobility simply do not riot when something goes wrong in their community.

Short-term solutions yield short-term peace.

Time to pray—and get to work.

Who Will Step Forward to Lead a New Baltimore?

June 5, 2015, *The Baltimore Sun*

L et's begin with some sober observations about recent events in and around my hometown of Baltimore.

The tragic storylines playing out in West Baltimore are by now familiar: an arrest and subsequent death of a young black man in police custody; peaceful and not-so-peaceful demonstrations; burning and looting of automobiles and businesses; police lines backing up in the face of brick/bottle-throwing young men; deadline-challenged, breathless reporters from 24/7 cable news outlets; serial appeals for peace from an embattled mayor and police commissioner; and the aggressive and retributive promises of an ambitious state's attorney, who seems to be more interested in leading a populist cause against police than bucking up and improving her police department. A less newsworthy development was the temporary re-emergence of Prince—who wrote a song about our riots. The state's attorney was on stage for the debut.

Detached from the immediate news cycle and its incessant reporting of Charm City's considerable ills is an ongoing economic reality that many of us who grew up here know quite well: the loss of industrial-era manufacturing plants. For context, check out the demise of nearby Bethlehem Steel. Its Sparrows Point plant declined from a high of 36,000 (mostly blue-collar, skilled jobs) in the 1960s to zero today. The last remnant of the facility, a 32-story furnace built in 1978 and said to be the largest in the Western Hemisphere, was demolished in January.

The loss of such industrial era employment centers (one can add the old Bethlehem Steel shipyard, the General Motors Broening Highway assembly plant, the west side Washington Aluminum plant, and Eastern Stainless and Western Electric facilities to the list) significantly weakened Baltimore's financial position; former workers seek jobs elsewhere or find themselves under-employed or unemployed. Here's a fact sure to keep the Greater Baltimore Committee up at night: Baltimore lost $3.7 billion in taxable personal incomes between 1992 and 2011.

The foregoing figure comes from Travis H. Brown's website and 2013 book by the same name *How Money Walks*, which interprets IRS tax migration data. Baltimore is not alone in this predicament. The New York City metropolitan statistical area lost $79.3 billion during the same time period; Los Angeles, $42.2 billion; and Chicago, $25.5 billion. Our nation's three largest cities lost nearly $150 billion combined in taxable incomes during periods of both economic growth and recession.

This dramatic loss of high-paying manufacturing jobs is a primary contributor to a sense of hopelessness on the street. But other social maladies are deeply rooted and equally destructive. These include the familiar litany of too many dysfunctional schools, too many high school dropouts, too many pregnant teenagers, too many single parent/no parent households, too many missing fathers, and a value-less drug culture.

A portion of the ugliness has quieted for now. The National Guard is gone. Preakness Week came and went without incident. Pastors ask for calm. Beat cops ask for a break—and support from "downtown." And some say it is time to heal.

But a broken city refuses to get on board. Record shootings and a rapidly climbing body count steal local headlines. Most of this crime is black-on-black—just not provocative enough to garner national headlines or attract high profile visits from self-appointed black leaders.

Which brings us back to this healing thing.

I, for one, wish to explore just what brand of healing is in store for us. You see, the same-old-same-old will not do. Indignant reactions to police-involved shootings followed by quiet indulgence of daily street violence is not acceptable. When Baltimore's mayor is asked about costly civil disobedience, the indulgence continues with promises that the un-arrested perpetrators will "have to answer" for their destructive behavior—presumably, next time. Not so the scapegoated police: a Department of Justice "approved" Baltimore Police Department will be tasked with the thankless job of patrolling some of the most dangerous neighborhoods in the country. "Black lives matter" should apply to every senseless death, including the overwhelming majority of deaths that are not police involved!

And enough of the familiar "not enough" spending mantra. We've seen a staggering $22 trillion in transfer payments since Lyndon Johnson's Great Society. Who among you believes that $25 trillion or $28 trillion would have done the trick in places like Baltimore?

It's time for something different. How about a radical reduction in local property taxes. Tax-free investment zones. Vouchers for kids in the poorest performing schools. A cultural reawakening concerning the epidemic of out-of-wedlock pregnancies and the central role of fathers in the home. And while we're at it, a long overdue apology from the city leadership to all those innocent people who were dragnetted by a city administration intent on "zero tolerance" policing in order to improve its crime-fighting statistics.

Either party can lead the healing process, but action must follow when the TV cameras pack up and go home; here, real engagement means candidates and elected leaders willing to take on lopsided odds and entrenched monopolies. Such is the hard part—and

I'm quite familiar with the hard part. Marketing the benefits of a healthy tax base, higher performing schools, community policing, and two-parent households is the easy part. Just look at what the alternative has brought us.

PART 2

* * *

The
Obama Era-Exacerbated
Economic Divide

CLASS WARRIORS THROUGHOUT THE AGES have utilized income inequality as a blunt instrument. The phenomenon's rather simple formula is impossible to miss: some people make more money than others (*much* more money in some cases). They say that this is a bad result and must be rectified. Favorite remedies are the vilification of wealth and calls for hyper-progressive tax increases. That's pretty much the formula, subject to special add-ons as required by particular practitioners of the art. The recent "corporations do not create jobs" indictment of businesses and entrepreneurship, as promoted by Senators Elizabeth Warren and Hillary Clinton, come to mind, as does the relentless union-dominated campaign to raise the minimum wage.

That this age-old criticism of capitalism has gathered momentum in the new millennium is without doubt. Wall Street scandals and a mortgage bubble-generated recession contributed to the gathering storm. The heavy media promotion of stories about the new class of "super wealthy" individuals also played a part. But it was the wholesale adoption of the "class warfare and income inequality" narrative by Obama Democrats that has moved the issue and ensuing debate forward.

It will not be lost on many of you that there is great irony to all this populist indignation, especially where the provocateur is stinking rich. But it has been liberal policies that have done so much to exacerbate the economic divide during the Obama era.

First, liberal Members of Congress played fast and loose with credit markets, promoting the notion that you too can buy a home—and forget niceties such as credit worthiness, assets, income, and the ability to make timely mortgage payments. This greed-laden merry-go-round eventually brought the entire economy to its knees, delivering a heavy blow to the portfolios of middle class Americans, while devastating the hopes and dreams of the working poor (the original sub-prime crowd). Add in an Obama-encouraged "easy money" Fed keeping interest rates at near zero for the last seven years (thereby providing a great lift to equities), and there you have it: a formula to benefit the rich while leaving the poor behind—or worse, punishing them with overwhelming debt. Yet Obama progressives seldom waiver from their middle class mantra. Man, these guys are good!

Our Limitless Debt

We continue to rack up millions each minute, but there are glimmers of hope on the horizon.

May 27, 2012, *The Baltimore Sun*

The U.S. debt clock is rapidly approaching $16 trillion. This year's federal deficit is in excess of $1.3 billion. These are staggering sums, mind-numbing in their sheer size. And for the 99.9 percent of us who were not math majors, almost impossible to get one's brain around. But comprehend it we must, as the deficit and what to do about it remain central to the outcome of Campaign 2012.

How did we dig a hole this deep? Well, that part of the equation is easy to understand. It's all about the "politics of yes"—that persistent, bipartisan disease whereby presidents and legislators seek voter approval through limitless federal spending. Here, every new interest group (and spending request) is received approvingly. It's easy: Just say "yes," tell the voters about your latest and greatest way to expand government, and cruise to reelection.

Both parties are at fault. Indeed, a guaranteed applause line in national politics is to point out that Republicans are the party of big government, while Democrats are the party of really, really big government. Enormous deficit spending over the past 30 years confirms this unfortunate laugh line. (By the way, the federal debt has grown by $2.3 million since you started reading this piece.)

It is an inconvenient truth (to borrow a phrase) that the politics of yes only works when the voters are complicit. On the left, there are precious few consequences for overspending taxpayer dollars. The mindset is familiar enough: The fact of unmet societal needs requires additional spending to meet those needs. For context, check out the rhetoric from the Occupy crowd—their list of needs is endless, as are their expectations for government services and new revenue to fund those services.

The end of the Bush tax cuts? Sure, but not enough. The Buffett Rule? Sure, but not enough. Major new taxes on capital and consumption? Sure, but not enough. (If this mindset begins to remind you of Maryland, you may be one of the many considering a change in residence in the near future—but that's another story.)

On the right, there is far too much situational conservatism. You know it when you see it: Cut all those other programs, just not mine. I had firsthand experience with this mindset as a congressional whip. It's not pleasant to watch, nor does it generate enthusiasm at the grass-roots level. Everyone has to be "all in" if we are to ever get serious about putting the brakes on our spending insanity.

Not so long ago, it was incomprehensible that America's credit rating could be downgraded. Not too many years ago, persistent annual deficits in the trillions were poisonous to one's political ambitions. At the beginning of this millennium, it was never contemplated that one four-year term could add $5 trillion to the national debt.

Yet, here we are, staring down the barrel of yearly trillion-dollar deficits and being lectured to *by the Chinese*.

But all is not lost. Everyone recognizes entitlement reform is the key ingredient in deficit reduction. And now two leaders have proposed a substantive plan to reform the most difficult entitlement, Medicare.

Rep. Paul Ryan, a Wisconsin Republican, and Sen. Ron Wyden, an Oregon Democrat, are of different political persuasions. Mr. Ryan is the steadfast conservative, Mr. Wyden the unreconstructed liberal. Yet both recognize the program is on an unsustainable fiscal path. Accordingly, their reform plan would allow seniors to either stay enrolled in traditional Medicare or qualify for a government subsidy to help pay for private coverage.

That both took a considerable political risk to lead a movement for reform of Medicare is an understatement. Mr. Ryan's rising star is diminished every time a Democratic-sponsored "Mediscare" campaign succeeds, as it did in last year's New York 26th District special election. For Mr. Wyden, it's worse. Many Democratic partisans view him as a turncoat. Their lament: How can we claim Republicans want to throw granny over the cliff when one of our most prominent progressives is leading the charge for reform?

The Ryan-Wyden proposal is not perfect. But it is a substantial proposal. It deserves due consideration if we are (finally) serious about putting an end to the politics of yes.

Surprise: When Taxes Go Up, Taxpayers Go Elsewhere

Robert Ehrlich says that in a mobile society, there's no reason for people of means to avoid tax increases by moving out of state.

July 1, 2012, *The Baltimore Sun*

Dyed-in-the-wool class warriors (including those whose opinions appear on the opposite page) should probably stop reading this piece *now*. The better to escape the dissidence that arises when economic facts of life are offered up against feel-good rhetoric.

Today's "Economics 101" lesson concerns tax increases, that favored weapon of class agitators everywhere.

And the primary takeaway from our journey into the real world of private-sector decision making is a familiar one: aggressive taxation of wealth through relentless income tax increases produces . . . less wealth.

Maryland's recent dismal walk on the wild side is germane, but only one of many recent examples.

The Free State's 2007 package of income tax increases (the largest tax increase in state history) was targeted to small-business owners and the 3,000 millionaires living in the state at that time. Twelve months later, there were 2,000 millionaires left in Maryland—and lots of red faces in Annapolis. You see, "The Powers That Be" are always shocked when taxpayers vote with their feet. Worse yet, TPTB got angrier when the millionaire's tax revenue numbers came in: A tariff that was supposed to generate $106 million in new revenue ended up losing $100 million. That a deep recession would exacerbate the damage was another missing factor in that messy narrative.

Fast forward to today: I wonder how many serious Marylanders expect the latest round of tax hikes to meet revenue expectations?

Similarly shocked were the tax hikers of the California legislature when 254 California businesses (26 percent more than in 2010 and five times as many as in 2009) abandoned the state last year. These moves followed the latest round of income and sales tax increases foisted on California employers. That state now holds the unique distinction of the highest personal income tax state in the nation and a sales tax that ranks in the top five. And tax revenue collections keep tanking. And a legislative analyst's office cautions that another round of wealth taxes might not meet revenue projections. And Lucy swiped the football from Charlie Brown again . . .

Another case in point: In 2009, New York revenue officials were sorely dismayed when revenues failed to meet expectations from the passage of a second wealth surcharge in eight years. Even liberal Gov. David Paterson acknowledged that repeated targeting of people with means can backfire, since those with second homes in less-taxing states can easily give themselves a tax cut by simply moving.

The notion that every economic class should pay a share of their income for government services is a cornerstone notion in any civilized society. Of course, "fair" will always be in the eye of the beholder, but I would bet that most taxpayers view marginal tax rates in excess of 50 percent as unfair.

Nevertheless, and despite our growing opposition to confiscatory tax measures, we on the right must recognize that government can be excellent: The United States Marine Corps, Seal Team Six, NASA, and our national parks system are a few examples of such excellence. For local context, think about the Maryland State Police and the Howard County school system. Few complain when government produces the results taxpayers have a right to expect.

On the left, it should become apparent at some point that the "go to" option of repeatedly fleecing producers often leads to less wealth and less revenue. Simply put, people who can afford to flee . . . often flee. And I'm not talking about the wealthy here, either. It is also a middle-class phenomenon. For any doubters, take a leisurely drive up I-83 north to Pennsylvania or Route 404 along the Delaware line any workday morning. You will see plenty of attractive new developments, many within a stone's throw of Maryland. But the collective wealth you see will not end up in Annapolis's coffers. Similar to so many tax expatriates in other states, these folks have simply had enough.

A final observation: Class warfare rhetoric is easily transformed into political ads. Thirty-second messages often speak to the "greedy" corporations and those evil rich people attempting to escape their "fair share" of the tax burden. But the real economic damage occurs after the election, when voters tend to pay less attention. It is during this time that businesses and homeowners make their economic decisions. Today, increasing numbers of business people (and families) have grown weary of being viewed as the progressives' own personal ATM. All of you advocates of millionaire (and now thousand-aire) tax increases should take note. Beware the more mobile society.

Mr. President, Nobody Else
"Made That Happen"

*Bob Ehrlich says Obama's words betray his lack of regard
or understanding of entrepreneurship.*

July 22, 2012, *The Baltimore Sun*

"If you were successful, somebody along the line gave you some
help. There was a great teacher somewhere in your life. . . . Somebody invested in roads and bridges. If you've got a business—you
didn't build that. Somebody else made that happen."

—PRESIDENT BARACK OBAMA
Speech, July 13, 2012, Roanoke, Virginia

Remember when Massachusetts Democratic Senate candidate Elizabeth Warren charged that "there is nobody in
this country who got rich on his own—nobody"? That
gratuitous shot at American individualism generated a storm of
criticism that continues to this day.

But a recent series of speeches by President Obama has trumped
Ms. Warren. The president's aggressive rhetoric (as recently
repeated in the above quote in Roanoke, Va.) likewise asserts that
Horatio Alger stories are indeed a work of fiction: that nobody is a
real self-made man (or woman) because everybody needs help along
life's long and winding road to success.

The president's obvious enthusiasm for this narrative provides insight into how he views American enterprise circa 2012.
More importantly, such language provides further context into

why and how the president seeks to transform our market economy and culture.

Of course, no person achieves success in a given field or endeavor without some help from the greater society. To paraphrase Hillary Clinton, it's all about the "village." And Barack Obama's village (and career) was filled with older mentors and friends willing to take young Barack under their wing. That these individuals were of a far-left mindset is a matter of fact. The likes of anti-war activist Bill Ayers, Professor Derrick Bell, poet Frank Marshall Davis, and the Rev. Jeremiah Wright are but a sampling of those who mentored or influenced the charismatic young lawyer with serious political aspirations.

The resulting Obama worldview interprets "help" in an expansive way, not the short-term safety net role a majority of Americans still see as government's appropriate role. Such is the value system of so many academics, clergy and community activists. These folks recruit others of like mind in order to bring about cultural change to a "broken" America they see as chauvinistic, racist, imperialistic, and greedy. The Lions Club it is certainly not, but more like a bunch of countercultural enthusiasts with a burning desire to expand federal power into every nook and cranny of the U.S. economy. For them, it's less about an even playing field and more about guaranteed results. The comparisons to a European Social Democrat economic model follow rather easily.

What is absent in this world is the romantic notion of good old-fashioned entrepreneurship, of self-reliant individuals willing to take a risk in order to live the American dream. This more traditional narrative emphasizes individual initiative and a demonstrated willingness to lose, the better to get back up and try again. The thought that simply entering the arena is enough to generate a reward or a guaranteed result is antithetical to this crowd; it (generally) views government as an impediment to success, not a preferred option whenever life throws us a curve ball.

All of us are formed by our life experiences—most particularly, our youthful ones. Most of these lessons remain with us throughout adulthood. They help form our viewpoints and opinions, our philosophical leanings and partisan identification.

And so this president arrived at 1600 Pennsylvania Ave. with a healthy regard for social activism and governmental power, but not so much for the role of individuals in creating wealth and upward mobility. The invective regularly directed against the role of private equity is one result. So are the not-too-subtle attacks directed against Mitt Romney's personal wealth. And so is the false narrative regularly launched against the small business owners of our country. Most make good money but are not rich. They work hard and expect others to do the same. And they kind of identify with ol' Horatio's stories, too.

Millions of small business people took huge risks to live the American dream. Their stories offer hope to so many with little more than a dream—and an idea. The president should think twice before he (again) degrades the very people who pay the federal government's freight.

The Fight to Win Over the Middle Class

New social contract has upended old assumptions about economic status in America

September 15, 2012, *The Baltimore Sun*

Question: What is the most guaranteed applause line in American politics today?

Answer: Anything that allegedly benefits that fine group of Americans known as the middle class.

Want proof? Well, just about every other sentence uttered at the Democratic National Convention paid homage to this esteemed socioeconomic group. Ditto for the GOP in Tampa, where speaker after speaker spoke of the virtues of the middle-income worker.

From a political perspective, the drumbeat makes sense. The middle class tends to vote in large numbers. This fact is not lost on aspiring office seekers. Further, a wide swath of Americans view themselves as middle class; they enjoy the direct messaging from their elected leaders.

Opinion polls reflect this expansive definition as well: The Pew Research Center recently found that about half of all adult Americans define themselves as middle class.

Of course, life's realities provide context; age, vocation, family history, number of kids, and cost of living all have a direct impact on one's economic self-identity.

Changing "collar" identities contribute to the expanded definition, too. It used to be oh-so-simple: White collars meant professional jobs making good money. Blue collars signified less education—and typically less income.

But these old stereotypes are less true today. Post-recession, large numbers of white-collar professionals (especially lawyers and investment banker types) find themselves on the street. A sustained bad economy has forced many to take far less lucrative jobs. Some young professionals have even moved back home with their parents. These under-employed workers may continue to manifest a middle-class outlook, even when their diminished incomes do not match the moniker.

Conversely, technology has changed the economic environment for many blue-collar workers. Those who possess the technical skills needed to compete in today's tech-crazy world see lots of opportunity for upward mobility. Hence, your automobile mechanic may have dirty fingernails and a worn blue-collar shirt, but makes a pretty good dime. Indeed, six figures is not foreign territory for in-demand technology workers. For this group, green dollars trump blue collars.

The flipside is problematic. Far too many blue-collar workers lack necessary workplace skills. Accordingly, their entry into the middle class is postponed. An overwhelming majority of Americans see a secure job as the first requirement to qualify for middle class status.

For local context, think about Sparrows Point in the mid-1960s: an abundance of semi-skilled and lower-skilled jobs and a local population ready and willing to fill the positions. Both employer and employee knew that a work ethic was far more important than a high school or college degree. Many who failed to secure a degree were nevertheless able to buy their way into a middle-class life: marriage, kids, a house, and a comfortable quality of life were part of the bargain (if one survived the toxic and hazardous work environment).

This romanticized, but generally accurate, description died for good in the 1980s. Fat and happy management and labor played a part. So did unfair trading practices from foreign competitors. But it was technology that ended this industrial era chapter. Seemingly overnight, those semi-skilled jobs disappeared—never to return.

Today, a new social contract carries a far different message for entry into America's middle class. It is now all about education and marketable skills.

Which brings us back to the respective parties' pitch in this hotly contested presidential election.

Each has a plan that focuses on training and skills. (In Charlotte, you may recall President Barack Obama bemoaning America's 3 million unfilled jobs due to lack of marketable skills.) But the parties differ greatly on how to match prospective employees and market demand.

Progressives contend higher marginal tax rates on upper-income earners and more public sector jobs will grow the middle class. It's all about income disparity and sharing the (read: your) wealth. For conservatives, such thinking is nonsense. They see tax increases targeted to small business owners as anti-growth. Neither do they measure economic progress as a function of public sector growth. They believe they "built it"—and they wish to keep a fair amount of it.

A further note beyond all the ideological bickering: Middle-class status is as much a state of mind as an income classification. It's the conviction that one's hard work has paid off; that economic security and workplace contentment are at hand. Another observation: Salary increases, promotional opportunity and employer stability tend to make for happy (predominantly middle class) employees. Happy employees are also happy voters—a point well understood on both sides of the aisle.

"Occupy" Fizzled Because It Got America Wrong

Robert Ehrlich says protesters failed to realize that most people would like to join the 1 percent.

September 24, 2012, *The Baltimore Sun*

Some pundits are bemoaning the unremarkable one-year anniversary of the Occupy movement's entry into American politics.

Indeed, it was not so long ago that daily street protests were the object of intense media coverage. For many progressives, hopes were high. Some viewed the angst-ridden movement as a convenient adjunct for the president's re-election campaign. The timing seemed perfect. Here was another opportunity to attack capitalism and all those wealthy folks who never seem to pay their "fair share." And to do so during an election year; things don't get much better for the class envy crowd.

Occupy supporters were even more pumped after the president himself signaled solidarity with the cause. Finally, a leader who was all about redistribution of wealth!

But the momentum has died. The remaining encampments are small. Media coverage is sporadic at best. And the political class is attempting to understand why.

Here's a thought: While there is a real and increasing sense of economic angst among many Americans, the demonstrators of Wall Street fame did not (and could not) capture their frame of mind.

The reason for the disconnect is readily apparent when middle class values are compared and contrasted with the words (let alone the slogans) of the Wall Street malcontents: The rent-a-cause protesters' abhorrence of all things market-driven and capitalistic is antithetical to the hopes and dreams of so many Americans who aim for higher economic status. To borrow a phrase, a clear majority of working Americans have skin in the game—they work hard and expect that their hard work will elevate their standard of living. They do not, however, expect a guaranteed result from the government.

In today's political jargon, it's difficult to get the 99 percent to resent the 1 percent when much of the 99 percent wishes to join the 1 percent.

The purveyors of class envy rhetoric may disapprove, but upward mobility and wealth creation remain primary goals for most Americans. For the angry crowds of Wall Street fame, not so much. They recoil from the notion of all those entrepreneurial capitalists who wish to take a risk, start a business, and make a buck. Maybe even buy an SUV.

Each "side" also has a quite different take on the nature of "demands" made to reach their respective cultural and economic goals.

From the occupiers' perspective, demands are expensive and expansive: green jobs, mandatory wage scales, a "living wage," free health care, retirement security, gender equality, limitless welfare benefits, etc. These entitlements constitute the familiar building blocks of an egalitarian society.

Conversely, those worried but unimpressed with the Occupy crowd understand government is unable to guarantee most of the foregoing agenda because it does not possess the ability to create the wealth required to secure the demands. Accordingly, their agendas are more intangible (balance the budget, pay down the debt, live within one's means), but achievable.

The resulting clash is predictable: the latter does not see the government as a guarantor of particular results. And that's not good enough for an Occupy movement desirous of a large and ever-growing government presence in our lives.

Consider: One group demands ever-more tax revenue from the "rich"; the other wonders why their "take-home" pay is so much lower than their salary. One group demands government subsidies from cradle to grave; the other craves individual initiative and success. One group demands additional stimulus and a "hands off" approach to entitlements, while the other sees Obama-era spending and regulatory excess as major factors in the economic malaise. One group demands a new political class that will impose greater economic equality, while the other asks for a new political class that understands how such government intervention helped fuel our economic upheaval.

Despite a disparate platform, Occupy's central themes are clear: limited economic horizons, progressive taxation, and aggressive government control of the economy. Indeed, a market economy with its inherent winners and losers is alien to the "social justice" agenda. Theirs is a justice born of seemingly limitless government-provided entitlements—benefits that seek to level the results of marketplace competition, if you will. But this ultra-progressive definition of social justice has little to do with our traditional (middle-class) view of freedom from government, competitive opportunity, and wealth creation. Hence, their relatively quick exit from our daily media reports.

Occupy may make a comeback bid. A compliant media would welcome it. But the odds will be stacked against them so long as the movement's leaders misinterpret the (still) viable wants and desires of middle-class America.

A Washington Poker Game with $16 Trillion in the Pot

Robert Ehrlich says that with fiscal cliff approaching, it will no longer be possible for either side to bluff.

December 9, 2012, *The Baltimore Sun*

Every kid knows that falling off a cliff is never good, but what about a "fiscal cliff"—how would that feel?

Americans may indeed find out, if Congress is unable to pass a budget plan prior to Jan. 1. So, what's at stake if such an event occurs? Plenty.

First, some background.

Members of both political parties have spent beyond the nation's means for many years. This economic fact of life is a bit more embarrassing for Republicans, since most GOPers at least try to talk a good game of fiscal sense. Not so much on the other side of the aisle, however. Today's progressives advance an unending list of needs requiring government intervention—with little consideration given as to how to pay for it all. For context, Senate Majority Leader Harry Reid hasn't even bothered to pass a budget for three years running.

Republicans consistently promise to slow the growth of government but fail. Democrats continually . . . promise, and succeed. The result is a $16 trillion (that's 16 followed by 12 zeros) federal debt, and counting. Annual interest in fiscal year 2012: $359 billion.

Last year, leaders on both sides struck a deal (the Budget Control Act of 2011) to the effect that automatic spending cuts of $1.2

trillion ("sequestration") would be tied to the termination of $500 billion in tax cuts (including Bush tax cuts and expiration of the payroll tax holiday), unless a budget agreement could be worked out. Such was the advent of the fiscal cliff; a scenario concocted in order that real discussion about real pain caused by real budget realities could be put off until after the 2012 presidential election.

And so here we are: three weeks until drastic spending cuts and tax increases lead to what most economists assure us will be another deep recession.

You've heard of the World Series of Poker. Well, this is the world series of budget negotiations—with $16 trillion in the pot.

For Republicans, it's no longer acceptable to sketch out a rough proposal for a flatter, slimmer tax code without identifying the specific deductions and tax credits targeted for elimination. For an American middle class addicted to tax preferences, this promises to be a difficult exercise. You see, many right-wingers are only situationally conservative; they're fine with a tighter code so long as their favorite preferences are preserved.

Another difficult hurdle: Most House Republicans have signed a pledge to refrain from tax increases. An agreement to raise marginal rates would be a clear violation of this promise. But what about a plan that would maintain present rates, eliminate certain preferences, and produce more revenue? This is precisely what House Speaker John Boehner put on the table last week, to howls of protest from some corners of his caucus.

On the other side, the vast majority of congressional Democrats are certified liberals intent on protecting (and expanding) the welfare state. They always want tax increases. One problem, though: "Tax the rich" is not a plan—it's a campaign slogan. The reality of ending the Bush tax cuts would produce about $800 billion of new revenue over a decade, or about eight days' worth of what it takes to run the federal government in each of those years.

Yet another problem: Increasing taxes on those making $250,000 a year hits small business owners hard. While small businesses may be the primary job creators in America, many of these entrepreneurial types have their business income taxed at individual rates. An income tax increase combined with Obamacare's new mandates and tax hikes will not produce the new jobs required to stimulate a sustained recovery.

Reminder to all class warriors: What sounds so populist in the heat of a campaign often does not work so well in the real world of profits and losses.

Which brings us to the real dilemma of entitlement reform on Capitol Hill, a topic that usually sends the left into fits of hysteria. Just witness the grief inflicted on Sen. Ron Wyden of Oregon (one of the most reliably liberal Members of the Senate) for his co-sponsorship of a serious Medicare reform proposal with Congressman Paul Ryan. And that bill simply provided seniors a chance to opt out of traditional Medicare for a better deal in the private market!

The fiscal cliff debate brings together all the ingredients for ugly—a down-in-the-mouth GOP pushed to find new revenues in addition to difficult budget cuts, and a newly energized, progressive president all dressed up to spend, but facing a fiscal cliff (and debt ceiling increase) that will force him to rein in heretofore sacrosanct entitlement spending.

Stay tuned . . . this could be more entertaining than "Lincoln."

Obama Economics: More Government Means More Growth

Robert L. Ehrlich says the president's response to a failed stimulus is to double down on it.

January 20, 2013, *The Baltimore Sun*

There is an old but rejuvenated movement in the country these days. It's a far-left take on Keynesian economics: a school of thought intent on raising taxes and expanding the public sector—*as a way to jump-start the economy.*

Yes, you read that correctly. The progressive intelligentsia (with a recent assist by the Congressional Research Service) are all hot and excited by the prospect of higher taxes on upper-income taxpayers, the better to spur economic growth.

The model is supposed to be the Clinton era, wherein income tax hikes coincided with strong economic growth, a surging stock market, and three consecutive years of a federal balanced budget. (Seems these adherents forget about the Clinton-era cut of almost 30 percent on capital gains, but I digress.)

The underlying rationale: Pumping more money into the public sector spurs economic growth through public investments. If that theory sounds a lot like the arguments in support of the $1.1 trillion Obama stimulus, well, that's exactly what it is.

But that massive stimulus has proved to be a bust; many of the hard-core unemployed have stopped searching for work, as unemployment has hung around 8 percent; and some economists are predicting yet another recession if profligate federal spending is not addressed in the short term. Sure seems like a long time ago since Joe Biden was promising 9 million new jobs if only those old supply-side Republicans would get out of the way.

Despite this state of affairs, the unreconstructed progressives at the White House will continue to sell the Kool-Aid of "high taxes and a large public sector equates to high growth" for as long as they control the reins. And the president is a willing cheerleader. Remember this quote from the 2012 campaign,

". . . The private sector is doing fine. Where we're seeing weaknesses in our economy have to do with state and local government. Oftentimes cuts initiated by, you know, governors or mayors who are not getting the kind of help that they have in the past from the federal government and who don't have the same kind of flexibility as the federal government in dealing with fewer revenues coming in. . . . If Republicans want to be helpful, if they really want to move forward and put people back to work, what they should be thinking about is how do we help state and local governments . . ."

What some saw as a rhetorical misstep was actually a reaffirmation of the "higher/higher" hypothesis. And now, a second term roadmap is in play.

Step one was the recently concluded fiscal deal, wherein the president used his strong hand to make an already progressive federal income tax code even more progressive (witness the return of the 39.6 percent tax bracket, new limits on deductible expenses on upper-income earners, and a new 20 percent capital gains rate).

Step two will take place in March at the next fiscal cliff showdown. The president is on record with his baseline approach: no new spending cuts without new taxes. It's as if any dose of budget cutting on one end must be made up for by additional dollars into the federal Treasury on the other. This is no way to make progress in paying down the debt. But remember the new paradigm: More government equates to more growth—and don't worry so much about all that debt ($16.455 trillion as of Thursday evening).

Last week's presidential press conference may have set a record for Executive Branch hubris, as the man who crucified President George W. Bush for pushing a debt limit increase in 2006 (and who voted against it) excoriated the GOP leadership for daring to tie the sacrosanct debt vote to additional spending cuts.

The last 3½ years have seen sluggish growth, historically high unemployment rates, low consumer confidence, and an additional $5.4 trillion added to the national debt. All this despite a $1.2 trillion stimulus, a Fed that has pumped in excess of $2 trillion into the economy, interest rates close to zero, low inflation, labor peace, and a slimmer, more efficient private sector with trillions in excess cash to burn.

The bottom line: The left's dangerous love affair with ever-higher taxes and public sector expansion is a formula for economic "malaise." Sad to say, that's not the only thing going on in Washington that reminds me of Jimmy Carter.

Disability Insurance Entitlement Explodes Under Obama

Robert Ehrlich says it's no coincidence that so many more Americans rely on SSDI under this Administration.

March 3, 2013, *The Baltimore Sun*

Those of you paying attention have noticed that the Obama Administration is actually doing what it promised: transforming America into a gigantic welfare state. And there are plenty of takers willing to cash in on it and "get mine." Numbers don't lie. Forty percent of the population was on some form of public assistance when the president took office; today, that number stands at 55 percent. And fraud is rampant.

"Exhibit A" is the Social Security Disability Insurance program (SSDI), a classic Washington entitlement that chews up tax dollars while (often) negligently providing for unqualified beneficiaries, an increasing number of whom are wont to remain on the public dole for . . . well, forever if they don't get caught.

Make no mistake—rapid growth, lax standards, and an increased cultural acceptance of long-term nanny state benefits has gotten SSDI into big fiscal trouble.

The 2012 Social Security trustees report shows that SSDI is on schedule to be exhausted as early as 2015, making it one of the first federal entitlement trust funds to go bust. Rapid expansion of the program has coincided with the tenure of the Obama Administration. Coincidence? Nope! The facts speak for themselves:

- Since President Obama's 2009 inauguration, 5.9 million people have been added to SSDI, a 23 percent increase over the last five years (compare that to 2.5 million new jobs created during the same time period);

- SSDI rolls have swollen to almost 11 million recipients (translation: 1 in 14 U.S. workers);

- in 2011, only 3.6 percent of enrollees exited the program due to "medical improvement";

- also in 2011, the program cost taxpayers $128.9 billion (18 percent of *all* Social Security spending) and generated a deficit of $25.3 billion.

As with all federal programs, SSDI was created as a social safety net to serve a legitimate purpose: to provide income assistance to vulnerable individuals unable to find work as a result of a disability. Most Americans support the sentiment, but compassion has its limits. We draw the line at those who game (defraud) the system in order to secure benefits.

How bad is the problem? Just ask any occupational therapist or nurse practitioner. They will regale you with myriad stories of minor ailments ("I need a handicap tag for my car—there are no close parking places at the golf course!") and demands for unfounded and outrageous disability ratings with excessive paid time off (". . . or I'll find somebody else to certify me!").

Think this is a heartless, right-wing indictment? Think again. The liberal Center for American Progress has opined that "the program provides strong incentives to applicants and beneficiaries to remain permanently out of the labor force, and it provides no incentive to employers to implement cost-effective accommodations that enable employees with work limitations to remain on the job. . . . Too many work-capable individuals involuntarily exit the labor force and apply for, and often receive, SSDI."

The supporting numbers are disheartening at best: In 1983, 163 per 1,000 SSDI beneficiaries terminated benefits and left the program. Today, that number has plunged to 74 per 1,000. A Heritage Foundation analyst reports that the increase in SSDI rolls accounts for one-third of the drop in U.S. labor force participation from 2007 to 2011, its lowest level since 1981.

The most egregious result of all the fraudulent awards is that some applicants legitimately in need of assistance may wait as long as two years before their files are completed.

But hope may be on the way. A 2012 Senate subcommittee's probe into the program revealed what an informed outside observer might already have assumed: Federal hearing examiners are often poorly trained, render inconsistent decisions, fail to follow required medical criteria, and use outdated occupational data to identify job openings for clients with partial disabilities.

The same congressional report presents solutions, including the required attendance of the government's agency representative at evidentiary hearings, a stronger review process, an expanded (expert) consultative process, and an updated job and medical guideline vocational list.

SSDI has experienced excessive growth for a number of reasons. Large numbers of aging baby boomers certainly contribute to the expansion, and additional qualifiers translates into more applicants. But there is more to the problem than numbers. An anemic recovery has contributed as well—hard times can compel those predisposed to public benefits to turn to the disability rolls.

Fortunately, common-sense remedies do not constitute heavy lifting. They can and should be adopted by a political class (allegedly) in the business of protecting and securing Social Security for future generations. Hard-working taxpayers deserve no less.

How the Welfare State Has Grown—And Sapped America's Economy and Culture

Despite claims by Franklin Roosevelt and Lyndon Johnson to the contrary, the New Deal and Great Society have produced a nation of dependence.

April 7, 2013, *The Baltimore Sun*

"I predict future happiness for Americans if they can prevent the government from wasting the labors of the people under the pretense of taking care of them."

—THOMAS JEFFERSON
From a letter to Thomas Cooper, November 29, 1802

My recent column on the challenges associated with the Social Security Disability Insurance (SSDI) program elicited numerous and very personal stories from readers about how individual (disabled) recipients depended on the program for daily maintenance. And, many asked, how dare I (and others of my ilk) question such a vital program? Have I no sense of compassion?

My support for SSDI's fundamental mission is clear. I said so in the piece. But what should be equally clear is that the program is in a state of disrepair during a time of rapidly declining trust fund balances.

I note this phenomenon in advance of the extended piece that follows. My purpose is to analyze the considerable carnage inflicted on our country by a too large and too intrusive federal government. A topic well worth revisiting now that a re-elected President Barack

Obama has restarted his campaign to expand federal jurisdiction over so many aspects of our lives.

New Deal and Great Society

We begin with President Franklin Delano Roosevelt's New Deal, a seminal movement that forever changed the way Americans interact with the federal government. Henceforth, the federal government would assume many of the social support mechanisms that had been the province of state and local governments, civic and religious institutions and individuals. That even FDR recognized the cultural dangers inherent in such federal intervention was evident in his 1935 State of the Union Address:

> Continued dependence upon relief induces a spiritual and moral disintegration fundamentally destructive to the national fiber. To dole out relief in this way is to administer a narcotic, a subtle destroyer of the human spirit. . . . We must preserve not only the bodies of the unemployed from destitution but also their self-respect, their self-reliance and courage and determination.

Your irony meter may be on overload, but try to control yourself. At least the alphabet soup of New Deal agencies that sprang forth during FDR's tenure helped pull us out of the Great Depression (although the outbreak of World War II certainly played a major role as well).

Now, spring forward to the second monumental expansion of the federal government in the 20th Century: President Lyndon Johnson's Great Society. Here the size and depth of the modern welfare state began to take shape during a most fractious time in American history.

It was the mid-1960s, and social unrest was the order of the day. A young and vibrant president had been assassinated. The Civil Rights movement was gaining momentum. An aggressive anti-war movement was beginning to blossom on college campuses. And a sexual revolution was changing American mores and morals.

Against all this societal turmoil came LBJ's grand plan to conduct a "war" on poverty through a large package of bills that sought to expand the depth and scope of federal power in unprecedented ways. New legislation came fast and furious. Forty programs dedicated to the elimination of poverty, 60 bills aimed at improved public education, and so many of the federal programs that constitute a modern federal safety net: Medicare, Medicaid, Job Corps, Head Start, the National School Lunch Act, the Department of Housing and Urban Development, the Food Stamp Act, the Urban Mass Transportation Act, and the Older Americans Act.

These and other new laws spawned the hiring of tens of thousands of new federal employees. The grand premise: the best and brightest minds in Washington, D.C., knew best how to cure what ailed America. Vast improvements in failing public schools, poverty rates, urban decay and health care for the poor and elderly were the promised deliverables.

Again, a president's high sounding, articulate rhetoric (and well-intentioned policies) were pedaled to an American public eager to listen:

"Every dollar spent will result in savings to the country and especially to the local taxpayers in the cost of crime, welfare, and of health and of police protection."

And:

"We are not content to accept the endless growth of relief rolls or welfare rolls."

And:

"Our American answer to poverty is not to make the poor more secure in their poverty but to reach down and to help them lift themselves out of the ruts of poverty and move with the large majority along the high road of hope and prosperity."

And:

"The days of the dole in our country are numbered."

Thus was rekindled what has become a relentless effort to build a European-style welfare state.

Failed Promises

Fifty years and $17 trillion later, many of the promised (positive) deliverables failed to arrive. Individual empowerment and self-reliance have faded, but the federal government's growth and influence has exploded. And results on the ground—where it counts—tell a story of ineffectiveness at best and societal devastation at worst.

A brief review of current conditions:

- *Food Stamp Program:* The landmark federal nutrition program has been wracked by fraud and inefficiency from day one. One in seven Americans now qualifies for benefits, up from one in 50 during the early 1970s. A program that began with a half million enrollees (at a cost of $75 million) now serves 48 million recipients (up 20 million since 2007) at a cost of $80.4 billion. Enrollees have increased an average of 11,133 per day under the Obama Administration. Interestingly, participation rates continue to increase despite a gradually recovering economy.

- *Single motherhood:* It's not politically correct to discuss illegitimacy rates these days, and that's part of the problem. You see, the relationship between out-of-wedlock births and poverty is beyond question. And rates have exploded since the '60s. Today, 29 percent of white babies, 53 percent of Hispanic babies and 73 percent of black babies are born to unwed mothers. And 71 percent of all out-of-wedlock babies are born into poverty. Sadly, single parents who are able to rise above difficult circumstances and achieve are the exception and not the rule. Most face daunting odds in their quest to climb out of dire economic conditions.

- *Medicare and Medicaid:* These health care programs for the elderly and poor are popular pieces of the federal safety net. Yet failure to modernize 1965-era delivery systems has led to fraud, abuse, and just plain old malfeasance. Costs are out of control, and cost projections are notoriously inaccurate. Two cases in point:

In 1965, the House Ways and Means Committee projected that the hospital insurance portion of Medicare would cost $9 billion by 1990. The actual cost that year was $67 billion.

In 1967, that same committee calculated the entire Medicare program would cost $12 billion by 1990. The actual cost in 1990 was $98 billion.

Another interesting note: Medicaid spending nearly doubled from 2001-2010. Yet a central thrust of Obamacare is to expand Medicaid coverage: Up to 11 million more low-income folks are expected to qualify. And don't worry about the bill; a broke federal government will pick up the entire tab—at least for three years. This despite many of our best physicians dropping out of the programs due to low reimbursement rates.

The irrefutable bottom line on entitlement spending: interest on the debt, Social Security, Medicare, and Medicaid will consume 100 percent of the federal budget by 2025.

- *Education:* Despite the commitment of billions of federal dollars, high school graduation rates remain unchanged since the early 1960s. Today, three out of 10 ten students fail to secure a diploma. Secondary school graduation rates for Latinos, African Americans, and Native Americans average just over 50 percent. The respected National Bureau of Economic Research says that the "[family plays a powerful role] in shaping educational outcomes" and that "the growing number of disadvantaged families promises to reduce productivity and promote inequality in America." You think?

Space constraints do not allow for discussion of additional measures of societal denigration. Suffice it to say a culture of dependency and a hugely expensive welfare state have been accompanied by significant spikes in drug use, domestic violence, crime rates, and incarceration rates, most notably for young African American youths. This latter group being the most victimized of all demographic groups over the past 50 years.

One conclusion is inescapable: waging war on poverty is big business for big government. This year's federal budget contains more than 70 federal welfare programs alone. Combined state and federal spending on social programs now approaches $1 trillion per year. Total social welfare spending since passage of the Great Society totals $17 trillion. Yet the nation's poverty rate remains unchanged from 45 years ago. What has changed is the dramatic decomposition of the American family and culture.

If you are at all bothered by the foregoing statistics, or you believe that our over-reaching regulatory state is antithetical to America's creed of individualism and self-reliance, you might begin investigating the voting records of congressmen and senators who continually expand the behemoth that is today's federal government (and all too often are returned to Congress by a complacent and ill-informed electorate).

The Great Society turned out to be considerably less than great; in fact, it crumbled at the twin poisons of dependency and bureaucracy. But America can do better. Hopefully, sooner rather than later, voters will demand an end to profligate spending, preemptive government intervention, and counter-cultural values—before it's too late.

Did We Learn Anything from the Subprime Loan Crisis?

Robert Ehrlich says the government's foray into risky lending practices suggests we have not.

April 21, 2013, *The Baltimore Sun*

A dangerous confluence of recent business stories have been attention grabbers. First, the Obama Administration announced an initiative to ensure more home loans for those with weak credit. Then, a number of prominent economists issued forecasts reflecting a slowing economy over the next several quarters.

For the public, it's déjà vu all over again: an all-knowing federal government again pushing its way into the housing market against the backdrop of a softening economy. Yet again, we hear calls for banks to facilitate more home loans to mortgage seekers with less-than-stellar credit. And all in the name of helping young people and those with poor credit histories secure a house.

But the ink still isn't dry on the bad (mortgage) paper and lawsuits generated as a result of the government's last attempt to manipulate risk. How quickly we forgot about that five-year recession brought about by government-sponsored risky loan practices. The downturn has been referred to as the greatest economic calamity since the Great Depression. The president said so himself!

The various villains who played significant roles in producing our historic mortgage meltdown are described in Chapter 6 of my book, *Turn This Car Around*. In no particular order: Republicans and Democrats who sold the romantic notion that *everybody* should own a home, regardless of income or credit history; progressives who perfected the art of using the Community Reinvestment Act (CRA), a federal law aimed at race-based redlining practices to leverage banks; negligent Wall Street rating agencies; greedy Wall Street investment firms; and a too-late-to-the-party Securities and Exchange Commission.

All played a significant role in the monumental crisis. Many have paid and are continuing to pay large fines, penalties and legal awards to an unending list of plaintiffs—most notably the federal government. And some of the worst (individual) actors have ended up in the clink. It's all there, including the few (mostly Republicans) who had the foresight to scream bloody murder during the heady days of the mortgage-backed securities boom. Alas, these select few were rewarded for their diligence with charges of racism by certain Members of Congress and the progressive left. It's a familiar narrative to congressional observers: Simply oppose any extension of the CRA, then get ready to defend yourself against accusations of racism and redlining.

That politicians, regulators, and private-sector investor types played prominent roles in the underwriting of so many bad mortgages is widely acknowledged. But another group deserves equal attention: the community activists (ACORN and its progeny) who engaged in regular "outings" of banks unwilling to write riskier loans in marginal neighborhoods. It was economic development by shakedown—underwrite even more subprime loans in return for community peace and a passing report on your CRA review. Unfortunately, too many banks complied.

There are just so many bad loans that can be rolled into new investment instruments (subsequently sold to the world) before things go south. In this case, "south" is defined as an economic crisis so severe that it erased almost 20 years of accumulated consumer wealth, according to the Federal Reserve's "Survey of Consumer Finances."

But now the feds wish to revisit "subprime lending land." Government again wants to substitute its judgment for the market's. (Seems those old community organizer habits are hard to break.) And yet again, it will be federal taxpayers on the hook for the inevitable cascade of newly mined bad loans.

One piece of good news for mortgage originators: Obama housing officials are asking the Obama Justice Department to reassure banks that they will not face severe legal consequences if (and when) large numbers of the newly issued loans turn out to be bad. Wow— bet everyone feels secure with their "get out of jail free" card.

Banks have suffered bad karma, and bad publicity, since the mortgage crisis began. Reports of obscene bonuses from Wall Street investment houses did not help. Neither did the generally successful but wildly unpopular TARP. And tighter underwriting standards in the post-crisis lending world have made life much more difficult for small business and the American consumer.

So, taxpayer beware: The government must be hyper-careful in reengaging banks in the subprime market. Indeed, mortgage creditworthiness should be a function of rational economic calculation and little else. Such is the hard (but familiar) lesson of our recent economic woes.

Note: As my column addresses issues of national importance, it is appropriate to add my condolences, thoughts and prayers to those of a nation grieving lives lost and lamenting the physical and emotional injuries inherent in the cowardly attacks of April 15. Please join me in expressing gratitude to American first responders for their extraordinary courage and selfless sacrifice in the face of danger every day. God bless America.

There Is Hope Yet for American Steel Manufacturing

Plants like Sparrows Point will never return, but new, high-tech plants are flourishing.

August 18, 2013, *The Baltimore Sun*

T he huge, idle steelworks is impossible to miss as one travels across the Key Bridge. More than once, my boys have asked about the giant plant at Sparrows Point. "What was made there?" "How many people worked there?" "How come nobody works there anymore?"

The answer is complex; the full explanation as to why hundreds of acres of prime industrial land are now shuttered goes far beyond one plant located in Sparrows Point, Maryland.

I thought about this Ehrlich family discussion while watching the uproar generated by the New York Metropolitan Transportation Authority's decision to allow a subcontract for the steel decks of the Verrazano Narrows Bridge project to be built by a Chinese steel fabricator.

The contract spurred the usual condemnations from political types. U.S. Senators Chuck Schumer and Sherrod Brown, Democrats from New York and Ohio, respectively, cried foul in an angry letter to the general contractor. Steel workers union leaders joined the chorus. Emotional calls for an "even playing field" on trade practice sounded a familiar theme.

But the chairman of the MTA issued a swift response that took me back to my children's questions about that big old plant. Seems that the MTA did attempt to locate an American source, but to no avail.

Per the MTA, "Not a single American fabricator had the capacity, the experience, and the willingness to tackle the job. . . . The American steel industry has not focused on the process of fabricating orthotropic steel decks for projects of this size and complexity, while fabricators in other countries have specialized in it."

And so another (American) steel opportunity goes by the boards.

The Verrazano Narrows Bridge story and the demise of Sparrows Point speak to the continuing woes of our steel sector. The contributing causes are familiar:

- Industrial era production methods were heavily labor intensive. Bethlehem Steel employed 35,000 people at its zenith in the 1940s. It was the world's largest steel mill. The well-compensated (but dirty and dangerous) jobs spurred local growth, especially the development of Dundalk and Sparrows Point. But technological innovation soon made it possible to produce more steel with far less labor. Employment at Bethlehem Steel subsequently dwindled during the last two decades of the millennium. Formidable socioeconomic challenges to the solid working class neighborhoods of Eastern Baltimore County soon followed.

- Unfair trade practices played their part. Dumping of heavily subsidized steel from Europe and Asia hit domestic production hard. Large scale foreign government support made it nearly impossible for once profitable sectors of the domestic industry to manufacture at competitive prices. Many of these unfair trade practices continue to this day.

- Management and labor grew fat and happy. Both acted as though the party (and profits) would never end. Until they did . . . with a thud. One-industry towns simply do not survive once the one industry hits the skids. (See "Detroit bankruptcy" for context.) Most U.S. steel communities have yet to recover from this economic catastrophe.

Today's headlines are depressingly familiar to this former Member of Congress representing Dundalk, Maryland. Weekly, I read of yet another probe into allegations of illegal steel dumping from China, Russia, Taiwan, Ukraine, or South Korea; yet another complaint filed with the International Trade Commission; yet another steel town heading toward economic ruin; yet another politician demagoguing about the "good ole days" of American steel supremacy.

But all is not lost. There *is* cause for optimism for a post-industrial American steel industry.

New high-tech specialty mills are a hot commodity. And they're popping up all around the Midwestern "rust belt."

These new factories are high-tech marvels. Their state-of-the-art technologies reduce carbon emissions and increase productivity. The workforce more often than not is non-union. The work weeks are shorter. Workers share in their health care premiums. And a 401(k) (rather than the old defined benefit pension) is the sole retirement vehicle offered.

Gone forever are the large blast furnaces with the small profit margins; such venues are just too capital intensive for a new age. So too are the ultra-dirty, ultra dangerous working conditions of yesteryear. That construct (which has generated thousands of tort claims in our courts) is never to return. Fortunately, this generation of American steel workers can expect to retire without the specter of environmental disease.

What emerges is a more diversified steel sector targeting viable niches such as automobiles, construction, appliances and oil and natural gas exploration, employing a computer literate and well-compensated labor force.

Most importantly, the new mills are proving generally profitable. As such, they will continue to play an integral role in America's post-recession recovery. And they just might save the manufacturing backbone of the American economy to boot.

HUD Latest Vehicle for White House Power Grab

Robert L. Ehrlich Jr. questions value of Obama Administration's housing proposal

August 25, 2013, *The Baltimore Sun*

There are so many things to say with regard to the federal Department of Housing and Urban Development's proposed rule entitled "Affirmatively Furthering Fair Housing." And since this proposal lands on the hot buttons of race and class, I'm going to ask all of you to take a deep breath, put aside your preconceptions about federal housing policy for a minute, and simply give some objective thought to the size and scope of this latest missive from Washington, D.C.

First, it is worthwhile to revisit a historical fact: Discriminatory housing practices were predominant in this country for a *very* long time. For context, check out metropolitan Baltimore housing patterns over the better part of the 20th century. The specter of such overt discrimination necessitated the passage of the Fair Housing Act of 1968. Henceforth, affordability was to be the determining factor in purchasing a home, not the color of one's skin.

The principle of affordability rather than race in choosing a home was far too long in the making; nevertheless, old patterns of lily-white suburbs and black inner cities began to fade with the impact of the new law and increasing black wealth. Few would disagree that housing discrimination has significantly declined over the past 50 years.

But what about more subtle forms of discrimination, such as redlining and residential "steering"? The remedy for these abusive practices came about in the form of various government empowerment programs that sought to accelerate desegregation through housing voucher resettlements. First, Section 8 certificates were made available to qualifying poor families in making rent payments for private apartments. Then, a series of controversial programs to transplant the poor to homes in upscale neighborhoods so that they might be exposed to homeownership in a safer setting. All of which did not sound reasonable to the neighbors (black and white) who had worked hard for the opportunity to live in those neighborhoods.

In fact, it's safe to say that suburban Baltimore's reaction to such programs was rather negative. Vociferous opposition and well-attended, high-profile protests became the order of the day. Liberal observers (including editorial writers from this newspaper) screamed "racism"; conservative opponents screamed "social engineering." Ultimately, the most unpopular of the voucher programs ("Moving to Opportunity") was quietly defunded by Maryland's junior Democratic U.S. senator.

Fast forward to today, wherein an ultra-progressive Obama Administration is on a second-term rampage to federalize just about everything in its sight (see my column of Aug. 11).

To wit, HUD's present push to impose a new regulation that would empower the feds to "track diversity in America's neighborhoods and then push policies to change those it deems discriminatory [by compiling] data on segregation and discrimination in every neighborhood." In plain English, this proposed rule empowers the federal government to arbitrarily judge discriminatory housing intent ZIP Code by ZIP Code, and then take the appropriate remedial action against the offending neighborhoods.

The implementing mechanism is to be HUD's "discrimination database." This vehicle would in turn seek changes in (local) zoning ordinances, housing finance, infrastructure policy and transportation in order to remedy the alleged segregation. Note the Obama

Administration's typical modus operandi: an aggressive federal power grab with few specifics on how it's all to go down in the real world of neighborhoods and communities. (If all this reminds you of Obamacare's reliance on an overarching regulatory bureaucracy, you are not alone.)

A further note: This latest Administration initiative sounds remarkably similar to the (anti-redlining and easy credit) federal housing policies that fueled the subprime mortgage meltdown that ultimately caused the "worst economic crisis since the Great Depression" (per President Obama).

Some of you dismiss these programs as nanny state "hand-outs" from the federal government. Others see them as a "hand up" to the economically depressed. Regardless, at this point we simply do not know if the proposed rule will prove to be as draconian as conservatives are predicting or as helpful as liberals wish it to be. It's all about the implementation.

But this is what I do know. Many years ago in Arbutus, Bob and Nancy Ehrlich taught that God helps those who help themselves. They also impressed upon me the notion that people tend to appreciate what they earn far more than what they are given. Independently, but in the same moral vein, Martin Luther King Jr. was teaching a racially divided nation that the content of one's character is far more important than the color of one's skin.

All fundamental values to live by.

Wonder how these words of wisdom would be framed in the Federal Register?

The Real Culprits of the Housing Crisis Go Unpunished

Economically illiterate policymaking in Washington set the stage for the subprime mortgage meltdown.

October 20, 2013, *The Baltimore Sun*

Those of you who read my first book ("Turn This Car Around") will recall my indictment of the many contributors to our historic mortgage industry meltdown and worldwide recession, AKA "The greatest financial crisis since the Great Depression," per President Barack Obama.

The guilty (and greedy) included Wall Street rating-houses that regularly awarded sub-prime or otherwise risky mortgage-backed products their coveted AAA rating; the (formerly) powerful government sponsored enterprises, most notably Fannie Mae and Freddie Mac, that lowered their underwriting standards in order to purchase ever more low quality mortgages; brokers and other middle men who helped to steer marginal credit clients into obviously unaffordable mortgages; naive (or worse) consumers who freely secured unaffordable mortgages; and, of course, the big Wall Street investment banks that put together and sold toxic mortgage products to the world.

That these key players were instrumental in America's economic downturn is without question. Also without question is the significant damage (public and private, monetary and reputational) inflicted on so many of the industry's key players. It seems as though every week includes a new Securities and Exchange Commission investigation, Justice Department probe, or multi-billion dollar settlement relating to a major Wall Street player.

But there is one group of miscreants who beat the rap. Not one of their ilk has been targeted for investigation. Neither has the media attempted to explore the depths of their culpability in significant detail. In fact, with precious few exceptions, these conspirators have been rewarded for their nefarious deeds.

I speak of government regulators and politicians. On the regulatory side, there was the 1990s era Department of Housing and Urban Development (HUD), the federal agency tasked with attaining so-called affordable housing goals. This they did, far too well in fact. An original portfolio goal of 30 percent sub-prime mortgages had increased to 56 percent prior to the economic collapse of 2008. And there was no more powerful Washington player than Fannie Mae. Their well-compensated lobbyists were always around the House and Senate banking committees. Members of all stripes paid attention to their concerns. Their clout was unmatched where housing policy issues were at stake.

But the most influential promoters of affordable housing/sub-prime mortgages were the Members of Congress who sold a willing public on what everyone seemingly wanted to hear—home ownership was within reach, necessities such as annual income, assets, and credit worthiness notwithstanding. In fact, three-quarters of all sub-prime/low quality loans were on the books of federal government agencies during the summer of 2008.

The brave few (mostly Republicans, and most notably Rep. Mike Oxley and Sen. John McCain) who sought to raise objections to the indulgent shenanigans of the political crowd were dismissed as obstructionists, racists, or both. I should know. I was a Member of the House Banking Committee with a front row seat to the daily indictments (primarily race and class-based) that were lodged against Members of Congress who questioned the endless leveraging of dollars into mortgage finance. Accordingly, few dared trek down that path.

Indeed, the champions of this crusade were progressive Democrats, most notably the outspoken chairman of the House Banking Committee, Rep. Barney Frank of Massachusetts. Witness this beauty from a 2003 committee hearing:

> . . . [in] my view, the two government sponsored enterprises we are talking about here, Fannie Mae and Freddie Mac, are not in crisis. . . . I do not think at this point there is a problem with a threat to the Treasury. . . . I believe that we, as the federal government, have probably done *too little* [my emphasis] rather than too much to push them to meet the goals of affordable housing and to set reasonable goals. . . . I think we see entities [Fannie Mae and Freddie Mac] that are fundamentally sound financially and [could] withstand some of the disastrous scenarios. . . . The more pressure there is [on these companies], then the less I think we see in terms of affordable housing."

A few years later, Fannie and Freddie were belly up.

History will record many recriminations from the great financial crisis of the new millennium. Missing will be the long list of public officials who pedaled an economically illiterate version of the "American Dream" to millions of gullible consumers.

Yet a re-elected Obama Administration has the usual suspects at it again. Fannie and Freddie are alive and looking to make new friends. The big bad investment banks continue to be regularly demonized by their former co-conspirators on the Hill. And new Administration housing finance proposals have emerged that are eerily similar to the problematic "bad credit, no problem" programs of yesteryear.

Washington is pretty good at revisionist history. But the primary contributors to our housing bubble and subsequent sub-prime meltdown are obvious to all who care to look.

We ignore the lessons of the recent past at our own (considerable) peril.

Desperate Course Correction

Obamacare was a PR nightmare, yet no one associated with it has lost a job.

December 15, 2013, *The Baltimore Sun*

The $1 billion, three and a half year rollout was a public relations disaster. Consumer access to its website is the focus of nightly Leno monologues. Nearly 6 million Americans have lost health insurance. That promised $2,500 per family savings has gone the way of the dinosaur. Mandate fear inspires part-time job growth. Formerly happily insured employees face smaller networks and substantially higher deductibles in the new exchanges. Colleges curtail underwriting student insurance. Privacy concerns abound. Insurance companies are unsure of what benefit packages their insured have purchased. Sticker shock hits the young and healthy. Medicaid rolls soar. An imperial president unilaterally decrees canceled policies be brought back to life, to little avail. Red state Democrats run for the hills. The Supreme Court agrees to rule on an over-reaching contraception mandate. Presidential voter approval dips into the low 40s. And not one member of the Obamacare team has lost his/her job.

So, what does the "post-partisan president" (remember when the media trotted that phony mantra out at the very beginning of Obama I?) do to stop the bleeding?

He does what most deft politicians do when the wolves are at the gates—he changes the subject. In this case, a no longer Teflon president reaches back for the "go to" option for liberals of all stripes—class envy. This familiar tactic is a sure-fire base motivator; and there is no better practitioner of the art than the 45th president of the United States.

The latest iteration of the strategy is to exploit the specter of income inequality, that intractable divide between rich and poor so reviled by the world's progressives since . . . well, the beginning of time.

This byproduct of capitalist economies (and socialist economies for that matter) now assumes center stage in the Administration's full court press to turn the national conversation away from Obamacare's endless stream of negative reviews.

The course correction occurred during last week's presidential address. Full campaign mode was adopted. The usual sycophants were enlisted. Rent-a-mobs were assigned to fast food venues to protest low pay. Renewed calls to raise the federal minimum wage made media headlines. A so-called living wage (defined as whatever hourly wage labor union leadership wants it to be) re-entered the national debate. An extension of federal unemployment benefits (presently 99 weeks) was offered up by the Democratic leadership. And yet another Obamacare exemption on behalf of organized labor became national news—and another national embarrassment.

On the rhetorical side, the specter of "trickle down economics" (again) became the focal point of a class-warfare focused Obama Administration offensive. Nothing new here; it was all "you didn't build that" redux—this time with an added element of desperation inspired by the myriad public relations problems of the president's signal legislative accomplishment.

One interesting aspect to the class conscious initiative has generally escaped media attention: a worsening economic divide, an unprecedented increase in the number of adults who have given up looking for work, a "shovel-ready-less" and frightfully expensive stimulus, and a record number of people on food stamps have taken place during the reign of . . . Barack Hussein Obama. Simply put, it's getting more difficult to "blame Bush" for a rather dismal economic record as we operate in year six of an Obama presidency. The story does not end there. An adjunct to the "change the subject" strategy is "deny—and pretend otherwise." But "reality denial" is usually obvious; you know it when you see it. The president's renewed campaign to convince the young and healthy that substantially higher insurance premiums and less consumer choice is good for them is one example. Harry Reid's claim that the president never REALLY promised you could keep you insurance and your doctor is another. But even these exaggerations (I'm being charitable) are overshadowed by Democratic Congressional Committee Chairman Debbie Wasserman Schultz's claim that all Democrats will happily run on an Obamacare platform in 2014. (Recall such was not the case in 2010 or 2012.) And THIS from the person charged with electing Democrats in that pivotal year.

Of course, Majority Leader Reid's pronouncement directly contradicts the president's own mea culpa. (Perhaps Reid was rechanneling his daily rebukes to Senator Ted Cruz during the recent government shutdown.) As for Chairman Schultz's promise, we can only "hope"—'cuz "change" will most assuredly follow. Change in the Senate leadership, I mean.

Obama Never Quite Scratches the Economy's Itch

Despite a record of inadequate fixes, Democrats still believe the next government program will spur the economy and job creation.

March 2, 2014, *The Baltimore Sun*

Those of us of a certain age recall the scene all too well: Lucy pulling the football away just as Charlie Brown was about to kick it, visions of football glory dancing in his head.

Charlie Brown always fell for the prank, believing that Lucy would finally come through next time around.

Today's apologists for President Barack Obama believe (much like Charlie Brown) that the next policy or program will surely jump-start a tepid, jobless recovery. And, as true believers, they are always surprised when it doesn't, when Lucy pulls the football.

But the deficit spending, big-ticket item gravy train is over. Republican control of the House means no new spending binge (à la stimulus and Obamacare) for the remainder of the president's term.

All of which leaves us in "Year Six" of a sustained experiment in European-style social welfare-ism—with a fractured Congress and a frustrated president intent on taking matters into his own hands, unilaterally empowering government "with his phone and his pen."

Mr. Obama does this because it is what he knows: See a problem, create a government program; when the problem gets worse, throw more money at the problem and indict your political opposition as lacking compassion.

The problem, of course, is that the offered prescription never quite scratches the economy's itch. In other words, the menu of policy options presented is more about placating political constituencies and feeding government rather than growing the private economy.

A review of recent events reflects the inconvenient truth:

A $1.2 trillion stimulus guaranteed to energize a recession-riddled economy with "shovel ready jobs" proved to be more sizzle than steak. Today, few Democrats talk about this failed experiment in Keynesian economics other than to complain that it was too small of a spending package to do the trick. Vice President Joe Biden is famously associated with this school of thought, he of the "it's never enough" wing of the progressive movement.

Two major tax increases (the end of the Bush tax cuts and the new and expanded taxes of Obamacare) targeted to upper income earners made the progressive federal tax code more progressive— but without altering the divide between rich and poor. Income inequality has actually gotten worse during the Obama era. Seems that punishing wealth does not motivate the wealthy to start new businesses and provide opportunities for the not-so-wealthy—quite a revelation to the class warrior crowd.

Today's mantra is all about increasing the minimum wage, even mandating a so-called "living wage," which appears to be whatever organized labor wants it to be. Raising the minimum wage will surely help some marginal workers put more money in their pockets while others (the most marginal, low-skilled workers) will either lose their jobs or find their hours cut. Seems that even well-meaning Capitol Hill types haven't found a way to make unskilled workers more valuable through government dictate. But the real bottom line is that a minimum wage boost does nothing to stimulate employers into creating more jobs.

Obamacare is an employment black hole, as evidenced by the Congressional Budget Office's latest estimate that Americans will work the equivalent of 2.5 million fewer full-time jobs by

2024. Accordingly, the president has delayed the employer mandate another year in order to forestall additional political fallout prior to the midterm elections. This latest extension includes rules that empower the IRS to investigate why an employer reduced its workforce under the exempt cap of 100 employees. Hopefully, this Orwellian provision will not survive court challenge. One can further hope the Administration's latest mantra (allegedly miserable workers will be liberated from "job lock") will be quickly dismissed by a distrustful public.

Some perspective is in order.

Our housing bubble recession was wide and deep. Trillions of dollars of wealth was lost. Credit became scarce. Unemployment skyrocketed. Bad actors played a part, especially those within government who pretended that just about everybody should own a home, regardless of income.

The journey back from the precipice has been slow and bumpy, made more so by economic policies that fail to promote economic growth.

This perilous path is led by no-growthers, the heavy (protectionist) hand of organized labor, and the limited horizon crowd who welcome the gradual decline of a "greedy" super-power. (Recall Senator Obama bemoaning America's disproportionate share of energy consumption and wealth.)

The bottom line: This president does not see growth and wealth creation (let alone entrepreneurship) as a primary component of American culture. Diminished economic expectations inevitably follow. Elections do indeed have consequences.

In Trade Policy, Obama Needs the GOP

Protectionist Democrats are less likely to support the president's signature trade agreements.

April 27, 2014, *The Baltimore Sun*

Free trade has been instrumental in building the most powerful economy on Earth. In fact, 38 million U.S. jobs are a direct result of U.S. trade with the world.

Yet, it's not so easy to be a "free trader" in today's politics. Some view trade with less developed (read: low labor cost) nations as a one-way ticket to domestic job loss. Indeed, two decades after the North American Free Trade Agreement, it's still easy politics to criticize the real and perceived disadvantages of mega trade deals.

It is against this backdrop that President Barack Obama has begun his pitch for so-called "trade promotion authority" (formerly known as "fast track"). The stakes are high: Two significant deals (one with the European Union and another with over a dozen countries in the Pacific Rim) will make or break the president's trade legacy.

In light of our separation of powers, TPA makes good sense. The Constitution vests the executive with the sole power to negotiate treaties, but only Congress has the authority to pass laws. And so fast track has been offered as a way for Congress to register its policy objectives while the president goes about the business of negotiating terms and conditions. The first delegation of the power occurred in 1934 with the passage of the "Reciprocal Trade Agreements Act." The authority has been expanded numerous times since, most recently in 2002—an extension that lapsed in 2007.

121

The bottom line: Congress pushes its priorities for the president to pursue. In exchange, the president is assured of an up or down vote and no last minute Congressional amendments to undermine what the executive has negotiated—an incentive for our trade partners to deal in good faith.

But what was relatively easy for past presidents is proving quite difficult for President Obama.

First, there is Senate Majority Leader Harry Reid, a partisan laborite uninterested in forcing his vulnerable Members to cast trade votes that will alienate the party's union base. Hence, the leader's vocal opposition to the president's State of the Union plea for TPA. The recent special election in Florida wherein an underdog Republican won in a district twice carried by the president will further dissuade Mr. Reid from antagonizing his party's most loyal supporters.

Then there are (some) tea party Republicans, who present an obstacle more because they are distrustful of this president's promises than because they are latter day protectionists. A portion of the approximately 60 caucus Members could break with the GOP leadership on TPA. Still, a clear majority of Republican Members in both chambers are "yea" votes on a bill desired by both their base and their chief antagonist, the president.

A third branch of the opposition is more identified by their votes than their rhetoric. They are the phony free traders, always willing to spout the free trade line at the local Chamber of Commerce but never quite ready to cast a supporting vote when it counts. This bipartisan group uses the popular "fair trade" fallback when explaining away anti-trade votes. And although subject to negotiation, important "sweeteners" such as "trade adjustment assistance" (dollars for workers displaced by foreign trade) and counter-subsidies to currency manipulation (an important tool in the fight against cheap Chinese exports) are never quite enough. It's called wanting it both ways, an unserious posture if we are intent on eliminating trade barriers around the world.

Yet, even if the foregoing obstacles are overcome, there is the persistent issue of how to market free trade to the general public.

The problems are considerable.

Most private sector employees (and certainly most of those employees within the service sector) do not feel the direct impact of trade policy. Further, trade agreements can lead to job loss, particularly in lower technology sectors of the economy. Unions are expert in exploiting this phenomenon to their political advantage. Congressional Democrats in labor districts know this fact of life all too well.

On the flipside, American business is notoriously poor at marketing the advantages of trade, particularly where new openings to foreign markets lead to the creation of new jobs. In a media context, advocates have failed to make the positive aspects of trade tangible in the same way that opponents have personalized displaced workers in vulnerable sectors.

There is another issue in play: an isolationist trend in the U.S.— an attitude linked to the unsatisfactory conclusion of two expensive wars and a continuing tepid recovery that has failed to temper middle class anxiety.

Going forward, a weakened President Obama will be hard pressed to secure pro-trade votes from protectionist Democrats unhappy with Obamacare's drag on the party. As a result, the president will be forced to rely on GOP support to pass his signature trade agreements.

Trade bills make strange bedfellows indeed.

Building a Business Is Bad Under Obama

The Obama Administration has demonized wealth creation.

May 11, 2014, *The Baltimore Sun*

L et's imagine for a moment a woman (we'll call her Nancy) who had a job but saw limited opportunity for advancement at her place of employment.

So, Nancy began scribbling out unique product designs in her spare time—an exercise that eventually led to a patent for a brand new widget.

But Nancy faced a problem common to every startup entrepreneur—lack of capital. She attempted to secure a loan from a number of local banks but was turned down due to lack of collateral. Seems our lending institutions have raised the stakes in the aftermath of the worst credit crunch in decades. This was especially frustrating because Nancy had a businesswoman's spirit—that willingness to leap into the hyper-competitive world of commerce.

And she would not be derailed. Nancy borrowed money from her parents and cashed in a small portfolio of stock to raise the capital needed to purchase the required equipment. Then, she set up a small manufacturing line in her basement. Nancy's determination and talent for engineering soon produced a modernized widget, which in turn led to a marketing agreement with Home Depot.

Nancy's new contract allowed her to move out of the basement and into a small facility. She hired five new employees, and business grew so quickly that Nancy soon expanded into a larger facility. Today, Nancy employs 49 people. (Given her narrow margins,

Nancy is careful to keep her workforce under the Obamacare mandate.) Her gross sales exceed $10 million a year. The same banks that refused her credit not so long ago now line up to get her business. And competitor widget manufacturers have inquired into whether she would be willing to sell her growing company, to no avail. Nancy is determined to become a dominant player in the widget market.

Many of you may identify with this prototypical American success story. Indeed, many of my readers could easily change out "Nancy" for someone you know—a friend, neighbor or acquaintance—who had a dream to build a business from the ground up. FYI, fill in "Kevin Plank" and "athletic sportswear," and you have the beginnings of the magical hometown story of Under Armour.

Not so long ago in America this storyline was a guaranteed winner. On the campaign stump, candidates for public office would celebrate such entrepreneurial success—often with an electorate grown accustomed to Horatio Alger stories and an American opportunity society. Interestingly, the fact that the Nancies of the world could become wealthy in the process did not detract from the storyline. It was, in fact, seen as a product of what hard work and brains could achieve in the freest marketplace the world has ever witnessed.

Unfortunately, such narratives are out of favor in Barack Obama's America, where wealth creation is consistently made the object of scorn. (What better example than the Obama re-elect campaign's strategy of demonizing Mitt Romney's career in private equity?) And where the seemingly limitless desire for additional tax revenue ("resources") makes class envy the preferred strategy of the left.

Regular readers of this column recognize the relentless mantra of "more, more, more" in every tax and budget debate on Capitol Hill. What I hope you understand is that every time "more" is satisfied with another tax increase, it's not enough. It's never enough. There is always more demand for revenue—more government programs—more need to take from those who "built that."

Sometimes, these builders choose to leave the premises (reference California's and Maryland's experience with wealth migration over the last decade). At other times, the taxing burden is so onerous that it makes no economic sense to start a business. But most of the time, the builders grin and bear it—and wait for the next election cycle.

Today's polls reflect that this group has grown weary of grinning and bearing and being made to wear black hats. After all, it is they who create the jobs (70 percent of new American jobs are created by small business owners) that pay the bills that keep the entire enterprise going.

This anger appears likely to play out in November when many of those senators who voted to give us Obamacare and stimulus and higher taxes will be on the ballot. I hope so—the Nancies of the world (and their employees) deserve better than this. After all, they built that.

The GOP Is Divided Over Ex-Im

Tea party Republicans want to eliminate the U.S. Export-Import Bank while others want to protect it.

July 13, 2014, *The Baltimore Sun*

Most people have never heard of it. Fewer still understand how it operates. But it is the focal point of a (mostly) intramural Republican fight playing out in the halls of Congress. Its ultimate resolution will have dramatic impact on a number of high profile American manufacturers—and the thousands of high profile jobs they represent.

I refer to the Export-Import ("Ex-Im") Bank of the United States. Its charter is to act as a lender/guarantor of last resort (where private sector investment is not available) on behalf of foreign purchasers of U.S. produced goods—mostly high-ticket airplanes and state-of-the-art energy generation equipment.

The heated debate over the propriety of such a financial entity is not new. Free market conservatives have sought to terminate Ex-Im for years. But the push for elimination ("de-authorization" in Congressional speak) gained momentum when newly installed House Majority Leader Kevin McCarthy, a California Republican, indicated his opposition to reauthorization once the bank's charter expires on Sept. 30.

Predictably, the debate splits so-called "establishment" Republicans from their more doctrinal colleagues on the right. The former view the bank as a legitimate financier in business to help protect America's industrial base. For example, Boeing Company's wide body jets are a prime beneficiary of the bank's largesse; the aircraft giant secured approximately two-thirds of Ex-Im's fiscal year 2013 long-term loan guarantees.

Supporters point to foreign finance entities that perform similar financing arrangements on behalf of foreign competitors. They ask why we would unilaterally disarm in the high stakes, high reward world of international trade—especially where the long-term future of the U.S. industrial base could hang in the balance. Also on the plus side is Ex-Im's unique status, which allows it to turn a profit. In fiscal year 2013 for example, the bank returned more than $1 billion in profit to the Treasury (out of a total authorization of $27 billion).

Advocates include a murderers' row of business interests with serious Washington push. Besides Boeing, General Electric Co., the National Association of Manufacturers, and the U.S. Chamber of Commerce are actively weighing in with Republican House Members.

The lobbying is intensely personal to boot. According to recent media reports, every Member of Congress will shortly receive an index card pointing out the businesses in their districts that enjoy Ex-Im support. The card will also reflect the jobs represented by these businesses.

Detractors within the GOP conference (including many tea party-affiliated Members) view the bank's operation as classic corporate welfare-ism. This group is particularly sensitive to "crony capitalism," whereby Uncle Sam plays Santa Claus by picking winners and losers with taxpayer money. Recall the Obama Administration's record of failed green technology start-ups for context. These fiscal hawks would rather the free market determine survivors without taxpayer subsidy and without giving rival carriers overseas (the sometimes beneficiaries of Ex-Im support) an undue advantage through lower finance costs.

The most prominent domestic critic in this regard is Delta Airlines—a competitor that often cites Ex-Im's finance cost subsidy as an unfair advantage in a hyper-competitive marketplace. The airline has even gone to court over Ex-Im's backing of several major airplane deals alleging the bank's failure to fully weigh adverse impact on other U.S. manufacturers.

Unlike most Washington policy showdowns, the battle over Ex-Im's future has been confined to the GOP side of the aisle. Relatively few Democrats sought to make hay of the issue, although then Sen. Barack Obama cited Ex-Im as a prime example of corporate welfare during his presidential campaign in 2008. Now the president supports it and wishes to expand its financing authority.

The ascension of the tea party within the GOP has brought the debate front and center; there is little reason to believe it will subside in the short term. Even some establishment figures such as 2012 vice presidential nominee Rep. Paul Ryan, a Wisconsin Republican, and House Financial Services Committee Chairman Jeb Hensarling, a Texas Republican, are on record as opposing reauthorization. But you can bet big business will continue to fight hard to protect this unique institution and its mission.

My prediction: A coalition of Democrats and mainstream Republicans will help Ex-Im survive this latest attempt on its life. The argument against unilateral disarmament and the reality of subsidized foreign competitors should carry the day. But serious reforms could be in play if the present uprising continues to gather steam. Stay tuned on this one.

PART 3

★ ★ ★

Conservatives at a Cultural Crossroads

"Keep the government out of my pocketbook—
and my bedroom."

SUCH IS A NEW LIBERTARIAN STRAIN SWEEPING THROUGH
America, most pronounced on our college campuses. For
context, check out the next Rand Paul appearance at a
university near you. The dialogue is all about the evils of
government and U.S. internationalism, and absent much
attention to the destabilizing impact of the formerly "JV"
terror team (per President Obama) known as ISIS. In older
circles, the position is portrayed as a moderate self-identity:
conservative on economics, but a social liberal. If only I had
a quarter for every time I have been offered this description
over the last ten years.

This latter identity is particularly popular with the fra-
ternity formerly labeled as Rockefeller Republicans, a once
thriving Northeast and Northwest GOP constituency now
almost out of business, but nevertheless maintaining a special distaste for the dreaded religious right. Membership in
this club requires regular condemnation of the pro-life, pro-
gun, pro-marriage, anti-immigration GOP base, albeit with
a special hostility reserved for the pro-life movement. Its bottom line is never far from the top of its talking points: We
Republicans need to stay away from "divisive" social issues.

This fracturing on the right could not have come at a
more inopportune time given the emergence of a strident

progressivism within the Democratic Party. Indeed, for the Obama left, it's "anything goes" time: abortion on demand, strict gun control, lax border security, profligate spending, and an end to American exceptionalism. Oh, and let's not forget wholesale federal pre-emption of just about every aspect of your life, most recently your local police department.

All of which leaves common sense conservatives at a crossroads, some might even characterize it as a "turning point." Either minimize cultural issues in order to attract independents or simply give in to the left. I reject this false dichotomy, jettisoning the withdrawal option in favor of a less antagonistic engagement in the culture wars. In other words, a declaration that our values (still) count—but a diversity of opinion is tolerated—even encouraged. I realize this degree of calibrated temperance is difficult to achieve, let alone maintain in the daily street fights of the culture wars. But this is a *real deal* American pluralism, appearing in stark contrast to the harsh speech codes, intolerant political correctness, and general valueless-ness of today's left.

The Father Factor

February 19, 2012, *The Baltimore Sun*

Epidemics typically generate an emotional response from the afflicted, especially where the disease brings about great carnage. Yet, one of the most gruesome conditions within contemporary America proceeds apace, with only periodic bursts of serious attention.

The epidemic in question is fatherlessness, and the cultural consequences are frightening. Here is a sampling of the damage taken from statistics researched by "The Fatherless Generation" project:

- 90 percent of homeless and runaway children are from fatherless homes;

- 85 percent of children who suffer from behavioral disorders are from fatherless homes;

- 71 percent of high school dropouts are from fatherless homes;

- nearly 60 percent of all children living in poverty reside in a single female parent household; and

- daughters raised without an involved father are 53 percent more likely to marry as teenagers, 71 percent more likely to have children as teenagers, 164 percent more likely to experience a premarital birth, and 92 percent more likely to get divorced.

It should not be lost on policymakers (and taxpayers) that all of the traditional markers noted herein (homelessness, runaways, dropouts, single-female-headed households) have direct links to poverty. They also have direct links to increased public costs through government assistance programs.

Of course, not all fatherless homes suffer impoverishment or produce troubled children. There are many hardworking single parents and guardians who overcome daunting obstacles to raise highly successful children. Often grandparents, extended family, mentors, and friends help in filling the void left by an absent dad. But cases of beating the odds are more the exception than the rule; fatherlessness continues to be an accurate predictor of adolescent difficulties.

The mere citation of the foregoing numbers can rile certain progressive pundits into hyper-defensive mode, as if the recognition of the problem and its awful consequences is somehow "insensitive." Well, the time for sensitivity has come and gone. A politically correct lens will not hide the damage brought about by this "disease." And time is of the essence. Every day without a renewed culture-wide commitment to active fatherhood means more kids placed at risk; every day produces more kids headed for a criminal justice system ill-equipped to handle the myriad of mental health problems carried by this troubled population.

During my tenures as governor, congressman, and legislator, I visited many of Maryland's juvenile and adult correctional facilities. Often, I left in a melancholy mood. These are no places for the faint of heart. The scenes are right out of "Scared Straight" and disturbingly predictable: jails full of mostly young men with little formal education. Dropouts are plentiful. Many are alcohol or substance abusers. Some suffer from mental illness. Few possess marketable skills. And a majority come from fatherless homes.

Our correctional system is expected to perform rehabilitative miracles. Unfortunately, far too many of our young offenders are received in damaged condition. Turnarounds are difficult (but not impossible) to achieve. And the task is made ever more challenging by the absence of an involved father.

Personal experience has further strengthened my views as to the pivotal role of fathers and male role models in childhood development. I have coached a youth football team for the last six years. This time has allowed me to watch firsthand the physical and emotional development of young boys from a variety of family backgrounds. My (reinforced) takeaway: Boys need father-inspired discipline. Any youth coach will tell you there are plenty of children without such influence. For them, the long-term prognosis is typically not a positive one.

So many social issues tend to break along liberal and conservative lines. This issue, however, stands alone: Young children require parental guidance, and fathers play an essential role in providing it. Despite periodic delusional messages from Hollywood to the contrary, this notion still represents a majority view. And everyone from President Barack Obama to Jay-Z to Pat Buchanan has said so.

Nevertheless, too much lip service and not enough actual fatherhood has produced too many problematic young people. Our cultural epidemic of fatherlessness is out of control. It reflects a weakening of our cultural values. And there is no one government program to save the day, either. It must be a collective effort to fix our culture, to make such results unacceptable in America. Failure to act will perpetuate our present desultory track, a truly unacceptable result.

A Letter to My Son: On Marijuana

Maryland's former governor tells his 14-year-old son why the teen should avoid pot.

February 16, 2014, *The Baltimore Sun*

Dear Drew,

I've been thinking a great deal about marijuana lately.

You can't turn on the television without seeing breathless reporters talking about a new cultural enthusiasm for legalizing weed. Two states (Colorado and Washington) have legalized marijuana possession for personal use. And it's probably only a matter of time before Maryland joins the party—pun intended.

You are now 14 years old. A high school freshman. Homework and sports dominate your life. Your goals are unlimited. Your mother and I think you are terrific, but not perfect. We also know you face the same issues and pressures any young person faces in today's permissive society.

So, this is not "THE TALK"—not in front of a couple hundred thousand readers, anyway.

But it is a reminder of what Mom and I have discussed with you since you were 7.

First, let's get every parent's 800-pound gorilla out of the way: No, I didn't touch the stuff. My reasons were pretty compelling: I was never interested in setting fire to something before I placed it in my mouth; smoking marijuana was (and is) illegal; and I knew better than to blow the scholarship opportunities that had been given to me.

I may have been more the exception than the rule for my generation, however. Marijuana was on every college campus in the 1970s, much like it is today. Many of my friends experimented socially, some smoked on a regular basis.

I did not think less of them for their actions nor did I lose friends in the process. Most did not develop a habit that led to harder drugs. But I did leave the room/dorm/area whenever the stuff began to be passed around. I didn't wish to pay the price for someone else's dumb decision making.

There is another, less direct connection I have with marijuana.

You know I have served in the state legislature, Congress and as governor. These positions gave me a chance to visit dozens of jails and prisons (juvenile and adult) throughout Maryland.

These are awful places. Many of the facilities are right out of "Scared Straight"—nasty, depressing institutions where dangerous people are housed in crowded conditions. (Thank God we have people willing to work in such environments.)

My most lasting impressions resulted from discussions with the inmates. They were white, black, male, female, poor, wealthy. Their previous stations in life didn't much matter—99 percent of the time their stories had a common denominator: addiction. Typically, an addiction that had led to the commission of a crime and then incarceration. And that habit seemingly always began with weed.

Often, we watch comedians or one or another of our cultural value makers poke fun at parental over-reaction to pot, A.K.A. "killer weed." These folks confidently point out that the "gateway drug" really isn't since so many people can handle their recreational drug of choice. I guess most people do handle it, just not the inmates I met in those Maryland prisons. I wish the image makers could experience what I've experienced. If they did, I don't think they would find marijuana quite so funny, or its legalization quite so clear-cut.

A few years ago, my friends in the Bush Administration got angry at my support of medical marijuana. They saw it as a backdoor step toward legalization. I saw it as one (merciful) option for those suf-fering from intense pain due to a dire or terminal condition. (An up-close experience with your 44-year-old, cancer-stricken uncle had only strengthened my conviction here.) Anyway, there is a world of difference between those suffering from devastating illness and those who simply wish to get high.

Parenting has a life cycle. The older you get, the less control I have over your life. This is as it should be. Indeed, college is all about exploring and grappling with newfound freedoms. It's called growing up.

Some kids will go wild. "Chains off" means "anything goes." The vast majority will survive, to their parents' everlasting relief.

Others will not be so fortunate. Here, bad decisions will lead to bad results—wasted opportunities—lost lives.

Mom and I want you to learn, explore, have fun. But when someone next month, next year or four years from now offers you a joint, we have one request: Think for a second about those kids I met so many years ago—the ones who couldn't handle it. Some looked just like you.

Voter ID Laws Uphold System's Integrity

Mixed-up priorities are revealed when purchasing allergy medicine requires a photo ID but voting doesn't.

February 24, 2012, *The Baltimore Sun*

Two recent bulletins place progressive outrage about voting rights in interesting perspective.

Item No. 1: The latest "Pew Center on the States Report" found 24 million invalid voter registrations and nearly 2 million dead people still on U.S. voter rolls.

Item No. 2: South Carolina has sued the U.S. Department of Justice—a result of the DOJ's decision to block the state from requiring voters to show government-issued identification in order to vote.

For many of us, this juxtaposition is a head scratcher. One might think the "powers that be" would focus on fixes to broken election systems around the country. Yet in South Carolina, the full power of the federal government is aligned against a state for having the temerity to require a reliable source of identification prior to exercising our most fundamental right. The government's rationale? Such a requirement is discriminatory against minority voters who may not possess the requisite documents. Justice may need more lawyers to handle its forthcoming workload, however. Fifteen states have passed photo identification laws over the past year, and the Supreme Court has recently upheld the constitutionality of a similar law in Indiana.

The issue has hit home enough with me that I wrote about it in my new book, where I recount how my seasonal allergies necessitate periodic visits to the local drugstore for Claritin D. My familiar face and name do not secure a pass from having to produce Maryland photo identification, however. (It seems a certain ingredient in this form of the medication can be used in the manufacture of meth-amphetamine.) Accordingly, I dutifully produce my driver's license. No big deal, you might say. A rational explanation for an ever-so-slight imposition.

Yet, on Election Day in Maryland and 19 other states, the experience is reversed; every time I produce that same Maryland driver's license to poll watchers, I am assured that no such requirement is imposed by the state. A rational takeaway: Our state and federal government value the regulation of my over-the-counter allergy medicine far more than the exercise of the most important individual right possessed by an American citizen.

Some excuse these mixed-up priorities on the basis that there are potential voters (mostly poor) who truly do not possess valid photo identification. Interestingly, this justification is offered during a time when it is becoming increasingly difficult to live in the United States without some form of reliable ID. And there is no shortage of documents that pass muster under state photo ID laws: driver's licenses, passports, naturalization papers, and student IDs, to name a few.

There are also options for the few who do not possess acceptable identification. Photo ID states typically allow provisional voting, so any potential voter can complete a ballot by supplying an acceptable form of identification before the election is certified. In South Carolina, the Department of Motor Vehicles will issue a free photo identification card to anyone who wishes to vote.

Religious freedom is also protected in photo ID states: Those with religious objections to being photographed need only sign an affidavit setting forth the reason they do not possess a photo ID.

As the debate over photo identification and voting rights rages in courts and state legislatures, it is illuminating that the proponents of "anything goes" voting fail to account for the interest of minorities in a free and fair electoral process that only counts legal votes. Voting rights are about access, transparency, and accuracy—requirements that have not always been guaranteed to African Americans and other minorities.

Ballot security concerns are heightened in so-called sanctuary states, where undocumented aliens are encouraged to live and work. It is a source of local embarrassment that Maryland and a few of its subdivisions have chosen this course. This "welcome wagon" for illegal immigrants may reflect a majoritarian view in progressive Maryland; nevertheless, it makes the realization of free and fair elections far more difficult.

The simple task of producing reliable photo identification at the polls should be a no-brainer. Every illegal vote cast and counted degrades our democracy. Lax immigration enforcement only magnifies the problem. Many of us in Maryland's significant political minority wish the state of South Carolina well in its battle against a misguided federal government.

Democrats' Insulting Play for the "Women's Vote"

Back-and-forth misses the point that gender should not be considered a predictor of political views.

April 22, 2012, *The Baltimore Sun*

The all-out battle for women's votes has begun in earnest, with the respective presidential campaigns each seeking to take advantage of real (and perceived) mistakes by the opposition and its acolytes.

The verbal volleyball match has been interesting to watch, as each camp seeks to prove how its candidate is the only true protector of women's rights.

A brief review: The Obama Administration commences a frontal assault on the conscience clause, that heretofore universally accepted exemption for religious institutions that prevented them from being forced to perform procedures and therapies contrary to their religious tenets. The Catholic bishops and other religious leaders raise strenuous objections, which lead the Administration to offer a hasty, so-called "compromise" exemption. Many religious leaders are not impressed with the more narrow conscience provision, however. Advantage: GOP.

Shortly thereafter, a major fundraiser for Rick Santorum publicly reminisces about the era when birth control meant an aspirin placed between a woman's legs. This statement was soon joined with the former senator's circa 2006 interview wherein he labeled contraception "harmful to women." Immediately, the Democratic

Party pounced: This was the "gotcha moment" operatives had been waiting for. Finally, a chance to prove the GOP's "war on women."

This alleged war has been in the Democratic National Committee's playbook for years. It's a favorite "go to" charge in the abortion debate, so it was no surprise that the mainstream media would run with it. Polls conducted after the Santorum flap reflected a widening GOP gender gap. Democratic fundraisers used the charge in their fundraising letters. Feminists rallied around the latest evidence of how out of touch the GOP is with today's women. Advantage: Obama Administration.

Next, another stroke of good luck for Democrats: Rush Limbaugh, the left's favorite punching bag, labeled a Georgetown Law student a "slut" and "prostitute" after her congressional testimony supporting the proposition that her (Catholic) university's health insurance should cover contraception. An empathetic President Barack Obama calls her to offer support, thereby further fueling the fire. Shortly thereafter, Mr. Limbaugh issues an apology after several sponsors pull their advertising from his show. The GOP presidential contenders are again forced on the defensive. Big-time advantage: Obama.

Alas, all good things must come to an end. This political good fortune came to a crushing conclusion recently when Democratic senior adviser Hilary Rosen spoke her mind about how she viewed stay-at-home mom Ann Romney, [who] "had never worked a day in her life." Ms. Rosen gratuitously included a shot at Ann Romney's husband, whom she dismissed as someone who "seems so old-fashioned when it comes to women. . . . He just doesn't really see us as equal."

The exclamation mark to Ms. Rosen's bad day was supplied by none other than Mrs. Romney herself, who responded with a point obvious to all who live outside the far left wing of Democratic Party feminism: Stay-at-home moms work as hard as anybody. The response was an immediate home run. It caused an embarrassed White House to quickly throw Ms. Rosen under the bus. It has, for the moment, placed the Democrats on the gender defensive for a change. Advantage: GOP.

The thrust of Ms. Rosen's remarks go to the selectivity of the progressive/feminist perspective. "Choice" has been the mantra of this group forever, except when women choose options contrary to their progressive litmus test. Witness the vitriol directed at Sarah Palin by the likes of former South Carolina Democratic Party Chairwoman Carol Fowler for her choice to deliver a disabled child. Witness the character assassinations directed toward conservative women such as Condoleezza Rice, Michele Bachmann, and Michelle Malkin.

Such antagonisms run deep. Gloria Steinem once dismissed Sen. Kay Bailey Hutchison as a "female impersonator," while Naomi Wolf notoriously castigated Ambassador Jeane Kirkpatrick as being "uninflected by the experiences of the female body."

That Ms. Rosen felt comfortable issuing the "mom-at-home" indictment was no surprise. It is by now a familiar charge. Political operatives at all levels should be careful in propagating this line of attack, however. The notion that women interpret the world from a single perspective is ludicrous and insulting to women—and men—who vote.

Here's a thought: Let's stop viewing gender (or race and ethnicity) as a predictor of one's political views. Now that would be advantage: America.

Key Demographics of the 2012 Campaign: Youth, Women, and Hispanics

Robert L. Ehrlich Jr. sees GOP opportunities in areas where Democrats claim an advantage.

May 12, 2012, *The Baltimore Sun*

Campaign 2012 is now joined. The darts that have been traded between the Obama and Romney camps now have extra-sharp tips. And it's going to stay this way through to Nov. 2. Most pundits predict a "razor close" and "particularly ugly" campaign. I concur.

So, which storyline is a political junkie to follow in light of the 24/7 coverage given to this race for the ages? Which subplot is most instructive with regard to the ultimate outcome?

A few thoughts for your consideration:

Youth. Young voters were a key part of the Obama constituency circa 2008, but far less so today. It's difficult under any circumstances to maintain a rock star status with any age group, let alone one (traditionally) least apt to show up at the polls. Four years of high unemployment have not helped in this regard. "Hope" and "change" have proved to be all of the former and none of the latter. Today, 54 percent of college graduates (many facing repayment of staggering student loans) are underemployed or unemployed. Still, the president's telegenic charm, youthful persona, and feckless charges of an alleged GOP plan to cut college scholarships present a significant challenge to the perceived "not-so-cool" Mitt Romney.

The Romney campaign's response to date has been predictable, but solid: Who better understands the dynamics of private-sector job creation? Here, the unapologetic capitalist enjoys a distinct advantage over the community organizer/law professor.

Women. The so-called war on women mantra is not new. It is a familiar indictment against the GOP and its candidates, even its female candidates. For context, recall Democratic operative Hilary Rosen's recent comment that former Governor Romney "seems so old-fashioned when it comes to women . . . he just doesn't really see us as equal." One problem, however: The indictment plays to mixed results with so many women (particularly those who are primary breadwinners) struggling along with this tepid recovery. Further, it is a fact of political life that not all women are pro-choice, liberal Democrats. Again, an opening for Mr. Romney to charge the president with an economy that cannot find its job-producing mojo. An unemployment rate in excess of 8 percent for 37 straight months is a huge obstacle for any incumbent president.

That a prohibitively expensive, haphazardly crafted stimulus has done little to improve our economy is yet another dagger in the president's economic record. Vice President Joe Biden's various public promises that the stimulus would solve our economic downturn will be grist for the Romney media folks.

A reminder for GOP'ers, however: The Obama campaign will continue to associate Rick Santorum's views on contraception with those of Mitt Romney. Do not allow the national debate to slip away from economic issues. Do not fall into the contraception trap. It will be the Romney campaign's fault if the tactic succeeds.

Hispanics. This Democratic-leaning constituency is a growing economic and political force—but this description does not begin to delve into the complexities of the Hispanic vote. For one thing, the influential Cuban-American vote is decidedly pro-GOP (hence the strong support for U.S. Sen. Marco Rubio for the Romney VP slot), while most other Hispanics lean Democratic.

Further, Hispanics have decidedly mixed views on immigration: Hispanic immigrants who followed the law and waited their turn to become American citizens are not so sympathetic to the cause of illegal immigration. Many believe immigration rates are too high. There is sharp division on whether illegal immigration has a positive effect on immigrants. Opinions are further tempered with the knowledge that many families are split up as a result of uneven enforcement practices.

Nevertheless, national surveys consistently reflect majority Hispanic support for the notion that immigrants should learn to speak English. A majority support making English the official language. Further, a bent toward traditional Catholicism and strong family values provides an opportunity for a Romney "values pitch" to this pivotal group.

But, like everything else this election cycle, it all comes back to the economy. Hispanic small business ownership has increased during boom times. Not so much during the Obama era. Hispanic chambers of commerce are a growing force in many communities. Entrepreneurship is a powerful goal with this group. Businessman Romney can play here, if he so chooses.

In D.C. Schools, Obama Chooses Unions Over Kids

President zeroes out funding for popular voucher program

May 20, 2012, *The Baltimore Sun*

Just when you thought the District of Columbia Opportunity Scholarship Program for poor, predominantly minority kids was fully protected from politics, here comes the Obama Administration with another broadside.

The popular program (which falls under congressional jurisdiction) allows impoverished children in the notoriously underperforming D.C. public school system to attend area private schools with vouchers of up to $12,000. Its contentious history includes full-scale support from congressional Republicans and the George W. Bush Administration. Unfortunately, but not surprisingly, it took but a few short months for a new Obama Administration to pull the plug on new applicants in 2009. The scheduled termination of the program was just another sop to anti-school-choice teachers unions from a union-friendly president.

Today's politics are marked by short-term, turbulent election cycles, however. And so the 2010 midterm elections brought a new House GOP majority to Capitol Hill. Shortly thereafter, pro-voucher Speaker John Boehner was quick to include $20 million (over five years) in voucher aid as an integral part of his 2011 spending deal with a still-resistant Administration.

Talk about the difference one election can make: one new House majority; one new House speaker; hundreds of poor, mostly

African American schoolchildren (again) provided the opportunity to choose quality over monopoly; and thousands of relieved, often tearful parents filled with gratitude.

This show of emotion is not surprising. The program is quite popular. Public opinion polls reflect clear majority support within the District. And there is a reason for such public support. Objective analysis from a variety of well-respected investigators (including the research arm of the Obama Administration's Education Department) reflects what common sense would lead one to suspect: Voucher recipients score better on standardized reading tests and enjoy substantially higher graduation rates, as compared with their peers in the D.C. public schools.

Simply put, the program works.

Nevertheless, now comes the Obama Administration with an election-year attempt to gin up its left flank by zeroing out voucher funding in its fiscal 2013 budget. The targeted beneficiaries: teachers unions and their anti-voucher allies in Congress. One especially troubling provision would prohibit students who were unsuccessful in the program's lottery from reapplying the next year. For anyone who has seen the raw emotional responses of parents to the news of their child's selection (or rejection) in one of these lotteries, this is a particularly nasty step in the wrong direction.

There are those public school advocates who oppose any form of public school choice. They view any option outside of the traditional public school setting as detrimental and in direct contradiction to the role of public education. Their answer to the many ills besetting so many of our underperforming school systems never changes: "Give 'em more money." And so we have, at every level of government.

But times are changing. Governments are stretched for cash. Taxpayers are demanding ever more accountability. The time for more money has come and gone. Dysfunctional school systems require fundamental change. Time has shown that good money after bad is not the answer.

Today, advocates of school choice come in many varieties: black and white, urban and rural, liberal and conservative, Democrat and Republican. They are increasingly willing to take a chance— to choose "all of the above"—when it comes to the education of our most challenging students.

In the District of Columbia, one of the "above" options is to give some poor kids a shot at a private school education. It is an opportunity to punch a ticket at a place that will nurture their intellectual skills. Of course, not everyone who applies is chosen; this one program is not *the* answer to our considerable educational challenges. But it is a part of the answer.

Anxious D.C. parents are awaiting the president's decision. Many rightly see the voucher program as their best opportunity to escape the pull of multigenerational poverty. Let's hope the leader who so convincingly talks about compassion will find some for a group of vulnerable kids living in his own backyard.

In a Gaffe, Obama's Worldview Is Revealed

The president makes clear that he views the nation's problem as too little government, not too much.

June 18, 2012, *The Baltimore Sun*

The political world is a-twitter about the president's recent statements on the condition of the economy.

You know, the one where President Barack Obama said the private sector is "doing fine." Well, that one was not received in the way it was intended. In fact, it generated so much ridicule that a few hours later the president again took to the public stage in order to correct his initial assessment. The subsequent damage control statement did little to calm the political waters, however. But it did a lot to illuminate this president's state of mind regarding job creation and the private sector.

It was in the second media hit that the president reminded us of his true worldview. To wit, that while there is hurt in the private sector, the real problems with our economy concern the austerity measures instituted by state and local governments over the past few years. In essence, the economy suffers because we don't have enough government in our lives. (And this despite a massive public sector spending binge pursuant to his stimulus bill.)

Such a non sequitur requires further investigation into the president's psyche.

That the president is an intelligent man is beyond dispute. That his life experiences are (almost) wholly outside the private sector is equally true. For those in doubt, recall the resume: college, law school, community organizer, law school lecturer, author, state senator, U.S. senator, and president. Private sector experience is limited to a part-time associate's position at a Chicago law firm while a member of the Illinois legislature.

His youthful and early adulthood associations have been well reported—if not so well analyzed. These included relationships with the ultra progressive likes of poet Frank Marshall Davis, anti-war bombers William Ayers and Bernardine Dohrn, Harvard Law School professors Derrick Bell and Charles Ogletree, and the infamous Rev. Jeremiah Wright. In 2008, such associations gave rise to dire fears within GOP and conservative circles. But these concerns failed to play out much beyond the Republican right wing. Indeed, the last presidential campaign was about hope and change, not so much about questionable friendships and ideology.

Four years later, we have a more complete picture of the man, his philosophical approach, and value system.

To his credit, the president has shown a willingness to jettison campaign positions when national security is at issue. Witness the Administration's turnaround on issues such as the closing of the prison at Guantanamo Bay, civilian trials for enemy combatants, rendition of terror suspects, and escalation of the drone campaign in Afghanistan. And the world's most notorious terrorist was brought to justice on his watch. In these particular instances, the president has rejected his left leaning advisors—to the country's benefit.

With regard to economic initiatives, a clear and consistent picture emerges: The president is an instinctively progressive politician prone to flights of hyper-partisanship when he doesn't get his way. He advances federal preemption and a large-scale entitlement state over states' rights. He possesses a European social democrat's disdain for market capitalism and its inegalitarian consequences. Most importantly, he has an intellectual knowledge but lacks a practical grasp of how jobs are generated in the private sector. And the foregoing statement about what's really wrong with the economy is a telling insight into how the president wishes the country (and economy) would operate.

The president's policy agenda is by now quite familiar: more Keynesian stimulus, more entitlement spending, more public sector jobs, and more taxes on the rich (and not so rich) to pay for it all.

So, after all the town hall debates, phone banks, mass emails, and seemingly endless accusations and counter-charges, it all comes down to a rather fundamental difference of opinion: The president's egalitarian instincts lead to calls for greater government activism, the better to create a more equitable distribution of goods and services. Mitt Romney's market instincts lead to calls for less government intrusion, the better to create more opportunity for profit and economic growth.

These contrasting views of right and left are as old as the nation itself. But today's stakes are higher than normal. We have undergone a deep recession and tepid recovery. Our debt rating has been downgraded. Entitlement spending is out of control. The president has increased debt more than every president from George Washington through George H. W. Bush combined. And the American Dream's promise that you will live better than your parents is increasingly at risk.

America's middle class is nervous. That attitude typically spells "big problems" for an incumbent president. And I bet most taxpayers do not see additional deficit spending as the first (or best) remedy for what ails us.

Whether It's the Economy or the Colorado Shooting, the Left and Right View the World in Predictable Ways

More gun control wouldn't have stopped the Colorado shooter, and more government interference won't fix our economy either.

August 4, 2012, *The Baltimore Sun*

The gulf between the American left and right continues to widen against a backdrop of high unemployment, weak growth, and high-octane cultural battles.

I got to thinking about this growing divide in the aftermath of the Colorado movie theater shooting spree that left 12 dead, 58 injured, and a nation in shock.

Once the gravity of the story began to sink in, my mind turned to an inconvenient (for some) thought: How many lives would have been saved if someone in that theater had access to a firearm of their own?

On the other side of the divide, gun control advocates raced to use the tragedy as an opportunity to expand federal gun laws. A group of usual suspects led by Sens. Chuck Schumer and Frank Lautenberg and Mayor Michael Bloomberg were the first to jump. Similar to the outcry in the wake of the parking lot shooting of U.S. Rep. Gabby Giffords, many on the left view additional gun control as the "go to" answer whenever a gun-related tragedy occurs.

The aftermath of the 9/11 attacks brought equally stark, diametrically opposed views to an important national security debate.

Everyone began from the same premise: new screening procedures were required at our nation's airports. But how to get it done?
On the right, the inclination was to work with the private airlines
in building additional security infrastructure. On the left, the reflexive impulse was to create a new federal agency to run airport security. (Seems that traumatic national events always lead to new
federal agencies and expanded federal power.) And so the post-9/11
debate gave birth to the Transportation Security Administration.
Whether the creation of the TSA was the correct call will play itself
out over time.

Congressional reaction to the recent mortgage crisis is another
example. Conservatives saw the meltdown as the result of inappropriate government meddling and regulation: first, encouraging
the notion that nearly everyone could afford a mortgage without
regard to credit history and income; second, ordering the lower-
ing of underwriting standards at Fannie Mae and Freddie Mac in
order that more sub-prime loan packages could be bought and sold;
and third, perpetuating a social justice approach to the application
of the Community Reinvestment Act, thereby leveraging banks to
approve ever-larger numbers of sub-prime loans on behalf of high-
risk consumers.

On the left, the meltdown was seen as the result of Wall Street
greed—of ever-hungry brokers knowingly selling toxic assets to the
world in order to generate huge fees and bonuses. The increasingly
infamous Dodd-Frank financial regulation bill with its enormous
costs and thousands of pages of rules represents a typical Congressional response.

Perhaps no present-day debate makes my point better than how
the respective sides view wealth. Conservatives tend to celebrate the
status, especially where one's personal wealth is the result of blood,
sweat, and toil. You know, that old "self-made man" thing. Even the
accumulation of great wealth is no cause for alarm—most wealthy
people exercise their moral responsibility to give back. Check it out:
Americans lead the world in philanthropic giving.

"Angst" is the more appropriate description of how many liberals view this same phenomenon. Even greater discord is produced when great wealth is accomplished. Here, only major tax increases serve to assuage the progressive mindset. That this view is less about tax policy (even a 100 percent marginal tax rate on income in excess of $250,000 a year would not make a dent in our $16 trillion dollar federal debt) and more about egalitarian social policy is increasingly apparent.

These disparate views of wealth also provide insight into why Democrats and Republicans disagree on the right prescription for what ails our economy.

Both see a jobless recovery, slow growth, gloomy economic forecasts, and a worried American middle class.

The Democrats' solution is predictable: additional stimulus, more public sector spending, and steep, progressive tax increases. Recall President Barack Obama's infamous assertion that the private sector is doing "just fine" amid his call for more public sector jobs to bolster the economy.

Across the aisle, Republicans respond in equally predictable fashion: less spending, entitlement reform, and a tax cut for small business owners.

The election of 2008 propelled a free-spending, doctrinaire progressive into the White House; a gigantic stimulus, Obamacare, and $5 trillion dollars in new debt soon followed.

Two years later, it was a quite different storyline as a tea-party inspired tide returned House control to the GOP. The president's domestic agenda has been stalled ever since.

Election 2012 will be the tiebreaker. One of the two competing worldviews will carry the day.

America Isn't Greece—At Least Not Yet

The founders' vision of limited government and individual initiative can be salvaged.

August 12, 2012, *The Baltimore Sun*

Unidentified woman: "Well, doctor, what have we got—a Republic or a Monarchy?"
Ben Franklin: "A Republic, if you can keep it."

My periodic public speeches around the country usually end with an extended question and answer period. I enjoy these sessions because the tone and tenor of the questions provides me insight into the public mood.

One question that pops up with increasing frequency is a modern day adaptation of Franklin's historic dare: whether our Constitutional Republic and free-market capitalism are salvageable. The issue is typically presented in a negative light, as in "Aren't we past the point of no return when it comes to the scope of government intrusion into our lives?"

Not surprisingly, the issue is more frequently presented in conservative audiences, where the Obama Administration is often Exhibit A for the "we're finished" crowd.

Well, the honest answer to this most distressing of questions is yes, and no.

With regard to yes, there is no doubt the federal government has grown inexorably large. Federal spending in 2011 was $3,603,100,000,000. The federal deficit for 2011 was $1.3 trillion. And federal debt is projected to be 70 percent of gross domestic product by the end of 2012. Today, Congress and an activist judiciary ensure that the federal government reaches into every nook and cranny of American life, from local public education to health care. And Congress meets every year, which means government grows every year.

A further disquieting point for conservatives: The wholesale expansion of federal power has been a bipartisan phenomenon. Republicans have far too often acquiesced to relentless Democratic attempts to expand federal jurisdiction.

So the commonly accepted view that Republicans are the party of big government and Democrats the party of really, really big government rings true in many respects.

Another popular indictment in particular audiences is that President Barack Obama is a closet socialist, which he clearly is not. Socialism contemplates governmental ownership of the means of production and distribution—a view never espoused by the president. A more accurate label would be "European style social democrat," a worldview reflected in the president's relentless campaign to make an already progressive federal income tax code more progressive and to expand government entitlements whenever feasible.

An unassailable conclusion presents itself: The rapid expansion of federal power shows no sign of slowing down. And each generation of Americans has grown increasingly more comfortable with a large federal presence in our lives. Accordingly, it is difficult to imagine any successful effort to walk back significant portions of the modern welfare state.

Now, for the good news. All is not lost. Jeffersonian ideals prosper in many parts of the country. A majority of Americans continue to value individual enterprise. We have no shortage of entrepreneurs ready and willing to take risks in order to be successful. A majority of our citizens still view government largesse as a temporary helping hand rather than a way of life. And, at least over the past few years, a number of successful governors have begun to turn the tide against perpetual government growth and the more radical elements of public sector unionism. Indeed, at least in America, a significant number of public sector employees recognize the need for more balance in their benefit packages. It is a trend that must continue if we are to avoid more of the bankruptcies hitting California's municipalities so hard today.

For context, examine the sorry state of so many European economies. Huge debt burdens, high marginal tax rates, low productivity, unaffordable public sector benefits, and an only recently demonstrated willingness to recognize pending fiscal crises, are pervasive.

In Greece, the head of the state power company employees' union claims that "people and their needs are far more important than the needs of the market." Such a sound bite sounds so wonderfully populist, until one realizes that it is a healthy, competitive market that produces the goods that feed the people and their needs. No wonder Greece's sharp left turn has been so disastrous. This is the face of real socialism. And it has produced the always guaranteed (but never quite expected) results.

We are not Greece, yet. A majority of Americans continue to value enterprise over entitlement, capitalism over socialism. But we had better pay attention to what truly produces opportunity and wealth before the comparisons become more accurate and we fail old Ben's wonderfully blunt instruction.

Bring on the Midterms: GOP Still Has Plenty of Opportunity for Gains

Bob Ehrlich says Republicans can win next time by focusing on immigration, gun law enforcement, and fiscal responsibility.

February 10, 2013, *The Baltimore Sun*

L ast week's column chronicled a dire set of circumstances regarding our economy and culture at the onset of Obama II. This status quo is complicated by an aggressive liberal establishment attempting to take advantage of the president's post-election momentum and an always compliant mainstream media.

And then there's the necessity of offering an inviting conservative message, attractive to the all-important swing voter—a vital constituency that supported the president by a significant margin in 2012.

The task is easier said than done, but not impossible.

Here are some planks (and tactics) as the midterm election cycle begins:

Gripe sessions: Post-election self-reflection summits can be productive, but enough of the Dr. Phil moments. Remember, your opponents live for incidents of self-abasement; try not to provide them further ammunition.

Gun control: Speaking of ammunition, it is time to articulate a more positive posture on the issue of gun violence. We know how the media loves to degrade pro-Second Amendment views.

We further recall how this president views our predilections (". . . they cling to guns or religion . . ."). Accordingly, we remain open to suggestions that will keep firearms away from criminals and mentally unstable people, including ways to strengthen the federal background-check database system.

We also stand behind initiatives such as "Project Exile," a federal/state partnership that targets felons in possession of illegal firearms. U.S. attorneys must target these prosecutions; bad guys understand "federal time" means mandatory time behind bars.

Further, we should emphasize the irony of most gun control measures: No gun law can force the bad guys to register their guns or subject themselves to a background check, since it's already illegal for felons to possess a firearm.

Immigration: Post-election polls confirm that ill-chosen rhetoric and Bush-era immigration debates have turned off Hispanic and Asian voters otherwise attracted to GOP fiscal and social messages. The present debate presents an opportunity to: 1) pass sound policy; 2) appeal anew to these very "gettable" voting blocs, and 3) put this issue behind us.

First, we must strengthen the border using the latest technology and enforcement techniques. We live in the age of low-tech terrorism. This is a bipartisan no-brainer.

Second, we should support a "path to legality." Sen. Marco Rubio (and a bipartisan group of senators) recently announced a sensible approach: Those already here must pass a gauntlet (register, pay back taxes and fines, pass a background check, demonstrate current employment, learn English) in order to qualify for probationary status, i.e., become eligible for a green card. This process creates transparency, penalizes previous illegal acts, and (re)generates respect for the rule of law.

Most importantly, it respects millions of immigrants who honored our immigration laws, since this group is assured of keeping priority status in applying for the card. One additional element:

The newly lawful "probationary immigrants" will be ineligible for federal welfare benefits.

Spending and deficits: This is a tough one. GOP attempts to engage the voting public over debt clocks and nearly broke entitlement programs generated a collective yawn last November. Yet, we know there is no more important issue. A sequestration process scheduled to kick in about three weeks from now (representing $85 billion in spending cuts) presents an opportunity to blaze a more sensible spending path. Please note that sequestration is neither thoughtful nor equitable. It's simply the only option currently available to the plurality of fiscal hawks in Washington, D.C.

Further, it's not as though President Barack Obama, Senate Majority Leader Harry Reid, and House Minority Leader Nancy Pelosi have offered any serious plan to rein in Washington's insatiable spending appetite. (Recall the president's recent insistence to Speaker Boehner, "We don't have a spending problem.") The bottom line: We have a spending addiction and few prescriptions to save us. But it is not required that we talk about it all the time, just that we act when the opportunity arises.

Single women: another tough one. Single women with children and limited economic opportunities are logically drawn to the party of government; many are reliant on that government for their sustenance. This group is not terribly attracted to notions of individualism, entrepreneurship, or the Second Amendment. Many just want to figure out how to pay the bills. So tell them we will help pay the bills, but that steps toward self-reliance are expected as well. And (putting aside the issue of abortion) we have no interest in limiting their access to contraceptive options, Democratic Party messaging notwithstanding. A further point: A renewed focus on fatherhood and male role models within single (female) households with kids is long overdue.

There you have it—a platform of serious immigration reform, gun law enforcement, fiscal sense, female empowerment, and positive messaging. Not so complicated. Let's get to it.

Seeking a Comeback for Catholic Education

Robert Ehrlich says the decline of Catholic schools in Baltimore is a tragedy for the city's young people.

April 15, 2013, *The Baltimore Sun*

As many of you know, I was born and raised in solidly working class Arbutus. My family's Protestantism qualified us as an anomaly; the majority of the neighborhood kids were Catholic. Most attended local Catholic schools such as Ascension, Our Lady of Victory, and St. Mark's. A majority of them went on to graduate from high school at Cardinal Gibbons, Mount St. Joe, or Seton.

This school experience provided parents an attractive "three-fer": religious instruction, challenging academics, and excellent athletics—at a reasonable price, to boot. These attributes drove enrollment to unprecedented heights in the 1960s when more than 5.2 million children attended approximately 13,000 Catholic schools around the nation. Solidly Catholic Maryland led the way.

There was another (demographic) aspect to Catholic education that gradually became known to me over the years, and one that should be central to the future of Catholic (and all parochial) education. I refer to the influx of mostly poor African American and Hispanic students into Archdiocesan schools over the past 40 years.

Shifting urban/suburban trends explained the phenomenon. Many Catholic schools are located in urban and inner-suburban neighborhoods negatively impacted by inner-city blight and middle-class flight during the '70s and '80s. As a result, the church began recruitment efforts aimed at a new demographic. The results speak for themselves: Black and Hispanic students accounted for 10.8 percent of total Catholic school enrollment in 1970, 19.4 percent in 1980, 29.8 percent in 2010, and 34 percent today.

This profound racial/ethnic shift brought a poorer, more challenging population of students along with it. What had been schools chock full of working- and middle-class children taught by nuns who vowed poverty (a huge break for the budgetary bottom line) now took in more kids from the lower end of the economic spectrum—and many more kids in need of financial aid. And this at a time when the church began to be hit with hundreds of millions of dollars in priest sex scandal judgments, a cash drain that has placed eight archdioceses in bankruptcy and many more in dire fiscal straits.

The combination of urban economic realities and extraordinary legal judgments impacted Catholic school systems as well: Between 1970 and 2000, there was a net loss of 3,595 Catholic schools nationwide. The trend continued in the new millennium; in 2005, 38 Catholic schools opened while 223 either closed or merged.

It was against this backdrop that I engaged in my well-reported skirmishes with the defenders of dysfunctional public schools in Baltimore in 2005-2006. I followed a two-pronged plan of attack: 1) Use the provisions of the federal No Child Left Behind Act to close, merge, or privatize the most dysfunctional 13 public schools in Baltimore; and 2) Ask/plead with the Catholic hierarchy to stop closing schools in and around the city.

I was less than successful on both counts. First, the Democratic leadership and city teachers union put a legislative stop to the remedial actions necessary to transform the problematic city schools. It was a familiar storyline: a powerful teachers union and Democratic party monopoly (desperate to avoid the black eye of failure) trumping poor kids—again. And to make matters worse, the Archdiocese continued to close schools. As one prominent church leader told me at the conclusion of a private meeting over the school closure issue: "These [city Catholic] schools are not a core mission of the church." My frustration was palpable, to say the least.

My unapologetic enthusiasm for Catholic education goes far beyond an appreciation of a disciplined and more rigorous academic environment. These schools are mini-economic engines and safe havens for kids in some of our more violence-prone neighborhoods. They support jobs, labor income, and business sales in tough places. And they save a lot of taxpayer money. The Sage Policy Group estimates that Maryland saved roughly $200 million in expenditures due to the presence of Catholic schools in 2008-2009.

In a perfect world, healthy public, private, and parochial schools would compete for prospective students. But we live in the real world, where so many poor kids continue to be sentenced to dysfunctional schools. The sad fact is that every Catholic school closure means more kids placed in too often dangerous and academically substandard schools. Society is left to deal with the less-than-stellar results—at a cost that too often goes beyond the financial.

Here's hoping that under Baltimore Archbishop William E. Lori's innovative leadership, Catholic education will once again assume the priority status it deserves in the church's new game plan. A lot of kids in our most challenging neighborhoods would benefit. The state (and country) would benefit, too.

Multiculturalism Is the Enemy of Democracy

Killing of a British soldier, apparently at the hands of Islamic radicals, reinforces the danger of separatism.

June 2, 2013, *The Baltimore Sun*

"You people will never be safe. Remove your governments, they don't care about you," said Michael Adebolajo, one of two men arrested in the murder of British soldier Lee Rigby on May 22, 2013.

Here we go again. Brazen and brutal attacks against British and French soldiers. In broad daylight. At the hands of homegrown Islamic extremists (Mr. Adebolajo is reported to have shouted "Allahu Akbar!" as he struck). European conservatives reflexively clamoring for a crackdown on Islamic fundamentalism. The left reflexively reminding us that the West is not at war with Islam.

This latest horrific chapter of Islamic radicalism brings me back to a topic I have often chronicled over the past 20 years: the specter of multiculturalism.

At the outset, it is important to distinguish between the ethnic and racial pluralism Americans celebrate and the multiculturalism we must reject. It is a distinction deliberately muddled by the progressive left. Accordingly, a vital societal goal is presented to the general public in confusing ways. Fortunately, the corrective is easily identified: re-establish the centrality of pluralism within a uniquely American culture. Failure to do so invites the hijacking of a commonly understood concept by a progressive movement intent on remaking American culture in its own image.

For Americans, pluralism means the co-mingling of different ethnicities and races in one place. Our experience has shown this dynamic environment leads to the assimilation of diverse peoples into a singular culture wherein common values are taught, protected and celebrated.

The American story is poignant in this regard: Most immigrants left their native countries to escape religious persecution or seek economic opportunity. Some came to explore a new frontier. Kidnapped Africans arrived aboard slave ships. Regardless of origin, almost all arrived in the new world with little money.

What bound most of these disparate early arrivals together was an expectation (although not immediately available to all) that freedom and opportunity awaited; that economic mobility could be achieved through hard work; that religious tolerance would rule the day; that no king would ever reign over them; and that the rule of law would be supreme, blind to one's formal education, economic status or bloodlines.

In return, the people recognized the laws, language, and customs of the new nation. This general recognition became the societal denominator; a commonality of interests emerged including religious tolerance, market capitalism, personal freedoms, baseball, and apple pie. A uniquely American culture was born and grew into the most successful democratic enterprise the world has ever seen.

But rapid assimilation is a source of great irritation to malcontents on the left who wish to remake our culture and our self-image. Many reject the notion of the grand experiment itself; the American melting pot is not their goal. Indeed, they vilify the Founding Fathers. They see America as the product of cultural cleansing and forced assimilation. They cultivate victims and demand governmental apologies and reparations. In some cases, they wish to claim independent status—independence from our Judeo-Christian heritage and American culture. And failing such lofty goals, they seek to create a truly multicultural society, where American exceptionalism is assailed and separatism is celebrated.

Fortunately, the forces of multicultural progressivism have lately been forced on the defensive. A 2006 Pew poll explains why: A shocking 81 percent of British Muslims viewed themselves as Muslims first and a citizen of their country second. Hence, British political leaders now acknowledge what (until the last five years) had been regarded as a cultural third rail: governmentally pedaled multiculturalism is a dangerous failure.

Accordingly, in February, 2011, British Prime Minister David Cameron observed "multiculturalism is dead" (thereby echoing views expressed by German Chancellor Angela Merkel in 2010 and Australian Prime Minister John Howard in 2006). These conservative leaders were ahead of the curve in their willingness to oppose the multicultural apologists who have preached (and practiced) separatism within the oldest pluralistic democracies the world has seen. The rise of Islamic fundamentalism certainly sped up British disdain for the anti-assimilation crowd, but it was inevitable that such social separatism would fail: It can only be a brief period of time wherein disparate ethnicities can co-exist (let alone prosper) without the emergence of common bonds and a commonality of interests.

In America, the incremental defeat of the tarnished concept is not easily accomplished. Progressive interest groups have too much invested in a far-reaching guilt trip narrative to simply retreat. They are in business to degrade the concept of a singular American culture. They are determined to maintain identity politics; it is their lifeblood. It is the primary tool in the multicultural playbook. And a proven winner with the mainstream media.

But the murder of a British soldier reminds us of our (cultural) high stakes challenge: continue to expose the emptiness of the multicultural agenda, while recognizing practitioners of the act will not give up without a fight.

In Obama's America, the Federal Government Comes First

Robert L. Ehrlich Jr. says the expansion of Washington's presence in our lives has been the hallmark of this Administration.

August 11, 2013, *The Baltimore Sun*

E lections have consequences. People who attain political power daily make decisions that affect citizens in myriad ways, some not so obvious.

For example, one of the more under-analyzed (but long-lasting) consequences of a re-elected Barack Obama is the ongoing expansion of federal control, overseen by an Administration intent on federalizing just about anything standing in its way.

No halfway-interested citizen can claim surprise. This president's life is a model of progressive activism, from Harvard Law School to (Chicago) community activist, to law professor, to candidate for public office. Even a brief private sector (law firm) stint was focused on civil rights and community advocacy issues. Further, his personal testimonies speak to the influences of uber-progressive friends and mentors such as Rev. Jeremiah Wright, poet Frank Marshall Davis, and anti-war activists/bombers Bill Ayers and wife Bernardine Dohrn.

The collective impact of these experiences and associations was a decidedly far left voting record while a member of the Illinois legislature and the U.S. Senate. It follows that our 44th president entered the Oval Office with a clear game plan to enlarge the federal presence in the lives of every American.

This preference for governmental activism is a political fact of life in deep-blue Maryland. We are home to tens of thousands of federal employees and countless thousands of private vendors dependent on federal largesse. Accordingly, we (almost) always vote Democrat over Republican in presidential elections. And we (almost) always do what the federal government tells us to do, regardless of its impact on state sovereignty.

But we are proving to be more the exception than the rule when it comes to acceptance of Obama-era interventionism. Indeed, increasing numbers of state legislators, governors and attorneys general are passing legislation or turning to the courts in order to protect their traditional 10th Amendment rights.

A sampling of recent activity:

- At last count, 37 states have entertained bills that would negate one or more aspects of federal gun control regulations (this according to the anti-gun Brady Center to Prevent Gun Violence).

- Since its unfortunate passage in 2009, 20 states have passed legislation to either challenge major provisions of Obamacare or simply opt out altogether. (If only it was that easy to escape the reach of this mammoth turkey.)

- Texas is known for its fierce sense of individualism, so it should come as no surprise that the "Lone Star State" has 18 lawsuits pending against the federal government. Although many of the suits pertain to alleged Environmental Protection Agency overreach, the state's attorney general has also sued over the Dodd-Frank financial services bill (dismissed last week) and federal pre-emption of state election laws—a hotspot for the Obama Justice Department.

- States have resisted the performance benchmarks and lack of flexibility set by the federal No Child Left Behind Act for many years, particularly those designations identifying "failing" or "persistently dangerous" schools.

- The debate has even reached to Federal Emergency Management Agency reform, as advocates attempt to redirect the agency back toward its original mission of handling catastrophic national emergencies and away from routine events traditionally handled at the state level.

Some of the state responses are more serious (and important) than others, but all focus on the pre-emptive use of federal power that usurps duties properly left to the states or local government.

In some instances, Republicans (and conservatives) must share the blame. Traditional state jurisdiction over issues of juvenile justice, medical malpractice, driving privileges, and local education have witnessed a GOP inclination to selectively ignore 10th Amendment strictures. (My former colleague Barney Frank of Massachusetts, much maligned on the right, regularly and gleefully went to the floor of the House to condemn these Republican violations of principle—much to my chagrin, since he was on target with his criticisms.)

But these GOP lapses are relatively minor in comparison to a Washington-centric Administration on a roll. There are no more elections in this president's future. He need not engage in any election year pretense to govern from the middle. Dodd-Frank, stimulus, Obamacare, new EPA emissions rules, challenges to state photo identification laws, broad new gun control proposals, and relentless calls for higher taxes reflect an enthusiastic preference for feeding the ravenous appetite of our Big Brother in Washington, D.C.

You should be uncomfortable with the country's present infatuation with federal power. History teaches how difficult it is to divest authority once legally obtained. Relatively few in Washington wish to counter this historical trend. And those that rebel are often subject to harsh treatment by the city's dominant left-wing media.

In light of our present course, there is little reason to believe "the drive to federalize" can be moderated over the next three years. Not a positive development for a country (and culture) that used to believe bigger was not necessarily better.

Nine Ideas to Revive the Republican Party

*Maryland's former governor offers his tips to win back
the White House.*

February 9, 2014, *The Baltimore Sun*

I've been running around the country hawking my new book,
listening to what people are saying, and scribbling notes about
what a new Republican platform should contain—at least what
one should contain if we ever want to win again.

Herewith, my top nine planks, offered for your consideration
at a time of continuing economic angst and rapid cultural change:

Reduce spending by half a percent

Seventeen and a half trillion dollars of debt and counting (not to
mention the hundreds of billions spent on interest each year). Both
parties are responsible, but the Obama era has been spectacularly
expensive with over $7 trillion in new debt added over the past five
years alone.

This fiscal approach is unsustainable—and immoral. And while
there is no silver bullet to cure our self-imposed spending dilemma,
some slowing of our spending pace is in order. I propose half of 1 percent. Such a cut equates to a savings of $18.9 billion next fiscal year.

I realize that even this minimalist proposal will excite those
who rely on federal largesse. In a word, they will go "nuts." Apoc-
alyptic predictions will dominate media coverage. But this would
not be the end of the universe as we know it. The federal government would still spend nearly $4 trillion dollars. The market would

respond in spectacular fashion. And for the first time in a long time, America's creditors (especially the Chinese) would see that we might be serious about a fiscal policy that sustains our super power status.

Real entitlement reform

Entitlement reform is long past due. The allegedly untouchable "third rail" may no longer be electrified; the burden of doing nothing is better understood today than in previous generations.

So, let's keep it real—and doable:

1. Increase the Social Security retirement age (from today's 66) phased in at the rate of two months per year. Those born in 1973 and later would be the first to plan for a new retirement age of 70 years old. The Congressional Budget Office estimates such a change would save $120 billion by 2021. We are living much longer than originally envisioned; our benefits should reflect this fact of life.

2. Increase Medicare premiums for the wealthy. This is a big revenue raiser ($50 billion in President Barack Obama's budget). One would hope that liberal purveyors of the "hands off Social Security" mindset might find this proposal too tempting to pass up.

3. Reform the Social Security Disability Trust Fund, presently scheduled to run dry within the next two years. A quadrupling of beneficiaries since the beginning of President Obama's first term reflects a broken program suffering rampant fraud, as evidenced by recent Congressional oversight reports. This should be the (politically) easiest trust fund to fix.

Immigration done right

The borders remain porous, and there are as many as 13 million people in the U.S. illegally. The Democrats have given up, finding it more politically expedient to ignore the law (sanctuary status, two tier drivers licenses) than enforce it.

Conversely, some Republicans want to round up the 13 million, dragnet style, and send them home. These folks do not live in the real world.

To borrow a phrase from my friend Charles Krauthammer, we need "radical fence building" followed by "radical legalization." We must build significant barriers (along with high-tech drones and anything else we can throw at the problem) that work—i.e., slow the flow to a trickle. Only after a successful security initiative will the country's leaders possess the credibility to institute a "path to legality." Then, the illegal millions will be placed in line behind those who have followed the law, but only after back taxes are paid, after passing criminal background checks, and after passable English is learned. Yes, it's a path—just not a free path.

Advantages abound: border security strengthened, out-of-the-shadows living (and paying taxes for millions), a potential path to legal status (green card) that could lead to citizenship, and a strengthening of the rule of law.

Obamacare: repeal, replace, repair

Thomas Jefferson once famously warned, "Great innovations should not be forced on slender majorities."

Yes, single party work products tend to be dysfunctional. They by definition have little room for error and enjoy shallow reservoirs of good will. But what to do about it?

How about "repeal, replace, repair." This approach would allow for the continuation of Obamacare's most popular provision: the elimination of pre-existing condition disclaimers. Prime candidates for repeal include "one size fits all" in the individual marketplace, the infamous "Independent Payment Advisory Board," the adverse selection doomed exchanges, and (count 'em) 22 new or expanded taxes, especially the ill-advised "medical device tax." Replacement provisions would be focused on market orientated ways to expand coverage, including writing policies across state lines, portability, health savings accounts, and protocols for state based tort reform measures. Most Republicans would support means testing of Medicare, too.

As it becomes more apparent that Obamacare's over-hyped promises were just so much baloney, the GOP must do more than watch this house of cards fall apart.

An urban New Deal

Long ago, the government decided to subsidize poverty—and got more of it. And not only more poverty—we got the dissolution of the nuclear family, high rates of addiction, gun violence run amok, and (more than a few) dysfunctional public school systems. More spending on a larger nanny state is not the answer.

Let's try freedom—hyper-freedom of the Hong Kong model— as in no tax job investment zones and radical school choice. Basically, Jack Kemp-style enterprise zones on steroids, and "all of the above" on school choice, targeted to our most decayed areas.

The establishment will explode. Urban political machines will fight to the last. Teachers unions will cry foul. And all to protect a crumbling power base that cheats the poor and powerless.

Freedom beckons—let's go for it. We can't do worse than the status quo.

An energy revolution

Not so long ago, our energy paradigm was so 20th century: wind mills vs. nuclear—"pick only one." Such false choices were brought to you by the church of environmental extremism, where even a hint of dissent about (man made) global warming was met with wholesale condemnation from the "mainstream" media.

As it turns out, man made modeling may not be 100 percent accurate. Worse yet, our next energy revolution will emanate from another fossil fuel, only this time the much cleaner (and domestically plentiful) natural gas.

All of which does not solve the ugly fight between the absolutist haters of all things carbon and the absolutist deniers of global warming. But new technology is leading us to cleaner energy independence. We just have to ensure government does its environmental due diligence, ensures our safety and then gets out of the way as the market does its thing.

Federalism can live . . . again

The 10th Amendment lives, at least according to a spate of recent Supreme Court opinions.

Accordingly, many of our divisive cultural debates are most appropriately handled at the state level. These include abortion restrictions, gun control initiatives, expansions on the right to marry, capital punishment, criminal justice reform, and election integrity.

Alas, easier said than done. The temptation to federalize is endemic to Washington, D.C. Violations bring few electoral consequences. Federalist principles can be revived, but only with the people's understanding that not every want and need is the federal government's business.

A fatherhood initiative

The evidence is in. The American family is sick. And widespread fatherlessness is the primary culprit.

We do not need yet another government program. Pro-dependence government programs caused this crisis. We need our political and cultural leadership to issue a clarion call for what used to be an obvious value: Children need fathers. Secondary message: Don't father the kid if you're not willing to pay the price.

An increasingly promiscuous society invited this cultural catastrophe. It has been especially devastating to the African American community. Only an "all in" response can reverse it.

Free Trade—Now

The Obama Administration, free trade Democrats, and the GOP agree: The president should have fast track authority to negotiate trade deals. But Majority Leader Harry Reid and organized labor stand in the way.

Two major deals are at issue: one with the European Union and the other with 11 countries within Asia and the Pacific Rim.

Free trade built this country. Success here means more jobs and lower prices for U.S. consumers. But what should be a no-brainer is made unlikely by the likes of protectionists like Senator Reid.

Freedom of, Not from, Religion

You do not have a right to control the religious practice of others just because it offends you.

June 1, 2014, *The Baltimore Sun*

One of my earliest childhood memories is going door-to-door at the Kendale Apartments on Maiden Choice Lane in Arbutus with Mom. The purpose of the exercise was not to solicit contributions on behalf of a political candidate, however. Rather, Mom and a group of like-minded volunteers were organizing in opposition to a woman by the name of Madalyn Murray O'Hair—she of the [un]holy crusade to ban prayer from public schools. Given my tender years, little did I realize that the Ehrlichs were fully engaged in a culture war that continues to burn brightly five decades later.

The issue concerns the parameters of our right to practice and follow religious traditions and customs in public places.

A brief historical reminder: The exercise of our sacred bundle of First Amendment rights is not unlimited. For example, Americans enjoy and take great advantage of freedom of speech. It's what allows you to read diametrically opposed viewpoints on this very page. Yet, one does not have the right to yell "fire" in a crowded theater. Similarly, for the people's freedom to worship according to their individual convictions. Here, the framers clearly had one such limitation in mind: avoiding the establishment of a "state" religion. Otherwise, a healthy diversity of religious practice was their goal. They got it right, too. Our grand experiment in religious freedom has been an unqualified success.

Another point of reference: The framers never used the phrase "separation of church and state"; the drafters of the Bill of Rights never entertained the notion that American citizens would be separated from religious expression. A central point emerges: The dominant culture possesses an expansive right to observe its faith-based traditions and customs. Further, religious minorities (and non-believers) do not possess an alternative right to be free from offensive practices.

Nevertheless, Ms. O'Hara and her progeny have successfully circumscribed religious practice in the public square. Prayer is long gone from the public classroom, and every Supreme Court calendar contains cases whereby an aggrieved party wishes to further limit public displays of religious conviction in one way or another.

All of this is by way of introduction to the Supreme Court's recent decision in the case of Greece vs. Galloway.

The facts were not in dispute. The little town of Greece, N.Y., had traditionally begun its town council meetings with a non-denominational prayer—usually (but not always) from a Christian minister. (Note: Greece is overwhelmingly Christian.) But the practice managed to offend two plaintiffs who thought it was a bit too Christian for their tastes.

The majority opinion noted that such opening prayers are an integral part of American civic tradition going back to the founding. No surprise there; check out the daily opening prayers in Congress, state legislatures, and most any town council in America. Further, the court noted a long line of precedent whereby prayer in public spaces has repeatedly been upheld. Writing for the majority, Justice Anthony Kennedy noted: "That the First Congress provided for the appointment of chaplains only days after approving language for the First Amendment demonstrates that the Framers considered legislative prayer a benign acknowledgment of religion's role in society."

A clear-cut case, right? Not so fast. The vote was 5 to 4, as the reliably liberal wing of the court (Justices Kagan, Ginsburg, Suter, and Sotomayor) held that any sectarian element in public prayer constitutes a governmental endorsement of religion. For these four justices, only generic, nonsectarian prayers would pass Constitutional muster.

Now fast forward to my daily activities wherein perfect strangers regularly seek to engage me in political conversation. On occasion, my new acquaintance will state that he/she does not vote because "the parties are all the same." It is on such occasions that I think about cases such as Greece vs. Galloway.

All elections count. But executive elections really count. Governors and presidents appoint judges, sometimes for life. Barack Obama has appointed 258 federal judges—two to the U.S. Supreme Court. The vast majority are activist liberals going about the business of legislating from the bench. The next Democratic president will do likewise—and likely have the opportunity to create a long-term liberal majority on the Supreme Court. Such a turn would be disastrous for our economy, and culture.

Just a thought for your consideration as you begin to think about the presidential election of 2016.

American Values Under Obama

Why Obama is viewed as weak

November 2, 2014, *The Baltimore Sun*

Two columns ago, I passed on a series of political observations from the heartland. Today, I'll give a snapshot of American values and viewpoints a decade and a half into the "new" millennium.

For my left-leaning readers, you have much to be pleased about as America enters the seventh year of the Obama presidency.

First and foremost, the populace has grown acclimated to an intrusive federal presence. The Obama era's "new federalism" has been a driver in this regard, wherein Congress increasingly invites aggressive federal regulators to "fill in the blanks" left by omnibus legislative vehicles. Accordingly, federal bureaucrats cranked out 2,185 regulations last year, 77 of the "major" variety. Obamacare alone has accounted for more than 20,000 pages of new regulations since inception. FYI: In 2014, American taxpayers worked from January 1 to April 21st just to pay the tax bill for government at all levels.

Closely tied to this cultural acceptance of really big government is a disinterest in the growth of the federal deficit, now exceeding $17.6 trillion. Indeed, clear majorities in blue state America constantly request additional spending and increased government activism while, periodically, the heartland registers a demand for fiscal discipline. For the most part, however, relatively few Americans view the size and expense of government as a major obstacle to progress, with one caveat: Americans still expect government to work. But a major recession and tepid recovery have rattled the middle class. And recent experiences with Obamacare's dysfunctional website, the VA's secret wait lists, a porous southern border, an ascendant ISIS, and an unprepared CDC have given Americans further pause about government preparedness and efficiency, at least in the short run.

Culturally, a profound leftward shift on marijuana, gay marriage, immigration, and access to birth control is most apparent among young people. Here, the Democrats' "war on women" campaign has prompted numerous GOP candidates to support over-the-counter birth control (a sensible position, in my view). Alas, Republicans are still charged with the gender offense if free birth control is not added to the program (not so sure this one has similarly caught on). Regardless, it's clear that America is more secular and progressive in the new millennium. That the foregoing successes have reduced the political effectiveness of the "Religious Right" is without question. Indeed, the vitriol that was previously reserved for religious conservatives is now redirected toward fiscal conservatives—the tea party.

But all is not rosy for America's liberals. A few prominent items on the Democrats' wish list have lost momentum—even regressed due to unforeseen circumstances.

The continued decline of private sector unionism is one such trend. Unions now account for only 11.3 percent of the U.S. labor force. A smaller, post-industrial era manufacturing sector is the primary culprit. Added to this diminution in union power is an increased willingness by blue collar Democrats to vote Republican. (For local context, check out Sauerbrey-Bentley-Ehrlich voting totals in Dundalk over the last 25 years.) Conversely, public-sector union membership continues to grow. These unions are all about courting Democrats in an endless campaign to expand the public sector. Yet even here, courts have begun to chip away at once sacrosanct pension benefits as municipalities seek to escape crushing retirement and health care obligations.

In the "shocking" category, the issue of public education—once wholly owned by Democrats and their teachers' union allies—has shown significant cracks. Increasingly, Democratic office holders are speaking up for "school choice" in our most dysfunctional communities. The most (politically) dangerous of these episodes occurs when legislative black caucuses team up with Republicans to produce more educational options for predominantly African American parents fed up with under-performing schools. Such momentum even extends to hyper-liberal California where an innovative "parent-trigger law" allows 50 percent of parents at under-performing schools to force staffing changes and even conversion to a public charter. Talk about power to the people!

Gun control has also lost steam. Not so long ago, gun control advocates sought to use the specter of mass shootings at schools and shopping malls as fodder for a renewed push for expanded federal controls. An anti-gun president and attorney general were fully on board. Yet, the advent of the Obama Administration brought gun sales to dizzying heights. Fear of domestic terror incidents such as the recent workplace beheading in Oklahoma and ax attack in New York City will only further strengthen gun sales around the country.

On foreign policy, a post-9/11 pro-war frenzy was replaced by a bipartisan isolationist approach during the Obama years. But a series of videotaped beheadings and new threats to the homeland find Americans still wary of boots on the ground in an unstable Middle East but equally wary of presidential indecisiveness in the face of a murderous ISIS onslaught in Iraq and Syria.

Finally, as presented on this page a few weeks ago, the truly "purple" issue of criminal justice reform continues to generate support across the political spectrum. A significantly reduced political fear quotient is bringing the parties together on alternatives to incarceration for nonviolent drug offenders, re-entry assistance, mandatory minimum sentencing reforms and executive activism on post-conviction relief (pardons and commutations).

The bottom line: American culture is increasingly secular and permissive, especially along the coasts. There exists majority acceptance of government activism, but Americans continue to recoil from government negligence—from leaky borders to leaky websites. And they don't like being lied to on matters that count (keeping your doctor and the JV army known as ISIS).

Cross currents, indeed.

Unforced Errors or Tactical Mistakes?

April 14, 2015, *The Baltimore Sun*

Political pundits like to label gratuitous political gaffes as "unforced errors"—mistakes that come out of right field without warning or reason.

These events are given extra analysis because they are unexpected and uncalled for—usually offhand or just plain unthinking statements or actions that enjoy a long shelf life in this social media and cable television driven world.

Many conservatives misinterpret the president's—and his surrogates'—consistent, predictable actions as examples of such unforced errors.

To wit:

"You didn't build that." was not a rhetorical mistake by the president, but rather an indictment of entrepreneurial America, those men and women who started a business only to become successful, and worse, *wealthy.* This group consistently finds itself in the president's crosshairs; their preference for independence, profit, and success drives veteran class warriors to distraction.

"Individuals will be empowered to make choices about their own lives and livelihoods . . . [they] would have the opportunity to pursue their dreams." The liberation theory displayed herein by White House Press Secretary Jay Carney followed the Congressional Budget Office's analysis that Obamacare would reduce the American workforce by 2.3 million full-time equivalent jobs by 2021. Mr. Carney further explained such job loss would free Americans to pursue their dreams, hobbies, and leisure activities without the burden of losing their health care. No solace was offered to those left to pay the tab.

Radical Islam. There, I said it—as do most Americans and Muslim leaders engaged in a battle against a bloodthirsty enemy. Question: If the Saudis, Jordanians, and Egyptians feel comfortable with the phrase, why not the president of the United States?

"Fore!" Nothing screams empathy from the leader of the free world more than 18 holes immediately following a press conference called to address the beheading of an American journalist. Now, I'm often the first to defend this president's desire to play golf. But where was the staffer in charge of "optics" on this one?

"Workplace violence." Technically, yes, the Fort Hood murders occurred at a working Army base. Still, most interpreted the incident as terror-related since the killer, Major Nidal Hasan, yelled "Allahu Akbar!" while gunning down 11 innocent people. But, then again, this Administration can't bring itself to call the war a war.

"If you like your health care plan, you can keep it." What was awarded the "Lie of the Year" by PolitiFact may have been a whopper and obvious to anyone who bothered to read the bill, but it nevertheless served its purpose—just enough voter assurance to pass the man-made catastrophe known as "Obamacare."

James Taylor singing "You've Got a Friend" to the French as an apology for the U.S. president, vice president, and/or attorney general not bothering to show up for a gathering of world leaders in the aftermath of a terror attack in Paris (no, not a "random target," Mr. President) was a low point of Administration "soft power."

"Sergeant Bowe Bergdahl served the United States with honor and distinction." National Security Advisor Susan Rice's infamous statement was dubious from the jump. But trading a deserter for five varsity terrorists *did* get the Administration closer to a major policy goal: closing Gitmo.

The Crusades and The National Prayer Breakfast. That the "moral equivalency" option was used to contextualize the ugliness of the crusades (11th through 13th centuries) in the immediate aftermath of the live burning of a Jordanian fighter pilot did leave many observers confused. But not me. The crusades had to have been the first thing a reflexive apologist would think of in the aftermath of such a monstrous event—what, you didn't see that one coming?

The president's "war resolution." Here, at last, is the presidential recognition that the "JV" terror squad ISIS constitutes a real threat to the U.S, but, per expectation, with the usual self-limiting notifications to the enemy (no ground troops and a deadline for withdrawal).

"We cannot kill our way out of this war. . . .We can work with countries around the world to help improve their governance. We can help them build their economies so they can have job opportunities for these people." State Department Spokeswoman Marie Harf's response to ISIS beheading 21 Egyptian Coptic Christians did not refer to the victims as Christians, but rather "Egyptian citizens." And then came the suggestion these barbarians will stop the slaughter and bloodlust if only they have a job.

This is what true progressivism looks like. The next time you can do something about these constant affronts is November 2016.

PART 4

★ ★ ★

The Disaster
That Is *Obamacare*

IT IS DIFFICULT TO ENCAPSULATE THE MYRIAD PROBLEMS generated by the health care reform initiative known as *Obamacare*. It is equally difficult to analyze the complexities of a magnum opus that is 1,300 pages in length and has generated 10,516 pages of interpretive rules (as of this writing) in the Federal Register. This monstrosity has and will continue to produce reams of critical analysis for the foreseeable future or until it is replaced with a more market-friendly rewrite that truly extends health insurance coverage to the working poor at affordable rates.

My twenty-year career in public life provided me the opportunity to learn a great deal about health care delivery in America. This knowledge was helpful in identifying a number of Obamacare's deficiencies at an early juncture in the public debate. I analyzed Obamacare through a series of columns aimed at the average person: that individual who is bright enough to negotiate life's daily challenges, but lacks the time-energy-patience to slog through a bill that many Members of Congress neglected to slog through in the first place. If they had done so, perhaps I (and so many others) would have been left with less to complain about. Alas, a careful understanding of what the bill actually did (and how it goes about the business of accomplishing its aims) was not in the cards. You see, this was the president's *signature legacy item*. Accordingly, Democrats were expected to do what they had to do—damn the torpedoes—and the political repercussions—and the proper statutory language.

Fortunately, so many of those who followed Speaker Pelosi's and Leader Reid's orders soon found themselves out of public office a mere two or four years later. This result may have provided a sound moral about the dangers of negligent, irresponsible legislating, but the damage had been done. The federal government's historic intrusion into health care delivery had been accomplished, and in a most harmful way.

Some say that Obamacare was simply a halfway endeavor given that Democrats did not have the desire to go "all in" with single payer—the goal of every true believing progressive. If accurate, God help us if and when a Democratic Congress ever has the fortitude (and votes) to complete the task.

Obamacare: The 2,300-Page Monstrosity

As Supreme Court takes on health reform, even the president's supporters are running away from it.

March 25, 2012, *The Baltimore Sun*

The most important six hours of recent American history will start to unfold on Monday. That day, the Supreme Court begins three days of oral argument on the legal challenge to President Barack Obama's health care reform law ("Obamacare").

The Court's decision will have a profound impact on the quality of American health care. The political repercussions will be equally strong: The decision will either reinvigorate an Obama campaign looking to make good on its signature legislative initiative or fuel a united Republican counterattack along the lines of "We told you so."

Casual observers may not realize there are 26 states and one business organization (The National Federation of Independent Business) acting as plaintiffs in the consolidated case. Separate suits (representing constitutional challenges to the law's requirement that individuals purchase insurance) have been filed by the state of Virginia, Liberty University, and the Thomas Mann Center. Numerous other court challenges have been dismissed, mostly on procedural grounds.

The political stakes are high and trending Republican: Obamacare's myriad complexities and federal overreach was the rallying cry of a midterm election cycle that saw Democrats lose their House majority and six net Senate seats. More recent polling reflects equally ominous news for the president. A February USA Today/Gallup Poll showed 53 percent of voters in swing states viewed Obamacare as a "bad thing." Only 38 percent of respondents approved. Among independents, the news was even worse: 35 percent said the law makes them less likely to support the president's re-election, as opposed to 16 percent who said it makes them more likely. Recall that substantial GOP gains among independents fueled the 2010 midterms.

My next 50 columns could be taken up with political analysis surrounding this 2,300-page monstrosity. Recall then-House Speaker Nancy Pelosi's plea to "pass the bill so that you can find out what's in it"? The good news: I will not devote my remaining 2012 columns to such a task. The bad news: You may not be so pleased to read what the president and congressional leadership blithely did to the health-care consumer in the name of "reform."

With regard to process, let me assure you the average Member of Congress did not follow the daily drafting process in great detail. The consumption and interpretation of 2,300 pages of constantly changing, arcane policy language is indeed a Herculean task. Most relied on "talking points memos" issued by the respective caucus staffs or bill-writing committees. Nevertheless, Speaker Pelosi's artless comment failed to convey a sense of order and competence rightfully expected by the general public.

Another bit of procedural news: The law's more than 700 pages of individual directives have already spawned 2,163,744 words (Fox News describes the volume as 2 1/2 times the size of the Bible) of regulatory interpretation (as of May) from federal agencies, mostly the Department of Health and Human Services. In other words, Obamacare is bureaucratic heaven on Earth; its regulations will be issued (and become the subject of countless lawsuits) for decades to come. This, of course, is one of the primary attractions for Obamacare's advocates, as federal health care policy gradually becomes more a function of government dictate than market-generated demand.

Alas, Obamacare dictates are not meant for all, especially those labor unions that were candidate Obama's most vociferous supporters in 2008. Indeed, the Obama Administration had granted 1,231 waivers of participation as of January, when political pressure finally ground the waiver mill to a halt. Labor unions received fully 50 percent of the Administration's largesse, a revealing fact in light of organized labor's enthusiasm for the bill. Two further anomalies: Nearly 20 percent of the waivers approved in April 2011 emanated from former Speaker Pelosi's district, while Senate Majority Leader Harry Reid secured a waiver for *all* insurers operating in the individual market in the entire state of Nevada.

Much of the analysis and politics surrounding Obamacare pertain to one overarching issue: the power of the federal government to regulate private economic behavior through the Commerce Clause. Progressives see a generally limitless connection, while conservatives advance the notion that private health insurance (particularly the decision to forgo such insurance) is a personal decision outside the reach of the federal government. In other words, the mere power of the federal government to regulate commerce among the states does not extend to forcing every American into the commercial insurance market. A possible complication for the GOP: Justice Antonin Scalia, a member of the Court's so-called "conservative majority," has (at times) adopted a more expansive view of Commerce Clause jurisdiction.

Nevertheless, I (and many other observers) believe it more likely than not that the Court will strike down the mandate. The Court could strike all or only portions of the statute. A divided Congress would then attempt to figure out what to do next.

A Death Knell for Employer-Funded Insurance

Ehrlich says Obamacare will impose great costs on society.

April 1, 2012, *The Baltimore Sun*

The Supreme Court directed a harsh spotlight on Obamacare this past week, but the problems with the law go far beyond the constitutionality of the "individual mandate." One of the great unknowns generated by the passage of Obamacare goes directly to the heart of health care choice: the notion that increased employer costs and regulatory burdens would cause employers to simply pay fines (and send their newly insurance-deprived employees to state-run exchanges) rather than continue employer-subsidized insurance. That some of the largest American companies would consider such a move has caused plenty of Democratic heartburn. In one scenario, AT&T estimated its health- care costs would drop from $2.4 billion to $600 million if the company eliminated employee coverage and paid the government-mandated fine instead.

A 2011 analysis by McKinsey & Company confirms what so many economists (not employed by the Obama Administration) had predicted all along: Obamacare will cause a drastic decrease in the number of employers who offer health insurance to their employees. A McKinsey analyst observed that such a change would impact "something in the range of 80 to 100 million individuals." The draconian consequences for the federal budget: Millions of new entrants into government-subsidized coverage mean billions in additional Obamacare-generated expenditures.

Today, employers are performing their cost-benefit analyses in anticipation of full Obamacare implementation in 2014, while the daunting notion of large employers willingly breaking the back of the nation's employer-based health care system is causing many sleepless nights in Washington. Readers may recall a pledge to the effect that those Americans happy with their health care coverage would keep it. This pledge was joined with a promise to maintain our long-established, employer-based system of health insurance. Both assurances became a familiar mantra during the national debate over Obamacare. Both look to be considerably less than accurate.

Obamacare's possible impact on employer-sponsored plans and constitutional questions surrounding the individual mandate have generated so much attention that it is easy to forget the legislation's 18 tax increases estimated to cost American taxpayers in excess of $500 billion over the next 10 years. Of course, these numbers are merely estimates. History has taught us that long-term revenue estimates are typically understated, while political consequences for often incorrect "guesstimates" are often negligible.

Nevertheless, Obamacare's tax provisions are wide, varied, and anti-growth. To wit, a brief sampling:

- annual fee on health insurance carriers

- increase in payroll tax for higher-income earners

- higher payroll tax on investment income for upper-income earners

- fee on manufacturers and importers of branded drugs

- excise tax on premium health insurance plans

- excise tax on manufacturers and importers of selected medical devices

- increase in adjusted gross income on medical expenses

One of the smaller revenue measures is also one of the most revealing: a new federal tanning tax. Yes, the federal government has invaded your tanning bed, to the tune of $2.7 billion. One wonders what Jefferson would say about this one.

The influx of Obamacare revenue into the federal coffers represents a monumental shift of dollars away from an employer-preferred to a government-subsidized health care system. On the left, such aggressive taxation adds to the program's attractiveness. Talk about a progressive win-win-win: $500 billion in additional tax revenue from the "rich" while the traditional employer-based system slowly ebbs away. Who said the president doesn't think "big"? Only one problem: Big means big regulation, big exemptions, big taxes, big spending, and a big loss of freedom. It's just a big loser.

As a former governor, I am acutely aware of Medicaid's fiscal upside and downside. The popular federal-state program pays 50 to 83 cents on each dollar spent on medical care for the poor. Coverage of certain base populations is mandatory, although states may choose to cover additional populations and provide additional services. And herein lies the rub, as the states have gradually expanded Medicaid coverage during good times and bad.

Some may conclude the states emerge the big winner: More of their citizens secure coverage, and the feds pick up 100 percent of the tab. No such luck, however. Obamacare requires states to maintain existing benefit and eligibility levels. The penalty for noncompliance? Elimination from continued participation in the program.

The macro impact of Obamacare's Medicaid expansion: What was a rapidly spiraling-out-of-control program will now be a wildly spiraling-out-of-control program. Only this time the federal taxpayer will be on the hook for an additional $2 trillion, on top of the previous $5 trillion in debt racked up during the Obama Administration's first four years in office.

Obamacare's authors most assuredly foresaw the millions of new Medicaid enrollees. As such, a program originally targeted to poor women with children will now cover in excess of 80 million Americans. A program so large and entrenched is nearly impossible to reform—yet another appealing aspect of Obamacare for the social engineers within the Obama White House.

Obamacare and Birth Control: Women's Health Isn't the Issue

Liberals in the Administration are trying to overturn a previously untouchable cornerstone of the abortion debate.

April 8, 2012, *The Baltimore Sun*

My 16-year career in two legislatures (eight in the Maryland General Assembly and eight in Congress) included many debates on the most divisive issues of our time: Capital punishment, affirmative action, war and peace, impeachment, entitlement reform, and abortion rights were guaranteed to generate partisan strife and emotional debate.

No issue generated more emotion than a woman's right to choose. Intense, emotional debates produced a unique lexicon, as legislators debated the merits and implications of "judicial bypass," "parental consent," "partial birth," and the many complexities attendant to Medicaid (taxpayer) funding under certain circumstances.

What was not an issue, even in hyper-progressive Maryland, was the guarantee of "conscience clause" protection. The notion that religious institutions would not be forced to provide abortion or other contraceptive services in contravention of their religious beliefs was the third rail of abortion politics. Similar recognition of a conscience exception was the norm in state legislatures around the country. Even the most ardent pro-choice legislators accepted conscience exemptions as part of any statutory regime. That is, until the secular progressives within the Obama Administration reversed this bipartisan embrace by requiring all health insurance plans to cover reproductive services, including some that many consider tantamount to abortion.

From all accounts, it appears that major Catholics within the Administration (particularly Vice President Joe Biden and former Chief of Staff William Daley) raised strong objections. Besides recognizing the shift as bad politics, these two gentlemen may have recalled the president's circa 2008 pledge to the National Conference of Catholic Bishops that the conscience clause would not be tinkered with in the interest of comprehensive health care reform.

Unfortunately, however, Messrs. Biden and Daley lost the internal debate: Valerie Jarrett and other like-minded liberals within the Administration carried the day. Indeed, such a rare opportunity to overturn one of pro-life's foundational principles could not be ignored.

Fierce reaction from the Catholic Church and other religious leaders moved the Administration to offer (almost) immediate, if unsatisfactory, compromise by limiting the exemption to religious groups that employ members of their own religion, i.e., churches.

Then, in a stroke of political good fortune, Rick Santorum's contraception comments took the conscience story off page one. Talk about fortuitous timing: Mr. Santorum's comments opened the door for the Democratic Party to dust off its "Republicans are anti-women" mantra. The four remaining Republican presidential candidates have been on the defensive ever since.

Still, the revised conscience regulation will be revisited during what promises to be an ugly, hyper-partisan general election season.

Accordingly, a few reminders are in order. To wit:

- Even in the absence of Obamacare, every private employer in America (including faith-based employers) is free to offer unlimited contraception services within their employer plans;

- The Administration's regulation was always about mandating medical service(s) employers must include in their employee health care plans, despite situations where an employer's religious convictions are to the contrary; and

- The Administration's compromise exemption is quite limited: All employers who serve people regardless of religious affiliation will be forced by the federal government to provide contraception, sterilization, and morning-after pill coverage to their employees. In other words, churches are exempt, but faith-based affiliated institutions such as hospitals, clinics, colleges, adoption agencies, and food pantries are not. A second federal mandate: Such services will be offered free of charge by private insurance companies.

The crux of this matter: Religious freedom under the First Amendment will now be so narrowly drawn that many employers who have been exempt will be subjected to Obamacare's contraception mandate.

The president's more partisan defenders contend this debate is about a woman's right to secure the contraception option of her choice. This, to guarantee younger female support for the president's re-election. They further understand the dire political consequences should the issue be viewed instead through the prism of religious freedom.

The bottom line: Individual freedom is the primary victim under the myriad mandates of Obamacare, and nowhere is this loss of freedom more pronounced than under this new and not so improved conscience clause exemption.

Hopefully, the Supreme Court will strike down Obamacare in its entirety. Any new health care reform package should leave the well-established conscience protection alone. Health care reform is difficult enough without (gratuitously) chipping away at this cornerstone of religious liberty.

Obamacare: Constitutional but Contemptible

Progressive base is pleased by Obamacare's survival, but the opposition is fired up too.

July 8, 2012, *The Baltimore Sun*

So much to say and only 800 words to say it. So let's break the Supreme Court's Obamacare decision down between the law, politics, and the real world.

The decision: A monstrous new social program was found constitutional. A mandate the president insisted was not a tax was found to be a tax—and fully constitutional under an aggressive interpretation of congressional taxing authority. It was indeed fortuitous for President Barack Obama that Chief Justice John G. Roberts Jr. read the mandate as such; the majority opinion made clear his opposition to such drastic federal intervention under the Commerce Clause.

Accordingly, a narrow majority of the Supreme Court continues to recognize some limitations to federal intervention in everyday commerce. Per Chief Justice Roberts, "[T]he Commerce Clause is not a general license to regulate an individual from cradle to grave, simply because he will predictably engage in particular transactions."

Interestingly, the justice whom conservatives were most worried about made clear his disdain for the majority's decision. Justice Anthony M. Kennedy's stinging dissent charged that the Court had "undermined" the "values" that should have guided its analysis: "caution," "minimalism" and "the understanding that the federal government is one of limited powers."

Nevertheless, the majority opinion was a win/win for the president; his mandate to purchase health insurance survives. If the costs borne by those now forced to buy insurance are construed as a tax (as I and many others believe they should be), they join with the other 18 (mostly) progressive Obamacare taxes to form the largest tax increase in American history. Lost among most of the analysis was another surprising result: Obamacare's attempt to cover more people under Medicaid was significantly limited; those states that refuse to extend coverage to new beneficiaries will no longer face the prospect of losing their existing federal payments. A small victory for the taxpayers on an otherwise bad day.

The politics: It was a great day at 1600 Pennsylvania Ave. Liberals of all stripes celebrated a surprising victory in a court they love to hate. Even the losing Commerce Clause argument could not ruin their day. But the old axiom, "Be careful what you wish for," is appropriate here. The decision reminded voters of an unpopular program that Democratic candidates ran away from in 2010. As periodic reports of Obamacare's exploding costs and adverse impact on job creation continue, one wonders whether marginal-seat Democrats will change direction to support the bill. Don't bet on it.

For conservatives, the decision was a reminder that there is no such thing as a "sure" thing. The Jets beat the Colts in Super Bowl III. Truman beat Dewey in '48. And a Roberts-led court has given its approval to (most of) Obamacare.

Within hours of the Court's decision, reports surfaced about an extraordinary surge in contributions pouring into the Romney campaign coffers ($4.6 million in 24 hours from 47,000 donors). In politics, it's usually about the aggrieved party, and aggrieved right-wingers now have added impetus to defeat the president. Look for a "repeal and replace" moniker to assume a higher profile in the Romney lexicon.

Public opinion polls reflect a majority of Americans remain opposed to a bill that is projected to cost $1.76 trillion (over 10 years) and has already produced 5,931 pages of arcane regulations. Opponents now understand that the only way to defeat Obamacare is a Romney victory and GOP control of Congress.

The real world: Over the past two years, the president has been able to tamp down speculation that large employers will drop their employer-paid health plans and simply pay an Obamacare-required penalty instead. Many corporate bottom lines would improve as a result, but not the well-being of millions of American workers. A spate of such decisions would set off alarm bells in the White House.

Regarding Medicaid, recall that even a Democratic Congress could not pass comprehensive single-payer reform; Obamacare's increased eligibility limits (up to 133 percent of poverty) are a consolation prize for the government-run health care crowd.

Obamacare's impact will be felt disproportionately by small business owners. Many are taxed at individual rates. They will pay more and find it more expensive to offer health insurance to their employees. Remember, the most influential small business group in the country (the National Federation of Independent Business) was a plaintiff in the case.

The bottom line: Just because Obamacare is a bad idea does not mean it's unconstitutional. Whether the president decides to run on what will undoubtedly remain an unpopular program is another question. His progressive base is pleased by the high court's blessing of this aggressive federal power play. The opposition is empowered, too. The days of worrying about the "too moderate Mitt" are over. "President Romney" is the last hope to kill Obamacare. One year ago, who would have thunk?

Injecting Obamacare into Economy Will Hurt—a Lot

Robert Ehrlich says health care reform will bring higher taxes, bigger budgets, and less choice.

December 30, 2012, *The Baltimore Sun*

It's difficult to catalogue all the negative impacts of Obamacare in one place. Nevertheless, my readers deserve to know a few of the uglier details as the new year rings in one of the most expensive, convoluted policy experiments in American history:

- Lost in the hysteria surrounding Obamacare's 20 new tax increases is the law's surcharge of 0.9 percent on wages and salaries and 3.8 percent on investment income. This is another levy directed at small business owners. You know— the ones who are supposed to ramp up hiring to spark our economic recovery. A reminder: Obamacare's taxes are estimated to raise in excess of $500 billion over the next ten years.

- Next year, the federal government will fine every American who fails to purchase a "Minimum Essential" level of health coverage. One Congressional estimate found that as many as 16,500 additional IRS agents will be needed to enforce this mandate. FYI: The services to be included in the ME packages will not be decided by consumers through the health care market but by federal regulators through rule making.

- Obamacare mandates a $2,000-per-employee fine for those employers (with 50 or more employees) who find it unaffordable to continue their employer-sponsored health plans. Employees of these firms will be steered into the state-run exchanges. But no worry. Generous subsidies will be provided to those making up to $88,200 a year. What a classic Obama-ite plan: Isolate the employee from the real cost of health insurance; expand government dependence deeper into the middle class; and send the tab to the federal taxpayer.

- A chilling Christmas season headline from *The Daily Caller*: "Will Obamacare Drive Little Sisters of the Poor Out of the U.S.?" Answer: quite possibly. Obamacare's frontal attack on the conscience clause requires employers who hire without regard to religious affiliation to offer insurance services (sterilization, abortion, contraception) they find objectionable. Dropping coverage is not an attractive option; recall the aforementioned $2,000-per-employee fine due the federal government. Accordingly, the Sisters are forced to choose between their religious convictions and serving the aged and infirm.

- A new 2.3 percent tax on medical devices (implants, prosthetics, pacemakers, stents, etc.) remains one of the most unpopular items in the Obamacare-tax inventory. This is the last sector of our economy that should be singled out for punitive treatment, as these are the inventions that extend and improve our quality of life. Even worse, the tax will be collected against gross revenues, regardless of whether the manufacturer generates a profit. The industry association representing device makers estimates that 43,000 jobs will be lost thanks to this new tax. A further insult: Many of the lost jobs will be moved overseas. A repeal effort in the current Congress garnered 36 Democratic votes. And two weeks ago, 17 Democratic senators and senators-elect requested a delayed effective date. Let's hope this bad idea gets jettisoned during fiscal cliff negotiations.

- Medicare Advantage covers a quarter of all seniors with privately managed plans. The program is well regarded in senior America, but Obamacare cuts MA reimbursements by $145 billion. A likely result: Many seniors will return to traditional Medicare at reduced benefits and additional expense. How ironic that the most adversely impacted groups will be lower-income black and Hispanic seniors who like one of the government's best-run programs. (I wonder how many of these seniors remember the president's pledge that Obamacare would not require anyone to give up or change his existing health care coverage?)

- Obamacare is a budget buster of biblical proportions. The nonpartisan Congressional Budget Office initially estimated its cost at $938 billion. The latest CBO projection is $1.93 trillion. Further, millions of Americans will be added to a Medicaid program that has been driving state budget deficits for years. Obamacare's bottom line is to provide hugely expensive new subsidies for health care coverage while drastically increasing the federal government's power over the way medical services are offered and delivered.

In 2008, then-Senator Barack Obama stated, "If I were starting from scratch, if we didn't have a system in which employers had typically provided health care, I would probably go with a single-payer system." A Democratic Congress refused to follow suit, but Obamacare's 159 new agencies, boards, and commissions represent a significant step down a socialized, government-sponsored path.

Obamacare is designed to make our federal government the primary determinant of health care quality and quantity, but it doesn't end there. A new, unaffordable federal entitlement is born. Individual freedom of choice ebbs away. Another step toward a European-style delivery system is accomplished. Not a healthy day for American consumers.

Lost Jobs, Higher Costs: Obamacare Hits Home

Robert Ehrlich says the truth about the misnamed Affordable Care Act is starting to sink in.

May 24, 2013, *The Baltimore Sun*

On this Memorial Day weekend, as we remember with deepest gratitude the sacrifice of America's military heroes, we also offer our thoughts and prayers for the victims of the Oklahoma tragedy.

I've dedicated a half-dozen columns to the single most dangerous federal law passed in many years, the (not so) Affordable Care Act (aka "Obamacare").

History buffs observe that landmark pieces of legislation typically pass Congress with some degree of bipartisan support. (See, e.g., the Voting Rights Act of 1965, the Civil Rights Act of 1964, the Social Security Act of 1935, and the Medicare Act of 1965). Obamacare, however, is the exception; it failed to garner a single GOP vote. The president's signature legislative achievement was strictly a 962-page partisan affair, chock full of provisions unfamiliar to most Members who voted to pass it. Recall the immortal words of then-Speaker Nancy Pelosi, ". . . we have to pass the bill so that you can find out what is in it."

Well, the American people are beginning to understand "what is in it." And many are none too pleased.

As the numerous complexities (latest Obamacare regulatory word count: 2,864,094), contradictions and costs of Obamacare begin to register with the public—most notably employers—increasing disgruntlement emerges from high profile Democrats:

- *A trainwreck*—Senate Finance Chairman MAX BAUCUS

- *Beyond comprehension*—West Virginia Sen. JAY ROCKEFELLER

- *Let's just make sure [Obamacare is] not a third world experience*
  —HENRY CHAU
  Chief technical officer in charge of implementing
  Obamacare's insurance exchanges.

The concern is easily understood: Obamacare's primary pillars are crumbling. Witness the following oversold promises:

- *If you like your health care plan, you can keep your health care plan.*—PRESIDENT OBAMA

Well, not really. Numerous surveys reflect that Obamacare will cause a drastic decrease in the number of employers who offer health insurance. Recent congressional oversight hearings confirm the worst suspicions of Obamacare opponents: Many large businesses are deciding to pay a fee rather than continue coverage; many are converting full-time employees to part-time status; and employees who are losing coverage are experiencing great difficulties in signing up for new state insurance exchanges.

- *[Obamacare] will cut the cost of a typical family's premium up to $2,500 a year.*—PRESIDENT OBAMA

Well, not really. Even Obamacare proponents admit that millions of Americans will suffer a steep increase in their health care premiums. This is especially true for young, single adults. Most studies forecast a 40 percent to 50 percent increase for this demographic, even after premium assistance is included.

The news is only slightly better for employees of small businesses. The large insurer WellPoint concluded (in an 11-state analysis) that Obamacare-mandated small-group premiums will increase 13 percent to 23 percent. But government subsidies for small-group participants are minimal. The bottom line: higher insurance premiums for up to 10 million employees in the small-group market. What—you believed Obamacare's community rating provisions (placing older, sick people in the same risk pools as young, healthier people) would not impact premiums? FYI: The few states that already use this type of community rating have the highest premiums in the country.

- *[Obamacare is] not only about the health security of Americans. . . . In its life it will create 4 million jobs, 400,000 jobs almost immediately.*—Ms. PELOSI

Well, not really. A recent U.S. Chamber of Commerce survey revealed that 74 percent of small businesses believe Obamacare will make it more difficult to hire new employees. More daunting is the Congressional Budget Office's estimate that the tax and regulatory burdens generated by the new mandates will lead to 800,000 fewer U.S. workers by the end of 2020. In the words of CKE Restaurants CEO Andrew Puzder: "[The ACA] explicitly makes labor more expensive. It is completely predictable that businesses such as ours will search for ways to take jobs out of existing restaurants to reduce that expense." None of this should surprise even casual observers; increased labor costs always lead to reduced employment.

- *[T]hese reforms would greatly benefit Americans from all walks of life, as well as the economy as a whole.*—PRESIDENT OBAMA

Well, not really. A new gross receipts tax on medical devices may be the single most damaging of Obamacare's 18 new tax hikes.

Congress has been inundated with industry requests to repeal the law. Several Democratic senators have requested delayed implementation. Major employers such as Welch Allyn, Stryker, Boston Scientific, and Medtronic have announced significant layoffs. The Advanced Medical Technology Association estimates the new tax will cost 43,000 jobs. This levy is the grand slam of bad policies: enhanced development costs, fewer (life enhancing) inventions, lost jobs, and the migration of manufacturing jobs overseas. A mighty bad outcome for American health care.

Oh, in case you forgot, Obamacare will likely require the hiring of thousands of new IRS employees. You may have heard of this agency; they have been in the news lately. And not on the side of the taxpayer . . . what a mess!

Here's What the House Is Thinking with Its Obamacare Gambit

A veteran of the '95 government shutdown seeks to explain the calculations by the GOP as it draws a line over de-funding the Affordable Care Act.

September 22, 2013, *The Baltimore Sun*

The GOP's attempt to de-fund the "Affordable Care Act" (aka "Obamacare") is somewhat complicated, but I will attempt to bring it together for you.

We begin with the fact of universal Republican opposition to the law. Not one Republican supported Obamacare's original passage. And generally negative reviews by a nervous public since that time have only encouraged continuing attempts to slow down its implementation.

At the other end of Pennsylvania Avenue, the Obama Administration has been quite liberal with waivers, exceptions and delayed effective dates but strongly opposed to any (friendly or unfriendly) attempts to amend the bill. And this despite loud and growing opposition from some of the president's most loyal allies, including the Teamsters and Treasury Employees Union.

Another easy to understand fact: Democratic control of the Senate means opponents have no chance to amend or "starve" the bill (by denying funding) through the regular legislative process.

All of which brings us to the House GOP leadership's plan to attach an Obamacare de-funding provision to a bill (a "CR," or continuing resolution) that keeps the government funded and open for business at the end of the fiscal year.

This strategy would normally have the blessing of conservative types who are "all in" when it comes to shelving the widely unpopular health care reform.

But not in this case. Grassroots conservatives fear this is simply another "show" vote meant to placate them rather than truly derail the law. They understand that the Democratic Senate will strip a "loaded" bill of the offensive de-funding language before being returned to the House—a House that would likely accept the "clean" bill since Members had (again) gone on record as opposing the law for public consumption back home. This "cover your backside" approach is the focus of intense criticism by tea party leaders and leading Republican commentators (Rush Limbaugh, Sean Hannity, Mark Levin) content to risk a government shutdown over the issue. They believe the president has been wounded by low approval ratings, his Syria misadventures, and negative public reaction to Obamacare's approaching effective date. In their view, leveraging this next CR is the last, best chance to kill the bill.

FYI: These Members are not afraid to back up their tough talk, either. Last week, they rejected a short-term (90-day) spending package that merely provided the Senate with the option of de-funding the president's prized legislative accomplishment.

The opposing view is grounded in the harsh reality of government shutdown politics. It recognizes the GOP will most certainly be blamed for yet another chapter of frustrating government dysfunction by an Obama-compliant press. I was provided a front row seat to these negative media repercussions during the 1995 government shutdown. Although it was no big deal for me given my safe seat, it was a very big deal for those Republicans from competitive districts with large numbers of government employees.

Further, advocates of the "no-shutdown" approach point to likely GOP gains in the 2014 election (incumbent presidents typically lose seats in their 6th year midterms) that would be put at risk by a more stringent approach. The pragmatic bottom line: Why lead with our chin on a shutdown strategy when there is no reason to believe Democrats will agree to de-fund Obamacare?

Some hardliners point to the GOP's short term "win" over the president during last spring's budget showdown as "proof" the president will cave in the end. But that skirmish was one of the very few times the GOP negotiators enjoyed a degree of leverage (because of sequestration) over an Administration fearful of that ultimate budget hammer.

Such is not the case here, however. The president would welcome the harsh anti-GOP media spin that would surely follow even a short-term government shutdown. And all the more so to take attention off of Syria. He would also seek to exploit the above-cited marginal seat Republicans who would likely have little enthusiasm for a sustained shutdown. What an opportunity for a president gifted at blaming Republicans for all that ails a broken Capitol Hill.

The foregoing presents a monumental test for House Speaker John Boehner. Many rank and file tea party-inspired Members are unsatisfied with yet another "symbolic" vote to kill a law that has begun to inflict great damage and confusion within the health care marketplace. They are encouraged in their opposition by feedback from influential activists who enjoy outsized influence in so many safe (GOP stronghold) districts. Accordingly, they demand a strategy that marries de-funding of Obamacare with a must-pass piece of legislation such as the continuing resolution. (The upcoming vote on raising the debt ceiling presents another such "marital" option.)

This is a difficult call for conservatives. The stakes are high. Wildly conflicting policy (and political) goals are at play. More than one political career has been made or broken in such circumstances.

Obamacare Is a Turkey Ready for Slaughter

Republicans should dig in their heels and continue the fight.

November 10, 2013, *The Baltimore Sun*

Obamacare = Prenatal and Mammogram Screenings for YOUNG MEN—FINALLY!

Hopefully, you now understand why I have devoted about a dozen of my Sunday columns to the trainwreck widely known as Obamacare. From the beginning, this mega combination of many poor (and a few good) ideas was destined to be problematic in the real world of a market economy.

Here are my indictments:

Scope: Prior to Obamacare, approximately 15 percent of Americans were either under-insured or lacked health insurance. And there were plenty of proposals around that could have been cobbled together in order to pass a truly bipartisan bill. Such initiatives included allowing insurance policies to be written across state lines, reforming state high-risk insurance pools (to deal with pre-existing conditions), expanding health savings accounts, and building protocols for state based tort reform measures. Yet, the president sought to remake all of American health care, thereby impacting 17 percent of the American economy and causing tremendous disruptions in the individual and group markets. And he did it with a bill that generated not a single Republican vote. No wonder Obamacare lacks even a modicum of good will during these ugly opening days.

"One size fits all": A classic progressive mindset is now an unattractive reality for those in the individual market. You see, the president never really meant, "You can keep your present health care insurance if you want to." What he really meant to say was, "We know better than you what you really want and need." Accordingly, Obamacare-generated regulations have terminated the vast majority of so-called "substandard" insurance policies previously operating within the individual market. (Approximately 19 million Americans could feel the brunt of this change.) There is positive news, however. The president wants you to feel good about your new, more expensive plan. But, a dirty little secret is attached: The additional benefits you will now be required to purchase (many of which you do not need) will help subsidize the older and sicker, many of whom will now qualify for taxpayer subsidies on the state exchanges. Note to those misguided young men who helped make Barack Obama a two-term president: Your required purchase of prenatal care and mammogram screenings is the logical result of your vote; you are the chosen cross-subsidizers of the misnamed "Affordable Care Act." Remember: elections have consequences.

"We'll take that": The transfer of wealth (rather than the creation of same) is another fundamental tenet of progressivism. And this prized value is well represented in Obamacare's 2,300 pages of text, 10,516 pages of regulations (as of Sept. 10), and 22 new tax increases. Total wealth transfer is unknowable, but assuredly monumental. The price tag represents the largest tax increase in U.S. history.

Single Payer: The president has been none too shy about his preference for a single payer system. (You might recognize this as the wonderful system that encourages so many Canadians to seek quality health care in the U.S.) Indeed, some believe Congressional Democrats will utilize Obamacare's notable shortcomings to seek this ultimate mechanism of federal control. This notion is bolstered by the one aspect of Obamacare that is functional: rapid Medic-aid enrollment. This costliest of entitlement programs is proving to be an attractive alternative to the new exchange plans; nearly 90 percent of Obamacare enrollees are new Medicaid sign-ups. And nobody can claim surprise. After all, something for nothing has been Obamacare's (and the whole of the Obama Administration's) core attribute from Day One. The problem only occurs when that nothing turns out to be something; a lot of something for those governors who decided to take the "free" federal money (for three years) and run.

Reduced choice: Higher insurance premiums and fewer pro-vider options are the marketplace realities of the new exchanges. You see, large provider networks were cut in order for exchange options to be even minimally competitive. And the notion of a $2,500 savings per family should be added to the growing list of Obamacare's false promises.

Memory loss: I have up until now been sympathetic to the president's persistent claim that he was "out of the loop" regarding major scandals. After all, it is impossible to be up on everything going down around a gargantuan federal government. Neverthe-less, the rapidly expanding list of "I didn't knows" from the pres-ident has become problematic: Angela Merkel's phone intercepts, illegal IRS targeting, Fox News D.C. correspondent James Ros-en's phone logs, Benghazi terror warnings, mass NSA phone taps, and the spectacularly not-ready-for-prime-time Obamacare web-site constitute a disturbing trend. Three explanations present them-selves: The president is too detached from a number of his most important tasks; the president's staff keeps him in the dark in order to maintain deniability when things go south; and/or the presi-dent is less than forthcoming when commenting on matters of great import. None of these explanations is particularly appealing to a country that instinctively wants to believe its president.

Clintonite tactics: You remember the Clintons' modus operandi: Destroy the accuser. The Hillary-approved tactic was employed whenever her husband suffered a "bimbo eruption," a not infrequent occurrence. Similarly, today's Obamacare defenders rant, rave, and blame the GOP for Obamacare's numerous problems. And, as always, there's a frequent hint of Republican racism to explain the party's united opposition to the bill. Well, enough is enough. Here's hoping Republicans will not back off. Many were sent to Washington to oppose Obamacare. Many of their predictions are proving all too accurate. We can do better, but not with this turkey. Scrap it now, before it's too late.

Obamacare Hurts More Than Helps

Ehrlich: Obamacare is the most hurtful legislation of my lifetime.

March 16, 2014, *The Baltimore Sun*

There is a reason I have written about the Affordable Care Act ("Obamacare") more than a dozen times (and why it is the most extensive chapter in my new book): The law is the most hurtful legislation imposed on the American people in my lifetime.

But shuffling through daily bits of negative reviews is confusing. And so, as a public service, herein the latest (major) impacts to date:

- We now know the Obama Administration never intended for those in the individual insurance market to keep their doctor, hospital, or insurance. Obamacare's purveyors were intent on forcing those individuals to purchase the insurance product the government wanted them to have, not the "garbage" products that met their needs and pocketbooks. A weak apology from the president for his repeated mis-representations notwithstanding, many of the afflicted were suddenly without insurance, while others were forced to pay for services they neither wanted nor needed, e.g., mammo-grams for men.

- The flip side of "one size fits all" in the individual mar-ket was less consumer choice. The long list of newly man-dated benefits required carriers to narrow their networks of doctors and hospitals. As numerous pundits have pointed out, the new menu was basically four HMO options forced on a population that formerly enjoyed real choice (13,000 different plans, according to eHealthInsurance.com). Alas, the public outcry has been so intense that the president announced a two-year delay on the cancellation of the formerly "inadequate policies." But half of the country's insurance commissioners have said they will not seek to revive policies that the original mandate killed.

- The young people who twice put Barack Obama in the White House have wised up to Obamacare's generational bait and switch. Their failure to participate in the exchanges has revealed the law's soft (fiscal) underbelly. The accompanying economics are easy to understand: Without these heretofore easy targets, the law's attempt to transfer wealth from young to old (and healthy to sick) does not work.

- Other (less sympathetic) victims are the insurance companies who bought into provisions that hold carriers harmless once medical claims exceed anticipated costs (the so-labeled "risk-corridor" program). Since the Administration's own numbers now show an older, sicker population is signing on to the exchanges ("adverse selection"), the companies are looking for the promised fix: a taxpayer bailout. But House Republicans (led by Rep. Eric Cantor) are attempting to peel away these rescue packages. Stay tuned on this one.

- The Congressional Budget Office originally estimated that Obamacare would bleed 800,000 full-time equivalent jobs out of the economy. Two weeks ago, the CBO released a new eye popping estimate of a 2.5 million job loss (by 2024). The White House has been in damage control ever since. In perhaps the most revealing demonstration of progressive illogic ever, the Administration offered that such impact was not significant since fewer workers will now be concerned with health insurance in their job seeking endeavors.

- The infamous medical device tax is the most easily understood of Obamacare's countless deficiencies. This gross receipts tax on medical devices collects dollars regardless of whether the product has produced a profit. As such, it discourages innovation in a field where research and development is already prohibitively expensive. The not so surprising result will be fewer life sustaining inventions and a substantial loss of high-tech jobs. Already, major manufacturers such as Stryker and Medtronic have announced significant layoffs as a direct result of the new levy. And let's not forget that these products lead to longer and more productive lives; not exactly the type of sector you might think the government would target. Republican-generated repeal efforts have attracted a number of Democratic votes in both houses of Congress.

- Last week, UNITE HERE (a major union) wrote a letter to congressional Democrats bemoaning the ACA's "threat" to the middle class, including "higher premiums, loss of hours, and a shift to part-time work and less comprehensive coverage." Just the most recent example of labor's opposition to a bill they once promoted (but were promised would never hurt them). Now, the hurt is becoming all too real.

Negative impacts from Obamacare have become a regular part of daily media coverage. The bill is causing great uncertainty within our employer communities and health care system. And it can't be fixed in its present form (witness another delay in the employer mandate—this time until after the 2014 midterm elections). Give credit where credit is due—the president promised a new era of transparency; this convenient political maneuver intended to protect vulnerable Democrats couldn't be more obvious.

The sooner Obamacare goes away, the quicker people of good faith on both sides of the aisle can collaborate on solutions that work.

Affordable Care Act Lies

Obamacare is a failure that should be repealed and replaced.

September 21, 2014, *The Baltimore Sun*

The man-made catastrophe known as the "Affordable Care Act" and "Obamacare" still lurks. And nobody should interpret the absence of daily negative headlines as a sign the law's myriad problems have been rectified, or that there is substance to Harry Reid's claim of "untrue" horror stories following the law's implementation.

So, how much damage has been inflicted now that gross ineptitude in foreign policy has replaced gross ineptitude in health care policy?

Let me count the ways . . . and lies:

Young people will love it. Not exactly. Obamacare requires insurers to charge the same premium regardless of medical condition and accepts everyone who signs up. This perversion of market economics requires lots of young, healthy people to be overcharged in order to cover the costs of undercharged older, sicker people. When young people said "no, thanks," the White House turned to its allies in Hollywood to change their minds. Plenty remain unconvinced.

Everybody will finally be covered . . . for less than $1 trillion. A single-payer-friendly president sold the dream of universal coverage. But this summer's enrollment numbers fell well short of coverage targets. Further, the Congressional Budget Office's (CBO) original projection of a $938 billion price tag (over 10 years) now surpasses $1.3 trillion.

Health care reform will have little impact on employment. Labor force participation is at its lowest point in 40 years. The recovery has been historically weak and protracted. And the CBO blew the doors off with a February report reflecting an Obamacare-induced projected loss of two million jobs (out of the labor market) by 2017—mostly from workers choosing to supply less labor. Now, three Federal Reserve banks report private sector survey respondents are either cutting jobs, shifting workers to part-time status and/or increasing the employee contribution to their health care plans—all as a result of Obamacare. The bottom line: Americans are working less and in more unproductive ways. Many predicted this response, yours truly included. (See page 195 of "America: Hope for Change.")

You can keep your insurance if you like. Not really. White House memos reveal the president's staff knowingly misled millions of policy holders within the individual market. Over 6 million Americans had their health coverage canceled as a result. Today, additional millions within the group market are finding it equally difficult to keep their physician, specialist, and plan. Once the 2013 "Lie of the Year" (per PolitiFact) was revealed, Obamacare apologists retreated to familiar ground. The always dependable "But our motives were good" and "The government knows better than you" were offered as though the misrepresentations used to pass the law should be ignored. Those Americans who have felt the sting of Obamacare continue to take issue with the notion.

The medical device tax as money maker. This one was *never* sold as good policy, but just another revenue source. And predictions of deep lay-offs in the technology sector have proven correct. A recent industry survey concluded that the tax caused companies to lay-off or avoid hiring 33,000 workers in 2013 alone.

Now comes news that revenue will fail to meet projections and that the IRS is having difficulty identifying which companies to tax. Repeal has bipartisan appeal. But Democrats must pressure the president to get it done.

A progressive conscience clause. The president's bullying tactics over religious liberty plays well for the "war on women" audience, not so much in the courts. The "Hobby Lobby" decision was a serious setback for the Administration's aggressive re-write of religious conscience clause protection. Looks like The Little Sisters of the Poor and similarly situated charities and schools will win their contraception mandate challenges, too. Seems *so* many years ago the president promised respect for religious liberty during a highly anticipated speech at Notre Dame.

The typical family will save $2,500 a year. The Administration is generally mum on this old campaign promise. The reality is some consumers have seen lower premiums, others higher premiums, and just about everyone is experiencing higher deductibles. I can find no incumbent Democrat running on this particular promise.

Nobody will deny you coverage due to a pre-existing condition. One of the few bipartisan provisions in the legislation could have been accomplished in a simple bill via the creation of federal risk pools. Alas, the provision was incorporated into a 1,200 page monstrosity. Only 107,000 people took advantage of this policy change over the first three years of Obamacare.

Obamacare includes a few good and many bad policies pieced together in order to fulfill a campaign promise. To paraphrase Nancy Pelosi, we now know what's wrong in the bill.

Going forward, we must repeal and replace this turkey. A universal tax credit for everyone and health savings accounts for those in high deductible plans is a good first step. So is making Harry Reid Senate *minority* leader in November.

Obamacare Is a "Varsity Stinker"

November 23, 2014, *The Baltimore Sun*

O K, I can't help myself. Over the past three years, I have written at least a dozen columns critical of Obamacare (a.k.a. The "Affordable Care Act") in this space and devoted an entire chapter to the topic in my book "America: Hope for Change."

Yet, here I am with another piece on this man-made catastrophe. The reason: recently published stories that run right to my thesis—it's a varsity stinker that must be repealed.

One storyline concerns shocking comments made by a key adviser in designing the ACA, MIT Professor Jonathan Gruber. The relevant comments were recently released on YouTube, and include the following:

- "This bill was written in a tortured way to make sure [Congressional Budget Office] did not score the mandate as taxes. If CBO scored the mandate as taxes, the bill dies. . . . Lack of transparency is a huge political advantage. And basically, call it the stupidity of the American voter or whatever, but basically that was really, really critical to getting the thing to pass."

    This cynical indictment of the president's signature legislative initiative is not brought to you by some partisan hack. This was the guy the White House turned to when it wanted to develop national health care reform, the guy whose ideas the president said he had "stolen ideas from liberally," who was paid $400,000 by the Obama Administration to tell them how much it would cost to overhaul

16 percent of the American economy. Now we are informed it was a task he purposefully made hyper-confusing for the average health care consumer. Rarely is the general public forced to consume such Washington hubris in one fell swoop. But here it is in all its glory. Reminder: Your tax dollars paid this guy's hefty fee.

- Another story concerns the Supreme Court's decision to hear the case of King vs. Burwell. Recall the clear language of the ACA: Health insurance purchasers are eligible to receive subsidies when buying from state exchanges, but only 14 states set up an exchange. As a result, the feds stepped in with their own exchanges—with subsidies—despite no authorizing language in the law. Mr. Gruber has stated publicly his view that citizens of states without a state exchange do not qualify for subsidies: "If you're a state and you don't set up an exchange, that means your citizens don't get their tax credits, but your citizens still pay the taxes that support the bill."

  Such was the carrot and stick approach used to encourage states to set up their own exchanges. And recall this is a critical issue since the ACA exempts individuals from its mandate if the cost of purchasing a policy exceeds 8 percent of the individual's income. Hence, millions of Americans who will become ineligible for subsidies will also be exempt from the individual mandate.

- Storyline three concerns the increasing number of institutions and businesses deciding to either drop health benefits or cut worker hours in order to duck the ACA's employer mandate—the requirement that larger employers provide health coverage to their employees working at least 30 hours per week or face a $2,000 per employee penalty. Accordingly, today's headlines are replete with stories of employers dumping previously covered employees on to the Obamacare exchanges or cutting work schedules for part-time employees under the new 30-hour threshold. Fewer hours equals less take-home income for millions of American workers.

Obamacare's numerous oversold promises will become the focus of increased congressional oversight now that Republicans have regained control of the Senate. Look for attempts to repeal the most damaging elements of the bill (including, but not limited to, repeals of the medical device tax and the employer mandate, and a return to an under 40-hour definition of "part-time" employment) as the 114th Congress begins.

None of this should be surprising for those of you who have followed my long-running analysis of the ACA. Still, all of you should take the time to read the widely disseminated video transcripts of Professor Gruber. The condescension is startling, as is the deception.

For conservatives, the good professor's admissions are simply one more example of Washington, D.C.'s elitist attitude toward "flyover" (read: red) America. Yet, maybe, the results of Nov. 4th show the average voter has grown tired of such treatment. One can certainly "hope" that such a "change" in attitude will extend beyond one election cycle.

On the other side of the aisle, the outing of Professor Gruber's cynical construction of Obamacare is a very public embarrassment. But nobody should be terribly surprised. This condescending attitude has been famously articulated by the president. Recall "they cling to their guns or religion or antipathy toward people who aren't like them" (on those opposed to immigration reform) and "they didn't build that" (on self-made entrepreneurs). These and other similar quips reflect the Obama Democrats' view that the great unwashed (that's you) really don't get it—you're just too ignorant to see that Washington knows best.

The ACA may indeed be one of the more damaging pieces of legislation passed by Congress in many years, but it sure has given us new insight into how and why progressives do what they do. Scary.

PART 5

★ ★ ★

Abiding by
Immigration Law

My former congressional colleague and friend, Sonny Bono, once answered a debate question about illegal immigration with a classic rhetorical response: "What's to talk about? It's illegal." Fast forward to Barack Obama's America where such a comment would be viewed in poor taste. Indeed, we have traveled a long and strenuously politically correct road since that famous quote was uttered in 1992.

The second decade of the new millennium has brought serious cultural chasms over immigration policy. The Republicans have the better side of the debate for a basic reason: They at least have *some* appreciation for sovereignty and the rule of law. Alas, all is not so grand with the GOP. Our love for country and respect for its laws can get us (and our candidates) carried away at times. Reference Mitt Romney's desire for "self-deportation" circa 2012. Others may cite the failure of a Republican-led Congress to offer a sensible immigration bill to the American public. Such actions provide fodder for those who find evidence of nativism in the GOP's public stances. Yet, it is difficult for *this* Republican to stray too far from Representative Bono's admonition. The law *has* to be more than a simple suggestion if we are to respect and abide by it.

Which brings me to that lost crowd popularly known as Democrats. How else to characterize a party that regularly pays the rule of law little more than lip service?

A transcript of a *Washington Post* debate between yours truly and Governor Martin O'Malley, circa 2010, includes

O'Malley referring to illegals as "new Americans" (count 'em) six times. My response made national news: "By the way, if somebody breaks into my house, is that a new member of my family that night?" (I never did receive a satisfactory answer to my inquiry.) The fact that O'Malley *won* the election reflects how much we have lost our way on such a critical issue.

But the insults do not stop with Mr. O'Malley. Witness Barack Obama (mockingly) asking a large crowd of Hispanics whether the Republicans would prefer a "giant moat" on the southern border, or the once unimaginable extension of executive amnesty to over four million illegal immigrants in a single order. *Audacious* is an appropriate term here, as is unconstitutional.

There is, in fact, a place in the post-Obama world for a sensible immigration policy—one that seeks to fix a system that is so obviously broken.

What It Will Take to Get the GOP
On Board with Immigration Reform

Many obstacles remain, but the ingredients for an immigration deal are there.

July 7, 2013, *The Baltimore Sun*

Attempting to narrow America's immigration debate down to an easily understood set of issues is no easy task. But that's why The Sun pays me the big bucks. So, with no further caveats, I offer comprehensive immigration reform in 800 words, more or less:

The politics: Not too complicated here: It has become a post-Romney article of faith in GOP circles that the lopsided margin for the president among Hispanic (71 percent vs. 27 percent) and Asian voters (73 percent vs. 26 percent) was the result of perceived GOP indifference (and/or opposition) to passing an immigration bill. Whether this public perception is fact based is almost beside the point; most GOPers understand that demographic trends necessitate better Republican performance in these growing voting blocs. And it's clear how good the Democrats have become at demagoguing the "anti-immigrant party." Major GOP Hispanic leaders (Sens. Marco Rubio and Ted Cruz and New Mexico Gov. Susana Martinez) help, but a substantive fix of a terribly broken system is required.

The border: Repairing a broken border is a threshold issue for Republicans but far less of an issue for Democrats. (Recall President Barack Obama making light during the campaign of the GOP's alleged plans for a moat at the Mexico border.) Most Republicans have been screaming for increased border security since 9/11. Most Democrats have been offering increasingly attractive incentives (welfare benefits, drivers licenses, voting rights) to immigrants in the country illegally over the same period of time. And Democrats have won the last two national elections.

It sure seems like a long time ago when my former House colleague, Rep. Sonny Bono, famously stated during a U.S. Senate debate, "When something is illegal, it's illegal. Enforce the law." (The year was 1992). But we have failed to enforce the law at our southern border. And a more progressive culture has not been overly impressed with Republican calls to strengthen border defenses over the past 20 years.

This one, however, remains *the* issue for conservatives, particularly the conservative media. Republicans in Congress will require serious, objective measures of border enforcement as a price of their support on final passage. And it will be Senator Rubio who will continue to play the role of conservative opinion leader (and deal maker) on this fundamental issue.

The price they will pay: Fortunately, most folks have abandoned the idea of a mass deportation. Which begs the next key question for lawmakers: How many tests/evaluations will the heretofore undocumented be required to pass before the new law will deem them "legal"?

There appears to be general agreement around the plank(s) of clean criminal background checks (no felonies) and payment of a fine ($500–$1,000). But much controversy continues to surround hot button issues such as access to welfare benefits and tax credits, (proof of) payment of back taxes, and the carrying of a biometric card to record exit and entry into the country.

These, then, are the primary hurdles previously undocumented workers will be required to jump through in order to gain legal presence. But once the hurdles are negotiated, what then?

Well, a "registered provisional immigrant status," so long as the foregoing requirements are met. Then, after some period of time (10 years in the Senate bill), immigrants could seek a green card and lawful permanent legal status—if taxes are paid, another fine is paid, they have maintained continuous presence in the U.S., and have learned English.

Work visas and the tech economy: It is a sad fact of life that American higher education fails to produce the engineers needed to fuel our new knowledge economy. Hence, the H-1B visa growth industry, a mini-tech immigration service that provides technology workers (primarily engineers) with temporary work permits in the U.S. The Senate reform bill would increase the annual cap on such visas from 65,000 to 110,000 and possibly up to 180,000 depending on domestic demand and the U.S. unemployment level.

The issues here are two-fold: (1) What is the appropriate number of such visas needed to feed the American economy? and (2) Are some firms taking advantage of these foreign workers (primarily from India) by placing them in lower wage corporate positions?

Although critics of the program argue that these workers take jobs from Americans, this issue is not particularly partisan or philosophical. But it is venue driven. Members (particularly in the House) are sensitive to the constituent needs of their districts. Hence, the presence of growth orientated high technology firms in Members' districts makes Republicans and Democrats favorably inclined toward expanding this program.

The Senate's passage of its reform bill signaled the end of Round One. Round Two will play out in the House, where provisions regarding border security and a path to citizenship will be beefed up. And Speaker John Boehner has promised that only a bill enjoying majority GOP support will be brought to the floor.

It's not yet half-time, but a long overdue immigration fix is in sight.

Immigration Reform School

First, secure the border; then agree on amnesty and a path to legality.

August 17, 2014, *The Baltimore Sun*

Time for a brutal assessment regarding the state of immigration reform in America. Extreme partisans on both sides of the aisle—you will not like what you read over the next two minutes. Hopefully, the rest of you will chew on it for a bit.

First, the GOP. The upside here is that a majority of Republicans seem to have at least some appreciation for the rule of law. In the context of immigration reform, this instinct plays out in a desire to enforce the law—just like every other civilized country in the world, especially Mexico.

Yet Republicans have fallen short of the mark. We love to praise Ronald Reagan but conveniently forget that he signed a real amnesty bill. You can look it up: Almost three million illegal immigrants were made legal under his watch.

Moreover, some of our more zealous candidates tend to advocate positions that might play well in primaries but are wholly unenforceable in real life. The proposal to round up as many as 14 million "undocumented" foreigners prior to consideration of immigration reform fits here. And I won't get into how such an untenable proposal sounds to people of good faith (particularly independents) who want viable solutions to our border problems.

And then there are the Democrats. The Party of FDR, Truman, and Kennedy now laughs out loud whenever the issue of border security is introduced. In states like Maryland, successful Democrats run on platforms that offer sanctuary status—a public position that assures people in the country illegally that the state is not serious about enforcing its laws.

Some of you more naive types might think that such an "open borders" policy would constitute an "unforced error" in a time of terror, but far from it. In reliably blue states, an open invitation to flaunt the law carries no adverse consequences. In fact, all the better to run up the score with Hispanic voters. You might have noticed the sitting U.S. president is of this ilk. Recall his cynical "maybe [the Republicans] need a moat; maybe they'll need alligators" line about border security from 2011. The fact that such unserious rhetoric actually works should remind everyone how far left a once proud blue-collar party has digressed.

Unfortunately, the respective parties have left us between a rock and a hard place. The Republicans are deathly afraid, and the Democrats don't really care. What to do?

Herewith, a plan:

First, hire as many additional border agents as needed to get the job done. Once personnel needs are met, complete fencing where it makes sense (remember fences *work*—just ask any West Bank Israeli). Then, utilize state-of-the-art drone technology to police difficult to defend places along the border. Finally, sit down with President Enrique Peña Nieto of Mexico to reiterate why America is getting as serious about border control as . . . Mexico. Play hardball if required, but President Nieto's active cooperation is a necessary element of southern border security.

Once objective, quantifiable security measures are up and running, serious people from both sides of the aisle can get down to work. Serious in this context means arriving at a working definition of "amnesty."

My view is to promote a "path to legality" for those who are here illegally but possess a clean criminal record, marketable job skills, at least some proficiency in English, and owe no back taxes. An additional military or public service commitment could be added here as well.

Still, the path will be narrow. These prerequisites mean the individual will become a legal, non-citizen, guest worker for a period of years. Welfare benefits will not be available, but the promise of a legal residency should help bring the "hidden millions" out from the shadows.

Important note: The politically thorny issue of ultimate citizenship can be worked out during negotiations. Some will insist that those who arrived illegally should never be rewarded with full citizenship. Others will offer that a fresh beginning requires a real shot at full legal status. Regardless of where one falls on this issue, it should be beyond question that those who followed legal process and did the right thing should be first in line for citizenship.

One last point. The humanitarian crisis of 2014 must be solved as soon as possible. Children who have a credible claim of persecution in their home country should be allowed to stay just like any other person seeking asylum. The remainder should be returned to their parents. Money required to fund both policies should be appropriated, quickly.

Why Obama Is Viewed as Weak

November 30, 2014, *The Baltimore Sun*

Two recent Presidential pronouncements reflect the essential Barack Obama. Each also explains why so many view him to be the weakest of American presidents.

Example one pertains to Mr. Obama's public reaction to the gruesome terrorist murders of five Jewish worshippers during morning prayers in a Jerusalem synagogue on Nov. 18th.

Those of you able to watch the president's reaction that afternoon may recall the unemotional monotone during remarks expressing American outrage at the carnage. But it was what followed the initial words of condemnation that revealed the inner Barack Obama—the one that seeks out a moral equivalence whenever America is engaged in the world (particularly where American diplomacy or military assets are at stake), and the Israeli-Palestinian conflict is no exception.

From this egalitarian predicate, the president held both "sides" jointly liable for the daily outrages that desecrate the Holy Land. As such, the president's calls for "mutual restraint" were targeted as much toward the defensive Israelis as the offensive Palestinians.

That this ambivalence with regard to Israeli policy has been exacerbated during the tenure of Bibi Netanyahu is without doubt. In turn, the Israeli prime minister understands this American president has been weak on Israel since his days in the U.S. Senate. Expressions of moral (or any other type of) equivalence by Mr. Obama only further strengthens this notion, particularly among the Israeli right.

It is here the former law professor prefers to intellectualize shades of gray where stronger leaders would see black and white—kind of like a law professor directing students to argue both sides of a case. But the embattled Mr. Netanyahu has no such luxury. His is a daily experience in survival—surrounded by enemies sworn to destroy his country, including the mislabeled "peace loving" Palestinians, a majority of whom vocally and often violently demonize the Jewish state (check out the media scenes of Palestinians celebrating news of the synagogue murders—even making sweets in order for their children to participate in the "good" times).

Example two concerns the facts and circumstances surrounding the president's groundbreaking immigration announcement that suspends the deportation of almost 5 million illegal immigrants. Herewith, five considerations as you digest this latest assault on the Constitution:

- Recall that the Democrats controlled all three branches of government during the first two years of Obama I. Accordingly, the president and Democratic leadership could have passed any iteration of immigration reform they wished; the Republicans were powerless to stop them. Yet, not one bill emerged from either chamber of Congress. Rarely is the president asked why he failed to press his advantage at the time.

- The media (particularly Fox) has run dozens of video clips wherein the president repeatedly voices his opinion that he lacked the power to sign an executive action of this magnitude. The pre-midterm interviews are replete with warnings about how such an action would be "unfair," "illegal," "illogical," and "not how we do things" in our system of government. Such disingenuousness is one reason why the president's credibility has slipped so dramatically over the past two years.

- In a well-timed ploy reminiscent of white-coated physicians descending on the Rose Garden to shower praise on

Obamacare, the White House released a list of (count 'em!) 10 prominent lefty law professors supportive of the executive action power play. (A number of the signatories have personal connections with the president.) In light of the president's long and undistinguished Supreme Court losing streak on matters of executive branch overreach, Mr. Obama will assuredly need all the professor-types he can gather.

• The last thing an American president should do is reflect any sense of understanding or empathy toward the Palestinian Authority until such time as it stops its determined effort to invite another intifada. A fragile Israel simply can't afford such indulgences into moral equivalence when so many guns are pointed at its head.

• Democratic apologists claim previous presidents issued similar orders. Yet, as numerous pundits (and law professors) have pointed out, this order is distinguished from previous directives since it does not interpret an existing law, is not done on a country-specific basis, has no connection to a humanitarian crisis in the country of origin, and is clearly contrary to congressional intent. Oh, and few if any serious observers believe a "dysfunctional" Congress is an appropriate rationale for such unilateral action.

For those of you inclined toward a different perspective, you might check out Professor Jonathan Turley's widely cited dissenting critique. The self-professed liberal academic is the lead attorney attempting to defeat this latest Administration power grab.

Footnote: The Department of Justice provided its legal support for the order with about one hour to spare. There was also a report that DOJ originally opposed the action—presumably before they were reminded who signed their paychecks.

Sanctuary Cities

August 4, 2015, *The Weekly Standard*

Sometimes, those of us left in the common sense majority ask how things could go so wrong—how consensually accepted notions of justice could be scuttled so quickly, and how respect for the rule of law could have fallen so low—that a major American city would find it acceptable to provide safe passage to an illegal alien who had been deported on five previous occasions.

Such is the reality check presented in the matter of thirty-two-year-old Kate Steinle, the mother of two brutally gunned down by one Francisco Sanchez, a Mexican citizen living freely on the streets because of San Francisco's self-proclaimed "sanctuary" status—a state of affairs that *mandates* lack of cooperation with federal officials charged with enforcing the country's immigration laws because . . . they . . . can.

The murder generated the usual and expected public outcry, albeit among major media and public officials it was mostly confined to Republican and conservative commentators and politicians. What, you thought MSNBC would moralize about its favorite progressive mecca?

Which brings us to a remarkable place in the evolution of progressivism in the good ole USA: *One of our two political parties is no longer concerned with immigration law.* Indeed, many of its elected officials go to great lengths to distance themselves from it and then market their non-compliance to politically active "immigrants' rights" groups. You may recognize practitioners of the art by their willingness to characterize calls for border enforcement as "anti-immigrant" or "nativist."

On the progressive side of the political universe, it's as though federal immigration law has been reduced to a discretionary set of suggestions to be either followed or ignored by the dictates of local office holders. And of all the sanctuary cities in the country, the wholly owned Democratic city of San Francisco occupies a special place in its disdain for U.S. sovereignty.

The facts of the Sanchez case speak directly to the hubris of the city's progressive leadership. You see, Mr. Sanchez was released from federal custody (wherein he was serving time for entering the country after deportation) and turned over to the San Francisco sheriff pursuant to an outstanding criminal warrant. Alas, the San Francisco district attorney declined to prosecute because the warrant was a decade old (drug) possession charge. But this is not the gravamen of the outrage. You see, ICE had previously filed a detainer requesting it be notified if the city intended to release Mr. Sanchez—a dangerous alien repeat offender. But San Francisco authorities failed to honor the detainer. Kate Steinle's murder was a horrific consequence of this premeditated and conscious failure.

The city's uber-progressive leadership shows no signs of retreating from its lawless policy. It's as if a certain level of collateral damage is discounted in order to maintain itself as the center of the sensitivity universe.

In the real world (outside of San Francisco and other similarly situated cities), however, there are calls to boycott sanctuary jurisdictions and even cut off federal funding.

I am far from convinced that the successful execution of these sanctions will change (bleeding) hearts and minds. Recall these are the politicians who long ago decided that repeated illegal re-entry into the country was a "no count." But now they are confronted with a far deeper level of condemnation attendant to Kate Steinle and other innocents hurt or killed by people who have no business being in the country in the first place.

Maybe, just maybe, law abiding Americans now finding themselves on the wrong end of the sanctuary city scam are beginning to care, and to count the victims. This status quo is unacceptable. An empathetic but law-abiding people must ensure that Kate Steinle's death is not in vain—the ruminations and excuse-making of the usual suspects notwithstanding.

Time to get a serious grip in The City by the Bay.

PART 6

A Weak Presidency
Leads to a More
Dangerous World

AN ABIDING IMPACT OF MODERN PROGRESSIVISM on the young Barack Obama is unfortunately reflected as much in foreign policy as domestic issues.

What other outcome was possible? The young law professor and politician was indoctrinated by a who's who of radical left, progressive, anti-war all-stars: Bill Ayers, Frank Marshall Davis, Derrick Bell, and that notable man of the cloth, Reverend Jeremiah Wright.

The resulting worldview screams "Dove!"—and much more. And it is the "more" that has given our friends and enemies alike plenty of reasons to view America as a declining superpower. You see, Barack Obama is an anti-war community organizer gone wild, influenced by a healthy dose of anti-colonialism and the hard left's profound animosity toward the projection of American military strength around the world.

And therein lies the weak link of the internationalist Obama—a leader more interested in ending wars as opposed to ending them on favorable terms—the U.S. president more interested in world public opinion polls (witness the president's June, 2015 claim that America is "the most respected country on Earth" under his leadership) as opposed to whether our allies trust us and enemies fear us. Throw in the naiveté of an academic, outsized ego, and a genuine distrust of the U.S. military, and you have a formula guaranteed to make the world a more dangerous place for America and its allies and those who rely on us to protect them.

This mindset embraces a familiar set of left-leaning principles. The projection of U.S. military might *causes* Muslim hatred of America; selling out Poland and the Czech Republic on missile defense will contribute to a happy "reset" with Russia; placating Putin will cause the Russian bear to back down on Ukraine; indifference to the "green" revolutionaries in Iran will bring the Ayatollahs to the nuclear negotiating table; the warmonger Netanyahu must be replaced by a Labor government. How else to convince Hamas to give up its terrorist ways?

I could go on but I'm certain you get the point. The smartest guy in the room believed his Muslim background, Nobel Peace Prize, and visceral distrust of military engagement would get the world to *like* us (and *him*), and in the process bring peace. After all, a de-fanged, reformed Uncle Sam had promised to lead from behind—way behind. Only one problem presents itself: When the single greatest force for good on the planet exits stage left, the resulting vacuum tends to get filled by lots of (now fearless and empowered) bad guys with evil intent, territorial ambitions, and time on their hands. And, if history is any barometer, such situations rarely lead to real peace.

Can Jewish Voters Be Sure of Obama's Commitment to Israel?

Iranian nuclear threat could undermine support for president

September 2, 2012, *The Baltimore Sun*

O ne of the more intriguing aspects of Campaign 2012 is the impact of Obama Administration rhetoric and policies on the Jewish vote.

Obama supporters dismiss any thought of discord among this vital Democratic constituency. They point to sustained Jewish support for Democratic presidential candidates in every presidential election cycle. Indeed, it is a rare occasion when the Democratic nominee fails to garner 65 percent of the Jewish vote. And this year's Republican ticket fits their preferred narrative to a T.

In Mitt Romney, they see a conservative Mormon businessman with a tea party favorite as his running mate. Democratic operatives are further enthused by the outrageous rape and contraception comments of Rep. Todd Akin. Such incidents play into the now-familiar indictment of an "extreme" party controlled by that most dangerous of constituencies, the Christian right.

This narrative is easily made and eagerly bought by a majority of progressive Jewish Democrats. It is sustained by a distrust of conservative Republicans on a wide variety of social issues, including abortion, school prayer, social welfare, and gun control. (Even the GOP's unshakable support for the state of Israel dissuades few from this popular caricature).

I know from whence I speak: A conservative Republican in deep-blue Maryland has a monumental task in changing Jewish hearts and minds outside of the predominantly right-leaning Orthodox community. The easily demonized likes of Akin, Sarah Palin, Michele Bachmann, and other prominent tea party leaders make the task considerably more difficult.

But Campaign 2012 may complicate the usual formulas. And I'm not referring to leftover political scars from then-Senator Obama's spotty voting record on Israel, or the president's past association with the likes of the Rev. Jeremiah Wright.

More recently, and more importantly, the Administration's (quickly retracted) position that Middle East peace negotiations must begin with pre-1967 borders gave further pause to those who question the president's real commitment to Israeli security. Israeli Prime Minister Benjamin Netanyahu's aggressive condemnation of the position to a visibly agitated president during a highly publicized Oval Office press conference reenergized concerns in Jewish circles. (Such incidents perhaps explain Mr. Romney's 2-1 polling advantage over the president in Israel.)

Despite these hiccups, recent polls show the president with a 35-point advantage over Governor Romney among Jewish voters. Old habits are indeed hard to break. And this old habit will likely bring about similar numbers on Election Day. That is, unless the nuclear ambitions of Tehran's ayatollahs force Mr. Netanyahu's hand.

It's a scenario few wish to discuss. It has not been a major topic during the presidential campaign. But a nuclear Iran, with the saber-rattling President Mahmoud Ahmadinejad at the helm, has profound repercussions for the world community—and the U.S. presidential election.

The Obama Administration's stated policy is clear: A nuclear Iran is unacceptable; "all" diplomatic and military options are on the table.

This presents an interesting question for those Jewish voters who can't quite shake their concerns about this president. To wit:

How would the Obama Administration respond if confronted with unilateral Israeli airstrikes against Iran's nuclear facilities?

In 1973, a similar situation was presented to President Richard Nixon. History records that his advisers recommended a wait-and-see posture at the very beginning of the Yom Kippur War. But the president disagreed. Israel needed assistance immediately, and American logistical support was soon on the way.

Forty years later, a reflexively dovish president in the midst of a difficult re-election campaign may be presented with a similar decision. Prime Minister Netanyahu has no doubt how Mr. Romney would respond. But can the same be said for America's 44th president?

An Israeli military action against Iran would set off alarm bells around the world. At least publicly, most of America's allies would condemn the actions. And a newly empowered Muslim Brotherhood would spark widespread protests throughout a tense Middle East.

The man who regularly voted "present" while a member of the Illinois legislature would not have a similar option here—a disquieting notion for Jewish Democrats concerned about the latest threat to Israel's survival.

As Middle East Burns, Obama Fiddles

Robert Ehrlich says the president has failed to show leadership in crisis.

September 30, 2012, *The Baltimore Sun*

Political consultants often use the term "optics" to describe how consequential events are perceived by the general public. With regard to the present Middle East crisis, the president's optics are way off course.

There was the Las Vegas fundraiser following the terrorist attacks in Benghazi, Libya. This was followed by a *Letterman* appearance while violent anti-American demonstrations were breaking out in Europe, Africa, and Asia. Then, instead of a defense of U.S. values, pandering messages to the Muslim world in response to an amateurish anti-Muslim video that almost nobody (including the protesters) has seen. Finally, a visit to *The View* rather than sit-downs with world leaders at the United Nations.

For an Obama campaign that up until this time was bent on marketing the president's foreign policy credentials (Osama bin Laden, drone warfare, the Afghan "surge"), such decisions make for bad optics indeed.

You see, this president began his tenure with an aggressive outreach to the Muslim world, including miscreant regimes such as Iran. (Recall candidate Obama's promise to sit down with the likes of Mahmoud Ahmadinejad "without pre-conditions.") And the president's message was as hard to miss as it was difficult to swallow.

America had been arrogant. We had followed a self-serving and imperial path. Our adventurism had come at a steep price in the Islamic world. But we now understood the gravity of our mistakes. We would be more sensitive and understanding in the future. (Interestingly, there was no mention of U.S. blood spilled to protect Muslim lives in Kosovo, and no mention of the American dollars spent on humanitarian missions in numerous Muslim countries.)

The Administration's new hands-off approach was subsequently reflected in the American response to civil wars in Syria. It was the rationale behind the Administration's decision to ignore the democratic uprising in Iran. And it provides disturbing context to the president's choppy relationship with Prime Minister Benjamin Netanyahu and the besieged state of Israel.

But these "good will" gestures have gone unrewarded. Accommodations from the intended beneficiaries are not to be found. Indeed, anti-Americanism is on the rise throughout a tense Middle East. Further, the president's decision to go "all in" on yet another round of appeasement may not play so well in an America focused on the sight of a murdered ambassador and violent anti-U.S. demonstrations around the world.

Americans are well acquainted with the murderous history of radical Islam. From the Marine barracks in Beirut, to our African embassies, to the USS *Cole*, to the 1993 and 2001 World Trade Center attacks, the last 30 years have borne witness to the death and destruction generated by this perverse interpretation of Islam.

Today, the presidential campaign provides voters context to re-examine the president's more respectful, indulgent approach. "Restarts" may make for good sound bites in the heady days of a new administration, but four years down the road, voters have a right to expect tangible results. And the results of the Obama restart have been unimpressive at best.

The celebrated Arab Spring has degenerated into an Arab Winter. The formerly low-profile Muslim Brotherhood is now ascendant. And American influence in this important part of the world is at a nadir.

It just might be time for a new (and aggressive) message from the Administration: a clearly articulated mission statement that reiterates America's right to protect its citizens and reaffirms our intent to hunt down terrorists wherever they may hide.

Speaking of timely messages, where is the voice of moderate Islam during this time of international crisis?

This is the moment for the silent majority of practicing Muslims to engage. A good start would be for prominent imams and opinion leaders (in the U.S. and elsewhere) to condemn the terrorists in a very public way.

Americans would cheer this development; we are quite weary of the relentless, radical venom directed our way. We are running out of patience with regimes that fuel anti-Americanism while asking for foreign aid assistance from U.S. taxpayers.

Today, radical Islam presents an existential threat to our country and our culture. Challenging times require a unified response. It's time for the leaders of one of the world's great religions to step up to the plate. America is waiting. The world is waiting.

The Obama Doctrine: Passivity Where American Leadership Is Needed

The president's hands-off approach in Syria makes it more difficult for other Arab states to help put an end to the bloodshed.

October 14, 2012, *The Baltimore Sun*

A new issue has popped up in the presidential race. Surprisingly, it has nothing to do with the state of the U.S. economy. It is about a new world order that has removed familiar (and in some cases pro-American) leaders from strategically important Arab countries. And the next tricky chapter concerns what to do in war-torn Syria.

The challenges are familiar. A despotic regime uses its loyal military to maintain power. Its allies prop up a terrorist-friendly dictator. Various sectarian factions fight the government (and sometimes themselves) in an attempt to break free. Some Arab governments remain silent. Others seek to assist the rebels. Israel remains nervous, since the country is always the scapegoat (and target) for the alphabet soup of terrorist organizations in and around the Middle East.

The issue is front and center in the race for president because it places a major Obama priority in context, i.e., the foreign policy "reset" that was supposed to convince difficult regimes to like us.

Further complicating matters is the recent terrorist strike on our embassy in Libya. A murdered ambassador and potential cover up as to the circumstances surrounding the attack have raised concerns about the resilience of al-Qaida and its affiliates at a time the president is claiming the terror group is "on its heels."

In Syria, the Obama Administration will most likely continue
to ignore the pleas of the rebels. Such is the modus operandi of a
president who has ended U.S. military operations in Iraq, established a timetable for withdrawal in Afghanistan, and happily led
from behind in the liberation of Gadhafi's Libya. Indeed, these
are the tangible planks of a permissive Obama strategy intent on
further disengaging itself from America's (alleged) Bush-era cowboy image.

A war-weary American public is not necessarily unhappy with
the foregoing policy decisions. A clear majority of Americans want
our troops home. They are tired of the endless sectarian and tribal
conflicts in this troubled corner of the world. Most importantly,
they have grown weary of the daily casualty counts from a war the
U.S. has decided it cannot win—a weariness present on both sides
of the political aisle.

Only one inconvenient caveat applies: The American people
want (and deserve) assurance that the terrorists will not simply re-establish operations that will again place us in jeopardy here at home.

This caveat is an important one. Americans understand that
while there are limits to American might, it is equally dangerous
to withdraw from or ignore strategic hot spots populated by dangerous antagonists. Indeed, Afghanistan is where al-Qaida fighters
trained to kill Americans. And it was not so long ago that anti-war
candidate Obama labeled the Afghan conflict "a war of necessity."

Underlying this consideration is the notion that a deferential
America invites trouble. The old adage applies: politics abhors
a vacuum. In an era of an ascendant Muslim Brotherhood and
American retreat, such vacuums are plenty attractive to bullies like
Vladimir Putin and Mahmoud Ahmadinejad—not to mention
Hezbollah in Lebanon.

Which brings us back to Mitt Romney and last week's campaign pledge to support the Syrian rebels. Hopefully, some may be
excited about the goal of saving innocent lives from Bashar Assad's
increasingly brutal death machine. The world cannot be reminded

often enough: History records that American soldiers are regularly engaged in humanitarian missions that save Muslim lives. But it is the clear departure from the president's passive approach to foreign conflict that makes this policy initiative so important.

Mr. Romney's Middle East pronouncement recognizes the very real limits to American power in Syria and much of the region. He does not advocate for boots on the ground. And he further understands that American-style democracies are far more the exception than the rule in a region accustomed to dictatorships and despots.

But this newly minted Romney doctrine recognizes that other (worried) Arab states are hesitant to move without strong American leadership. The demonstration of such leadership by a new Romney Administration will help re-establish American influence in a part of the world that could only benefit from a revitalized American presence.

Assertive but pragmatic is a tricky path for any challenger. But it's one worth pursuing for a fast-closing campaign looking to take advantage of a foreign policy in disarray.

Obama's Foreign Policy Reset Has Little to Show for It

"Apology tour" emphasized America's faults, played down its strengths

October 28, 2012, *The Baltimore Sun*

Four years ago, a telegenic, charismatic senator from Illinois cobbled together a New Deal coalition of labor, environmentalists, progressives, African-Americans, and young people to capture the presidency.

It was an exciting time. America had elected its first mixed-race president. Another glass ceiling had been broken. Even those of us who opposed his policies recognized that the election of Barack Obama conveyed a positive message about America to the world.

In D.C., a jubilant media speculated about a "post-partisan" Capitol Hill. Finally, there had emerged a political leader with the cross-party appeal to bring the partisans together in common cause. That these observers chose to neglect the hyper-partisan and hyper-progressive voting records of Sen. Barack Obama in two legislatures reflected the high expectations generated by this once-in-a-generation politician.

For American foreign policy, the election of the anti-war Senator Obama marked a new day. He had been an ardent critic of a Bush Administration that had involved America in two major wars. The newly elected president repeatedly cited America's "cowboy" image as detrimental to our strategic interests around the world—most especially our image in the Muslim world.

It was with this background that the new president embarked on a new-era mission in the spring and summer of 2009. It is a tour worth reviewing now that America's standing and image around the world have become a major issue in Campaign 2012.

To review, a sampling of the president's rhetoric and tone:

- "In America, there's a failure to appreciate Europe's leading role in the world. Instead of celebrating your dynamic union and seeking to partner with you to meet common challenges, there have been times where America's shown arrogance and been dismissive, even derisive." (Strasbourg, France, April 2009)

- "9/11 was an enormous trauma to our country . . . but in some cases it led us to act contrary to our traditions and our ideals. We are taking concrete actions to change course. I have unequivocally prohibited the use of torture by the United States, and I've ordered the prison in Guantanamo Bay closed by early next year." (Cairo, Egypt, June 2009)

- "There is also no question that Guantanamo set back the moral authority that is America's strongest currency in the world . . . Rather than keeping us safer, the prison at Guantanamo has weakened American national security. It is a rallying cry for our enemies." (National Archives Building, May 2010)

Detractors have characterized these and similar quotes as markers of a "world apology tour," a reassurance to our allies (and enemies) that America had learned its lesson and would no longer be so arrogant in its dealings with other countries—and other cultures. Of course, "Gitmo" remains open for business to this day. Such was the naivete of the freshman senator from Illinois so willing to sit down with foreign miscreants "without preconditions."

Unsurprisingly, Obama supporters in the press and elsewhere have responded that at no time and in no venue did the president use the word "apology." True enough—but nevertheless, it is a weak defense for a foreign policy reset that has proudly led from behind in Libya and produced precious few tangible successes with the likes of Russia, China, North Korea, Syria, and Iran (the latter of which is oh-so-close to acquiring a nuclear weapon).

Something important was missing from the president's published texts: reminders about the considerable American blood given to save Muslim lives in Kosovo, Afghanistan, Iraq, and Kuwait. A citation to American sacrifice in this regard would have gone a long way to mitigating the harsh criticism from the right that followed the president's tour.

None of us pretend the United States has been a perfect actor on the world stage. Strategic mistakes have been made by misguided presidents of both parties. We have experienced episodes of isolationism and nation building. And not so long ago, foreign policy makers possessed the notion that American values could be imposed on other countries and cultures.

But the world must never forget that American soldiers and resources have been regularly utilized in the pursuit of humanitarianism and peace. We deserve a president willing to make this point on foreign soil—and in front of hostile audiences.

Such is worthy of consideration as America passes judgment on Obama-era foreign policy.

France's Discomfort with Capitalism

December 2, 2012, *The Baltimore Sun*

Historians note the American alliance with King Louis XVI sustained the American cause during the darkest days of the Revolution.

The history is impossible to escape. But for the deal struck in February 1778, General Washington and his Continental Army would likely not have survived.

Nevertheless, and despite a successful alliance in two world wars, taking the French to task has become a popular American sport.

French resistance to U.S. foreign policy moves is one reason. Some may recall France's refusal to allow American fighter-bombers into its airspace during Reagan-era bombing runs on Moammar Gadhafi's Libya (this in response to Libya's role in the terrorist bombing of a West German discotheque in 1986). And who could forget the re-labeled "Freedom fries" (in lieu of French fries) served in Capitol Hill restaurants and snack bars in the aftermath of the French refusal to join coalition forces in Iraq?

Other examples of French opposition to U.S. foreign policy may come to mind; suffice to say France has proven to be a rather unreliable ally since the end of World War II.

But it's not just differences in foreign policy decisions that separate the two democracies. It's the intersection of economics and culture that represents the major chasm.

I was reminded of this phenomenon while reviewing media reactions to President Francois Hollande's plans to raise France's top income tax rate to 75 percent, a rate that would surpass Sweden as the world's highest. (Similar to Maryland competing with California for highest-taxed state, but I digress.)

One potentially dire consequence is also the most predictable. Media reports indicate some wealthy citizens are making plans to move, and (in some cases) take their businesses with them. It's a scene straight out of the 1980s, when former French President Francois Mitterrand's tax increases caused a number of prominent French citizens to leave for more friendly venues.

That France's corporate tax rate is a business-unfriendly 35 percent represents a double whammy for enterprising entrepreneurs. No wonder other European countries are posting the welcome wagon signs. Alas, it is a repercussion of no great importance, according to Mr. Hollande's new government.

And herein lies a huge cultural divide.

In America—despite the best efforts of countercultural enthusiasts to expand federal power into every nook and cranny of the U.S. economy and the constant progressive drumbeat against the inequities of capitalism—most still support an "up by the bootstraps" work ethic. It embraces hard work and sacrifice. At its core, it celebrates individual sweat equity and the wealth it often produces. Indeed, this focus on individualism and the attainment of pecuniary rewards is the primary reason President Barack Obama's "You didn't build that" narrative was abandoned on the campaign trail. It appears that even this ardently progressive White House recognized that many successful Americans cling to the notion "they *did* build that."

The contrast with French culture and economics could not be clearer. A prominent French tax lawyer phrased it succinctly: "French people have an uncomfortable relationship with money. Here, someone who is a self-made man, creating jobs and ending up a millionaire, is viewed with suspicion. This is [a] big cultural difference between France and the United States."

You think?

Americans (still) tend to place entrepreneurs on a pedestal; many of us continue to value risk-taking, success, and the attainment of wealth.

Across the pond, high tax rates support a gigantic government bureaucracy that promotes dependency and supervises an all-encompassing social safety net. Government promises are quite attractive to boot: guaranteed workplace benefits, extended vacations, and a generous pension. Oh, and any talk of givebacks or benefit cuts generates *great* political unrest. In 2011 it produced Mr. Hollande and his new tax regime.

Periodically, French voters try a conservative, such as Jacques Chirac. But the right-wing governments invariably attempt to control spending or cut taxes. And they always pay a steep price. You see, the decks are stacked against the French right. The bureaucracy is too large. The safety net too comfortable. The public unions too powerful. And the status quo soon returns—with a vengeance.

Fortunately, America remains strong, but trend lines are worrisome. The twin slippery slopes of dependency and entitlement are on the march. So, next time you hear a politician complain that America's increasingly intrusive welfare state is akin to France's, pay attention. It is not a comparison we should invite—or welcome.

Putting Benghazi in Context

Robert Ehrlich says Administration's actions point to a possible cover-up.

November 4, 2012, *The Baltimore Sun*

My initial impression of the murderous attack on our consulate in Benghazi, Libya, was probably similar to yours. A horrific incident. A security failure. Another example of radical Islamic overreaction to the most tepid of incidents—in this case, an amateurish, offensive video about Islam.

I believed Ambassador Susan Rice as she peddled the video story during her Sunday TV appearances on Sept. 16. I believed Secretary of State Hillary Clinton as she repeatedly cited the video as the incendiary element behind the "spontaneous demonstration," going so far as to condemn the video on a paid ad broadcast to the Muslim world. And I believed the president as he (also repeatedly) blamed the video before a worldwide audience at the United Nations. Parenthetical note: White House Press Secretary Jay Carney did not make this list. I typically do not believe much of anything from him.

I continued to carry these initial impressions into early October. But developments over the past month have convinced me that either something went terribly wrong in the chain of command, or there is an ongoing political cover-up, given the relevance of the story to the president's reelection campaign—or both.

We now know that in the immediate aftermath of the attack, the president of Libya believed it to be "pre-planned, pre-determined";

that three calls for assistance went up the chain of command during the attack; that a known al-Qaida affiliate took responsibility for the attack that very night; that a CIA drone fed the entire seven-hour firefight back to the White House Situation Room; that deadly mortar fire (not exactly a normal tool of "mobs") killed two Americans on a compound rooftop; that the father of slain American Tyrone Woods says Hillary Clinton told him that we would "prosecute [that person] who did the video"; and that many Members of Congress had serious concerns regarding the initial Benghazi briefing conducted by the, until now, untouchable CIA Chief David Petraeus.

In numerous recent columns, I have made the point that stories (either accurate or not) tend to enjoy extended shelf lives when they fit into a pre-existing narrative. Such is evident in the White House's relentless attack on Mitt Romney's "47 percent" comment; such a statement paved the way for the president's campaign to perpetuate the image of an un-empathetic corporate raider with little concern for the middle class.

Republicans have articulated a different narrative in the case of an Obama White House possessing a strong predisposition against using the phrase "terror war" or "terror attack"—even when the phrase clearly applies.

Witness the Administration's ridiculous attempt to label the Fort Hood shootings "workplace violence." Well, it was workplace violence—but conducted by a Muslim extremist who shouted "Allahu akbar" as he commenced the coldblooded murder of 13 Americans. Additional note: The shooter (Army Major Nidal Hasan) has been praised as a "hero" by the radical cleric Anwar al-Awlaki, he of Sept. 11 infamy.

Other Obama Administration storylines support the indictment: Homeland Security Secretary Janet Napolitano's appalling attempt to replace the term "terrorism" with a new, more politically correct phrase: "man-caused disaster"; the Administration's claim that al-Qaida and its allies are "on the run" despite overwhelming evidence to the contrary; the president's indulgent rhetoric during his 2009-2010 Muslim-centric apology tour; and the Obama/Clinton determination to "reset" relations with heretofore hostile regimes "without preconditions."

Piece it all together, and there you have it: a narrative that provides context to the administration's rapidly falling-apart storyline on Benghazi.

Some in the mainstream media have attempted to minimize the administration's Benghazi missteps as the product of understandable confusion given the "fog of war." Others see a Fox News hatchet job on a vulnerable Democratic incumbent president. Hopefully, most will at least ask themselves why a now-discredited explanation about a video few have ever seen was so feverishly peddled to the American public—and the world.

An American ambassador and three other Americans are dead. Inexplicably, one of the most dangerous consulates (and most vulnerable ambassadors) in the world lacked a Marine detail. A no-name amateur filmmaker is still being held in the Los Angeles Metropolitan Detention Center without bond. Hillary Clinton and Susan Rice remain silent.

The American people deserve the truth, Vegas fundraisers and important elections notwithstanding.

Benghazi: The Obama Spin Continues

Robert L. Ehrlich Jr. says the Administration is still misleading the American public about what happened at the consulate in Libya.

May 12, 2013, *The Baltimore Sun*

"**B**umps in the road," said President Barack Obama, on the unrest in Libya and elsewhere in the Middle East that included the deaths of U.S. Ambassador Christopher Stevens, an information officer, and two Navy SEALS.

"Crude and disgusting". . . "an insult". . . "blasphemy". . . "[its message] must be rejected by all who respect our common humanity," President Obama said on the infamous anti-Muslim videotape that was originally blamed for the Benghazi terror attacks.

Benghazi happened "a long time ago" White House spokesman Jay Carney said on May 2, 2013.

"What difference, at this point, does it make?" said Former Secretary of State Hillary Clinton (on the causes of the consulate attacks).

Readers of this column recognize I am not a fan of conspiracy/ cover-up theories. There are usually plenty of (substantive) reasons why a politician should be supported or opposed without getting into unsubstantiated allegations or unprovable theories. But the record reflects that the American public has been misled about the events of Sept. 11 in Benghazi, Libya.

So why does the Obama administration continue its campaign to minimize a terror attack on an American consulate that killed a sitting U.S. ambassador? And why the lack of repercussions from a populace that tends to draw lines in the sand when misled by the federal government?

Political pundits from the right and left have advanced different explanations, but I herewith submit four rationales for your consideration:

1. The attacks inconveniently contradicted the Obama Administration's campaign narrative about how the death of Osama bin Laden signaled the beginning of the end for al-Qaida;

2. The Obama re-election effort needed a convenient "sounds good when you say it real fast" explanation for Benghazi in the days leading up to what everyone envisioned would be a close presidential election;

3. The last thing candidate-in-waiting Hillary Clinton wants is to be continually reminded about her State Department's complicity in failing to protect an ambassador who had repeatedly requested additional security for his minimally protected consulate; or

4. Parts of all of the above.

On the basis of what we know today, I choose No. 4.

No. 1 fits the administration's initial post-bin Laden narrative about how al-Qaida and its progeny were "on the run" and how an Obama-approved drone campaign had reduced the terror organization to a shadow of its former self. Rhetoricians among you will note that the president eliminated the "on the run" line from his campaign stump speech in the aftermath of the Benghazi attacks.

No. 2 fits because the phoniness of the now completely discredited "disgusting video" cover story would not come to light until after the election. Indeed, the apologetic, remorseful tone of those early video condemnations from the American president and his secretary of state might look pretty silly today. (Recall Ms. Clinton's emotional promise to the father of slain Navy SEAL Tyrone Woods that the videographer would be "arrested" and "punished.") But everyone sure bought the storyline in the days and weeks after the attack.

Also, No. 2 falls well within the Obama-inspired effort to convince us that America is not truly engaged in an extended war against Muslim jihadists who wish to impose their bizarre interpretation of Islam on the world. (Remember the "workplace violence" moniker given to the Fort Hood killings, the goofy "overseas contingency operations" label assigned to what may be a nonconventional but nonetheless very real war, and the insistence that domestic terror attacks be handled within the criminal justice system rather than through military tribunals.)

No. 3 makes a lot of sense if Hillary is truly (quietly) putting together her 2016 presidential campaign. Recall her indignant responses (before House and Senate investigatory committees) to charges that the administration was dilatory in preparation and response to the attacks on the diplomatic compound. She also denied having seen repeated requests for additional security from her Libya team and any involvement in the crafting of Susan Rice's Sunday morning news show talking points memo in which the attack was linked to the anti-Muslim video.

So, the former secretary of state deems the matter sufficiently investigated and is now ready to move on. In one respect, she has a point: Post-Benghazi stonewalling and government negligence in failing to protect the lives of the U.S. ambassador and his senior staff proved to be a non-issue in the November election. But it shouldn't have been.

Last week's whistle-blower hearings showed that putting politics aside in political Washington is almost impossible. It was Republicans on offense and Democrats on defense, as expected. But maybe enough suspicions have arisen that we may finally receive the *whole* story on the Benghazi murders, including what the president and secretary of state actually did that day and night. Four grieving American families deserve it. The rest of us deserve it, too.

Obama Foreign Policy Follies Befuddle Right and Left Alike

President is fundamentally uncomfortable with projection of U.S. military might.

June 9, 2013, *The Baltimore Sun*

The young Barack Obama's early enthusiasm for anti-war progressivism is well chronicled in his autobiography. Friendships with the likes of anti-war activists/bombers Bill Ayers and wife Bernardine Dohrn, poet Frank Marshall Davis, and the notorious Rev. Jeremiah Wright, and brief stints as a public interest lawyer, law professor, and community activist deepened his appreciation for leftist thought—and action. Indeed, the young senator from Illinois rode intense criticism of Bush-era foreign policy adventures and domestic surveillance practices all the way to the White House.

This pedigree has played out in predictable form on the domestic front. The Obama era is all about growing the size and scope of federal jurisdiction. Accordingly, the national debt has doubled under the profligate spending practices of the Obama regime. The true damage inflicted by Obamacare and a failed $1.2 trillion stimulus will keep the Washington bean counters busy for years. And don't forget the distressing array of hard-left judicial appointees and regulators.

But it has been the mixed messages and policies on the military front that have tried the patience of both right and left.

First, the early trips to foreign capitals (disparagingly referred to as the "world apology tour" by some), wherein the American president set out to improve his approval ratings with the Muslim world. The message was clear: America had learned its lesson—no longer would cowboy-like arrogance dictate American adventurism around the world. A compliant press announced "mission accomplished" in the short term, but a less-than-enthusiastic response domestically was the result of the president's failure to highlight considerable American blood and money (Kosovo, Kuwait, Afghanistan, Iraq) spent in the name of saving Muslim lives.

Another early sop to the anti-war crowd was the administration's insistence on rather goofy reinventions of familiar terms, all in order to create a more offense-less dialogue with hostile regimes. Hence, terrorism became "man-caused disasters," an act of religiously driven terror at Fort Hood became "workplace violence," and foreign military campaigns became "overseas contingency operations."

Then, a McCain-like "surge" in Afghanistan was announced, but contemporaneous with a deadline for withdrawal of U.S. troops. The message to the bad guys was quite clear: "We're gonna try real hard for a while, then go home"—not exactly Kennedy-esque. Al-Qaida surely smirked while taking notice of both news bulletins.

Next came Campaign 2012, wherein challenger Mitt Romney repeatedly pointed out how closely Obama tactics paralleled Bush tactics in the campaign against terrorism (rendition, detention, drones, Gitmo). Although generally accurate, the indictment had no legs; even progressives disappointed with Mr. Obama's situational hawkishness supported the incumbent in record numbers. Indeed, recent polling reflects how some previously anti-war, self-identified liberals now support the very same policies they once bitterly opposed.

What has legs is the administration's dysfunctional response to the Benghazi terror killings. Now that the phoniness of the administration's various fibs and negligence is slowly but surely coming to light, what conclusion is the public to draw? Answer: either a huge cover-up to "get over" until Election Day, or gross negligence by an administration in campaign mode and a complicit State Department. Neither explanation leaves you with warm fuzzies toward the president or his foreign policy team.

A related item: the Obama pledge to assist the Syrian rebels once proof of chemical warfare came to light. But that famous "red line" has been crossed, with no American response in sight. The bad guys (again) most assuredly took notice of this consequence-less, empty threat.

And now, the latest chapter wherein the administration's aggressive drone campaign (far beyond Bush administration efforts) is found to have killed four Americans and an unknown number of "collateral" casualties. But the significant announcement was almost immediately followed with a War on Terror "reset" speech signaling further American disengagement now that al-Qaida is "on the path to defeat"—a dubious proposition, more campaign slogan than fact.

This attempt to have it both ways in the messy business of non-traditional warfare speaks to the president's fundamental discomfort with the projection and use of American military might. His base constituency is viscerally anti-military, and he knows it. Yet, he is the commander in chief of the greatest force for good on the face of the earth—the American military. (What, you think other countries possess the intelligence, means, and might to conduct the midnight raid on ol' Osama?) And he has (at times) shown a willingness to choose national security over campaign promises.

Today, the president's predisposition toward speechifying and "clean" drone strikes is predictable and in accord with America's neo-isolationist mood.

But wishing for terrorism's demise is a lot different from making it so. The people deserve more clarity (and determination) in the long-running war against al-Qaida and its progeny.

The Vacillator-in-Chief

Obama's unease with his role as head of the military has produced a dangerously disjointed foreign policy.

September 8, 2013, *The Baltimore Sun*

Observers and pundits of all stripes have not missed the unease with which President Barack Obama approaches his commander-in-chief duties. Indeed, Chicago-style "community activist" and "Commander of the United States Marine Corps" don't normally appear on the same resume. Accordingly, an aggressive use of his substantial military architecture does not sit well with the anti-war activist. This discomfort presents itself in a decidedly disjointed foreign policy record:

Israel: The president's stated wish to create "space" between America and Israel was followed by a historic and uncomfortable Oval Office dressing down by Prime Minister Benjamin Netanyahu. Then Mr. Obama made a hard rhetorical tilt toward Israel on the heels of the 2012 election (transparent, yet politically effective as Mr. Obama's re-election campaign garnered 69 percent of the Jewish vote). No wonder Mr. Netanyahu worries about what a notoriously guarded President Obama would do when Iran succeeds in securing a nuclear bomb.

Egypt: The Obama Administration distanced itself from the Mubarak regime on the eve of large anti-government protests, aggressively reached out to a Muslim Brotherhood-led Morsi government, made tepid criticism of a wildly unpopular, undemocratic

Islamist constitution and offered less than enthusiastic support for the (anti-Morsi) pro-democracy demonstrators during the summer of 2013.

Afghanistan: The president ordered a military surge fast on the heels of a promise to withdraw our troops by a certain date, followed up with few reports of progress but plenty of declarations about America's intent to leave the premises—on schedule.

Libya: Mr. Obama would not assist the Libyan rebels (even on humanitarian grounds) until a last minute decision to join an anti-Moammar Gadhafi, European-led coalition followed by little of consequence until a sitting American ambassador was murdered at our consulate in Benghazi. Then we got high profile misrepresentations (to be kind) about the cause of the terrorist attacks, followed by (embarrassed) silence and a stated desire to put the entire episode behind us. For anyone wishing to take issue with this statement of facts, recall the incriminating retrospective of former Secretary of State Hillary Clinton (in a decidedly defensive appearance before Congress) once the administration's "Muslim video" explanation for the attack had been exposed as phony: "After all, what does it matter?"

Syria: The administration's policy of non-intervention (even when the anti-Assad rebels included pro-Western elements) during the initial stages of President Bashar Assad's murderous campaign against anti-government rebels morphed into a promise to arm the rebels should Mr. Assad be found to have used weapons of mass destruction ("a red line"). Then the administration claimed that evidence of WMDs had not been produced despite the fact that our Western allies had confirmed their use, followed by an announcement (by a deputy national security adviser) that the U.S. would sparingly arm the rebels; followed by assurances to Mr. Assad and Russian President Vladimir Putin that any U.S. military response would be limited and not intended to achieve regime change;

followed by Mr. Obama's ludicrous line this week that the afore-mentioned red line was not his line, but the world's.

Russia: A Hillary Clinton initiated "reset" intended to distance the accommodating Obama administration from the "cowboy" George W. Bush, together with a (Russian requested) broken promise to Poland to station defensive missiles in that pro-Western country, produced nothing but relentless pokes in the eye, from UN vetoes to Edward Snowden to an aggressive and provocative support of the Assad regime.

Drones: The administration admitted that its hyper-aggressive drone campaign in Afghanistan and Pakistan (far beyond Bush administration efforts) included the targeted killing of four American terrorists and an unknown number of collateral victims. That was almost immediately followed by a highly promoted War on Terror "reset" speech wherein the president signaled further American disengagement now that al-Qaida was "on the path to defeat"—a dubious proposition, more campaign slogan than fact, but most assuredly a notion the administration wishes to perpetuate in the public consciousness.

Then there is the administration's insistence on politically correct reinventions of familiar terms and concepts in order to create a more benign dialogue with hostile regimes. Hence, terrorism morphed into "man-caused disasters," a murderous act of religiously driven terror at Fort Hood was identified as "workplace violence," and foreign military engagements became "overseas contingency operations." The constant theme here is leading from behind, allowing a philosophical distaste for military action and indulgence toward those opposed to U.S. strategic interests to dictate the terms and tenor of U.S. engagements around the world.

"Feckless," "vacillating" and "ad hoc" are not descriptors of an effective foreign policy. They are, however, a formula for distrust and confusion among allies and enemies alike. Such an approach carries real strategic costs, including the denigration of our ability to impose our will or, at a minimum, influence events in dangerous places around the world. It also calls into question a vital element of our national identity, a heretofore Kennedy-esque engagement in furthering the cause of freedom around the world. The president needs to up his foreign policy game . . . . *now.*

Drawing Insults, Not Fear, from Our Foes

A weak leadership has led America's foes to mock us.

March 30, 2014, *The Baltimore Sun*

S ome of you tend to suffer MEGO ("my eyes glaze over") syndrome when the topic turns to foreign affairs.

But you should do all you can to resist the temptation. The world remains too dangerous a place for America to divert its attention.

Today, two significant foreign policy challenges confront us: (1) Radical Islam and its many iterations; and (2) a resurgent Russia led by our favorite former KGB agent, Vladimir Putin.

I was reminded of the former during a recent trip to Europe. A shoeless one-hour wait at the security checkpoint at Heathrow Airport was a not-so-subtle reminder about the importance of continued vigilance. And, of course, there are the daily reports of terror attacks around the world, almost always with plenty of dead and injured. Seems there are simply never enough casualties for these cold-blooded killers. Here's hoping President Obama's targeted drone campaign continues to hit the mark(s).

As for the latter, it's been difficult to get Mr. Putin off the front page for the better part of the last two years. One problem, though: Much of the Russian president's activities have centered around poking a very sharp stick in America's eye—an activity that seems to bring him a great deal of satisfaction. The latest insult: "Tweets" from Deputy Prime Minister Dmitry Rogozin, such as "Comrade @BarackObama, what should U do to those who have neither accounts nor property abroad? Or U didn't think about it?" and "I think some prankster prepared the draft of this Act of the US President." Late night talk-show hosts have had a field day with the parodies. It would be funny if it weren't at the expense and peril of America's strength, reputation, and global stature.

So much for the short lived, wildly unsuccessful Obama/Hillary Clinton "reset" with the former Soviet Union. For that matter, so much for President Bush's mistaken observation that he could "look Vladimir in the eye" in order to conduct business.

America (and the West) is paying a steep price for these miscalculations. Russia has repeatedly violated the "Intermediate Range Nuclear Forces Treaty," per a January Barack Obama memo to NATO. There was no quid-pro-quo from Russia after we double-crossed Poland and the Czech Republic out of promised defensive missiles. Russian money and material continue to support the murderous Assad regime in Syria and the ayatollahs in Iran. Edward Snowden is living (what passes for) the good life in Moscow. And for good measure, Putin has taken to mocking U.S. foreign policy on the pages of the *New York Times* and now on social media. This is not what the president had in mind when he famously (not realizing his microphone was live) promised former Russian President Dmitry Medvedev that he would have more "flexibility" after his re-election.

But mocking insults are only a consequence of a larger problem. Such behavior occurs because our enemies do not fear us. They don't fear American boots on the ground, or our leadership.

Indeed, it was fear of our military might and willingness to lead that convinced Saddam Hussein to refrain from using his WMD in the first Gulf War, got Libyan strongman Moammar Gadhafi to give up his nukes in 2004, and convinced the Iranian ayatollahs to free 52 American hostages in 1979. Yes, such leadership can make even real bad guys think twice about provoking America.

Today, bad guys with evil intent follow the daily news. Here, they read of disappearing "red lines," historic defense cutbacks, a secretary of state who promises "unbelievably small, limited" military responses, and an American public grown weary of costly foreign wars. In a word, they know the sheriff is tired and planning to leave the premises. They also understand political vacuums tend to get filled rather quickly.

The public surely soured on bloody, expensive, and seemingly endless conflicts in Iraq and Afghanistan. As a result, they chose the anti-war candidate determined to charm even rogue regimes with his cult of personality.

But the world is proving to be far more difficult than the telegenic Barack Obama wishes it to be. This part of "hope" and "change" isn't working out so well. In fact, it's looking more like Jimmy Carter redux all the time.

Where's our Reagan?

Obama, Played for a Fool

Foreign leaders see the U.S. President's foreign policy talk as words without action.

May 6, 2014, *The Baltimore Sun*

Each president brings his own unique preconceptions to the job. Post-depression, FDR believed the American people deserved a "New Deal." John Kennedy felt Americans would willingly "pay any price" to spread freedom and democracy throughout the world. Ronald Reagan thought a strong national defense would bring the "evil empire" to its knees. A post-9/11 George W. Bush saw radical Islam as the single greatest threat to Western-style democracy.

As a candidate and as president, Barack Obama, too, has been quite clear about the fundamentals of his foreign policy—particularly America's approach to the world's dictators and assorted miscreants. He would sit down and talk with them "without preconditions." A new era of diplomatic engagement would emerge. An acquiescent America would generate a resurgence of good will among Muslim nations. Mr. Obama would convince the Israeli occupiers that "land for peace" could be achieved even if the Palestinians continued to oppose the very existence of the Jewish state. He would "restart" a bilateral relationship with the former KGB agent, Vladimir Putin. And all this would be made possible because the primary cause of America's negative image around the world—George W. Bush—would no longer be in charge. This president truly believed his considerable force of personality would bring the world's troublemakers to task. And why not? A fawning media was advertising the arrival of a "post-partisan president" capable of uniting a divided America and improving our (his) reputation around the world. Certainly the awarding of the 2009 Nobel Peace Prize to Mr. Obama did nothing to discourage these lofty expectations.

Yet bad actors have a way of spoiling even the most heartfelt attempts at high rhetoric and good deeds. And today's bad actors are deep into the process of dissolving the president's primary assumptions.

Clinton administration press secretary George Stephanopoulos once famously declared that "words are actions" for President Clinton. But six years into the Obama era, seemingly endless (and empty diplomatic) assurances lack the muscle that would otherwise make them count.

The latest shenanigans in Ukraine offer a stark example. Here, the president's weak sanctions and dismissive reference to Russia as a "regional" power ring hollow as Mr. Putin proceeds to dismantle eastern Ukraine one zip code at a time. A mocking response to U.S. and Western military actions only further makes the point.

Similarly, Mr. Obama's constant brow beating of Benjamin Netanyahu's conservative government in Israel has generated no good will with Palestinian President Mahmoud Abbas, who refuses to recognize any parcel of Israel as a legitimate Jewish state. Now, Mr. Abbas has agreed to form a unity government with terrorist-affiliated Hamas. Neither has tough talk dissuaded the rogue nuclear ambitions of Iran, where the Holocaust-denying Ayatollah Khamenei and alleged "moderate president" Hasan Rouhani have negotiated a bomb-making deal with the West on a slower timeframe, to the utter consternation of Israel, its moderate Arab neighbors, and many Members of the United States Congress.

Perhaps the most glaring example of ostensibly serious but ultimately meaningless words is the now infamous "red line" regarding Syria's use of chemical weapons against insurgent rebels. Repeated instances of chemical gas attacks against his own people has proven a consequence-less act for Syrian dictator Bashar Assad. Worse, the unserious threats morphed into an embarrassing incident when Secretary of State John Kerry stated that regardless of any violation, a U.S. military response would be "unbelievably small" and "limited."

So, what do Messrs. Putin, Abbas, Assad, and Rouhani have in common (besides an utter disregard for Western style human rights and democracy)? Well, they fully understand that mere words are *not* actions. And that mere words that lack credibility do not generate respect—or fear.

One quality that distinguishes a dynamic leader is the ability to change course (and preconceptions) midstream when it becomes clear that what you are doing is simply not working. But can a president prone to conflict avoidance recognize that his moral entreaties to bad people are simply ineffective? That his vast reservoir of charisma is lost on tin-horn dictators and murderous autocrats willing to do anything to preserve their power? I'll take the "under," as they say in Vegas. It took years for Mr. Obama to fully admit that "Obamacare" might have problems. What do you think it will take to get him to see that Mr. Putin and his fellow bullies might be playing him for the fool?

"No Soldier Left Behind"

The developing story of Bowe Bergdahl raises troubling questions for the country.

June 8, 2014, *The Baltimore Sun*

L ike most Americans, the Ehrlichs celebrated the return of a captured U.S. soldier from Afghanistan. What parent would not possess a degree of empathy for the parents of Army Sgt. Bowe Bergdahl, held by the Taliban since June 30, 2009?

A positive aspect of a returned U.S. soldier is the notion that the U.S. military, the greatest force for good on planet Earth, recognizes its obligation to rescue its own. It's what a civilized, just nation does in consideration of the risk assumed by its young soldiers.

Yet, this developing story raises troubling questions for a country committed to eliminating radical Islam as a threat to stability and freedom throughout the world. The first issue is rather obvious and applies to every prisoner exchange negotiation: What kind of precedent is set when a ransom is paid for a kidnapped victim? Some question if such a willingness to negotiate with the bad guys does not lay the predicate for more of the same in the future. Recall that al-Qaida in northern Africa is a regular participant in kidnappings in order to raise money for its terrorist activities. An equally important concern pertains to the high value of the returned terrorists.

Indeed, the detainee group at issue here was not exactly the junior varsity. This was a front line group of dangerous militants, per a 2008 Pentagon assessment (subsequently made public by our "friends" at WikiLeaks).

The Afghan five are:

- A founding member of the Taliban and liaison to al-Qaida leader Osama bin Laden

- A provincial governor during the Taliban regime "who continues to be a significant figure encouraging acts of aggression"

- A deputy minister of intelligence in the Taliban government "central to the Taliban's effort to form alliances with other Islamic fundamentalist groups"

- A former Taliban army chief suspected of personally supervising the murder of thousands of Shiite Muslims and believed likely to rejoin "in hostilities against U.S. and coalition forces in Afghanistan"

- A suspect in a joint al-Qaida Taliban cell in Khost and "one of the most significant former Taliban leaders detained" at Guantanamo

The credibility challenged Obama Administration assures us the five detainees pose no threat. (The freed Taliban members will be forbidden from traveling outside of Qatar territory for a year and their activities will be monitored by Qatari and U.S. officials.) Yet only time will tell whether one or more of these previously active participants will show up on a future battlefield. I hope the administration is correct in its assessment, but I have a nagging suspicion the world has become a more dangerous place with these five bad actors back in play.

A further cause for concern applies to the specific facts of this case. You see, it is not clear why Bowe Bergdahl wandered away from his post that summer night almost five years ago. Increasingly, it appears the young soldier simply deserted.

Further confirmation of this allegation (and an alleged anti-American email) will change the tenor of the story for many, particularly if it is shown that other soldiers lost their lives in rescue attempts over the last several years. Already, the families of these men (joined by a number of Mr. Bergdahl's former comrades in arms and some Members of Congress) are raising objection to the high price paid for a disillusioned soldier who may have willingly made himself available to the enemy. What is most likely not at issue are the actions of Bob Bergdahl, Bowe Bergdahl's father, in support of his son. Despite his changed appearance (a bushy, unkempt beard) and brief remarks in Pashto (the language of southern Afghanistan) during an uncomfortable White House Rose Garden appearance with the president, most people are willing to give desperate parents the benefit of the doubt.

Still, one wonders how the White House staff could have allowed the president to be placed in such an awkward situation—let alone to have National Security Advisor, Susan Rice, (of ALL people) assure the country that Sergeant Bergdahl "served with honor"!

Some on the right incorrectly see the Bergdahl chapter as an attempt to change the subject from the deepening Veterans Affairs health care scandal. They are wrong. This prisoner exchange was entirely predictable given the administration's very public commitment to close "Gitmo," leave two unpopular wars on schedule regardless of consequences and change America's image in the Muslim world.

Yet, despite all good intentions regarding "No Soldier Left Behind" and a desire to keep campaign promises, what this administration calls "overseas contingency operations" remains a murderous holy war for the jihadists of Radical Islam. Remember, they see war in terms of millennia, not years. And, unlike this president, they prefer not to provide us dates certain for their withdrawal.

The GOP Supports Israel More Than Dems

We must support the Jewish state in its hours of need.

August 24, 2014, *The Baltimore Sun*

Recently I was talking with a conservative friend of mine about the drama in Gaza. I knew this individual to be thoughtful about world events and staunchly pro-Israel in outlook. It was soon after our mutual condemnation of Hamas that our conversation took an unexpected and disturbing turn.

Seems my friend is frustrated with the Obama Administration's tepid support of Benjamin Netanyahu's government and the Jewish voters who re-elected the U.S. president, a soft-on-Israel candidate. In blunt terms, he asked why he should be concerned about Israel when it is apparent (to him) that so many Jewish voters aren't.

For context, recall Mr. Netanyahu's Oval Office dressing down of an American president, persistent U.S. criticism of West Bank settlements, Secretary Kerry's continuing efforts to insert "moral equivalence" in Palestinian peace talks, and a similar enthusiasm to accommodate Hamas demands during recent ceasefire negotiations. Throw in Israel's monumental concern over Mr. Obama's stance on Iranian nuclear negotiations and you have a pretty strong case for legitimate Israeli distrust.

I've been thinking about my friend's observation as Americans digest world reaction to this latest Israeli-Palestinian skirmish.

Actually, indigestion is a more appropriate term, as anti-Israeli sentiment (particularly in Europe) becomes more pronounced. It seems violent pro-Palestinian demonstrations and the trashing of Jewish shops is back in vogue in Paris. Indeed, taking batting practice on the Jewish state is again a favored pastime around the world.

Increasing disenchantment with Israel is also rising in more secular Jewish circles. A recent Pew Research study on American Jews reveals a weaker emotional attachment to Israel (and Zionism) and an increased willingness to criticize Israeli policies among reform and secular Jews. For this segment of the community, Israel is no longer the most vital issue. Some pundits have even argued that progressivism competes with Judaism (and trumps Zionism) as this group's religion of choice. I'll leave it to the social scientists to argue the merits of such matters. But it seems reasonable to conclude that secular Jews are not as intensively pro-Israel as others within the Jewish community.

Yet such divisions on the Jewish left carry few consequences come Election Day. The last dozen or so presidential election cycles make the point. There has been a persistent GOP pattern of failure to grow the Jewish vote since 1964: Goldwater (10 percent), Nixon (17 percent), Nixon (35 percent), Ford (22 percent), Reagan (39 percent), Reagan (31 percent), Bush 41 (35 percent), Bush 41 (11 percent), Dole (16 percent), Bush 43 (19 percent), Bush 43 (24 percent), McCain (22 percent), and Romney (30 percent).

The political result is a "hall pass" for lefties: Denigrate Israel (particularly right-wing Israeli governments) and reap strong Jewish support.

But it's the other side of the equation that remains more frustrating.

I refer to the perpetually strained relationship between the Republican right and the Jewish community. Putting aside a strong (but small) group of Orthodox activists who regularly support GOP candidates (including yours truly), the Christian right's stalwart

support for all things Israeli is nevertheless viewed with great suspicion (and, often, open hostility) by the larger community.

The issue of abortion is at the center of this divide, but other
social issues (guns, school prayer, gay marriage, right-to-die, affirmative action) play here as well. My many visits (over 24 years) to
Maryland synagogues confirm this list of grievances.

* * *

Which brings us back to my friend's disdain for Mr. Obama's
persistent Jewish support. Herewith, my respectful reminder to him
and others of similar mindset.

Israel is a tiny island of Western values surrounded by sworn
enemies. Hamas to the south, Hezbollah to the north, and Iran to
the east constitute a dream team of terror players intent on "liber-
ating" Palestine from Israeli "occupation." Nevertheless, it survives
and thrives as a model of pluralistic democracy in the perpetually
troubled Middle East. America must support this loyal ally in its
hour of need. And every hour is an hour of need for the Jewish state.

Alas, a political detente between social conservatives and the
non-orthodox community is unlikely. Just too many disparate values at play. Yet, why should these matters supersede the issue of a
critical democracy's existence?

The bottom line: Reflexive support for Democratic presidents
goes back to the FDR era, when there were many isolationist, anti-
Jewish Republicans. But this attitude has significantly changed, and
it should be recognized. Today, support for the state of Israel is
simply stronger among most Republicans than it is in the current
administration. And the availability (or not) of Jewish votes on Election Day should not be germane to our special alliance with Israel.
A hostile world dictates that the relationship be regularly nour-
ished—unrequited love notwithstanding.

How Obama's Made Sure to Leave Every Part of the World More Dangerous Than He Found It

May 11, 2015, *The National Review*

"I will meet with not just our allies and our friends, but I will initiate tough diplomacy with our enemies. That includes Syria, Iran, North Korea, and Venezuela. I would meet with them, and I would meet with them without preconditions."

—Barack Obama,
May 16, 2008

"On all of these issues, but particularly missile defense, this can be solved, but it is important for [Putin] to give me space. . . . This is my last election. After my election I have more flexibility."

—President Obama to Russian President Medvedev,
March 26, 2012

The former promise was uttered during Senator Obama's initial run for the presidency. It was intended for consumption by his anti-war base and to let the world know the zero-sum worldview of the Reagan-Bush era was (finally) extinguished. The latter was not intended for public consumption, but was nevertheless captured by omnipresent audio during an unguarded moment between the two principals. Both statements genuinely reflect the baseline foreign-policy values and reflexive passivity of our 44th president. You see, Barack Obama was always secure in the belief that the constant projection of American military power was the primary reason for anti-American sentiment around the world.

Alas, seven years later, a seemingly endless stream of apologies, attempts to placate the world's miscreants, and inappropriate stabs at moral equivalency are primary components of a spectacularly failed U.S. foreign policy. Seems the "cowboy" Bush and all those opportunistic militarists at the Pentagon are not the reason so many bad guys take issue with the U.S. Similarly, the infamous time-dishonored plea for time regarding negotiations with Russia speaks to a comfortable familiarity with weak negotiating positions. With regard to Putin, "flexibility" can be read as "I have to look tough now, but just wait until I'm safely elected to a second term—then I'll feel free to cut a deal—any deal." This "anything goes" desire to cut deals and refrain from antagonizing bad guys (and, in the process, finally earning that Nobel Peace Prize so gratuitously awarded in 2009) explains a problematic series of policy decisions that has worried our allies and allowed our enemies daily batting practice at U.S. expense. To wit:

- An early world apology tour, focused on the Muslim world, during which the newly elected U.S. president issued mea culpas for alleged inappropriate U.S. actions around the world; interestingly, no mention was made or concern evidenced of considerable U.S. blood spent to save Muslim lives.

- The expedient selling out of Poland and the Czech Republic on missile defense in the interest of an oversold "reset" with Putin's Russia.

- A quick and forceful condemnation of Egyptian president Hosni Mubarak in the aftermath of his country's "Arab Spring" street protests—to the benefit of the viscerally anti-democratic, ruthless, and anti-American Muslim Brotherhood.

- A missed opportunity to gain negotiating leverage with a weakened Iranian regime by failing to support the dissident Green Movement in Iran, circa 2009.

- A historic breach (complete with personal insults) with a sitting Israeli prime minister who has the fortitude to place Israel's security interest ahead of Mr. Obama's nuclear legacy.

- An infamous "line in the sand" when proof of Syrian dictator Bashar Assad's use of weapons of mass destruction against Syrian rebels was revealed to the world, but forgotten when the U.S. began relying on Iranian boots on the ground to fight the formerly JV army known as ISIS.

- The trade of five varsity terrorists taken from Guantanamo Bay (of whom at least three are suspected to have returned to the battlefield) for the AWOL sergeant Bowe Bergdahl.

- An opening to diplomatic relations with the repressive Raul Castro without securing the release and/or extradition of political prisoners and wanted U.S. fugitives.

- A framework "agreement" announcement on the Iranian nuclear deal, followed in short order by harsh condemnation by Ayatollah Khamenei and a host of unanswered issues, including schedule(s) for sanctions relief, a process for sanctions relief, conditions attached to periodic inspections, a schedule for unfreezing Iranian assets, and a framework for dispute resolution.

The bottom line: The president has never been a comfortable commander in chief when placing American lives and military assets in harm's way; yet, the reflexive peace candidate seems ever-ready, willing, and able to negotiate with the world's most notorious bad guys—always from a position of weakness, always leaving the world just a bit more insecure than he found it. When it comes to so-called "peace" negotiations with the world's tyrants, it seems America is always open for (conditionless) business, a legacy that has and will continue to make Americans—and the free world—less safe.

The Many Lies Paving the Way to Obama's Legacy

July 22, 2015, *National Review*

On the Iranian threat to Israel: "The danger from Iran is grave, it is real, and my goal will be to eliminate this threat. . . . Finally, let there be no doubt: I will always keep the threat of military action on the table to defend our security and our ally Israel."

On health care: "If you like your doctor, you can keep your doctor. If you like your health-care plan, you can keep your health-care plan."

On Syria's WMD: "We have been very clear to the Assad regime—but also to other players on the ground—that a red line for us is we start seeing a whole bunch of chemical weapons moving around or being utilized."

On capitalism: "If you've got a business—you didn't build that. Somebody else made that happen."

On religious freedom: "Let's honor the conscience of those who disagree with abortion and draft a sensible conscience clause and make sure that all of our health care policies are grounded not only in sound science, but also in clear ethics, as well as respect for the equality of women."

On immigration: "They're going to say we need to quadruple the Border Patrol, or they'll want a higher fence. Maybe they'll need a moat. Maybe they'll want alligators in the moat."

On world public opinion: "People don't remember, but when I came into office, the United States in world opinion ranked below China and just barely above Russia, and today once again, the United States is the most respected country on Earth."

On Benghazi: "Here's what happened. . . . You had a video that was released by somebody who lives here, sort of a shadowy character who—who made an extremely offensive video directed at—at Mohammed and Islam . . . making fun of the Prophet Mohammed. And so, this caused great offense in much of the Muslim world. But what also happened, extremists and terrorists used this as an excuse to attack a variety of our embassies, including the one, the consulate in Libya."

I don't believe him.

I understand he is the president of the United States, a position that should warrant presumptive trust regardless of one's philosophical or partisan identification. But I cannot start with a presumption of trust when it comes to this president, the former true-believing community organizer whose word has proven to be vapid or even patently false on so many important issues. You see, this president is the classic progressive—far more classic than the Clintons, for whom truth is purely situational: only good as long as it fits their purpose, and then on to Plan B.

What makes Barack Obama the real progressive is that he truly believes that his great willpower magically transforms his pronouncements. Indeed, his mere will makes them accurate, especially if he repeats them enough, despite overwhelming evidence to the contrary. All of which brings us to this week's deal with the world's most successful sponsor of terrorism—and its most persistent deluder.

The major provisions of the Iranian nuclear deal are by now familiar to many concerned Americans. The agreement contemplates enhancement of the regime's nuclear infrastructure and aggressive development of an intercontinental ballistic missile program. (Wonder at whom those ICBMs will be aimed?) It includes the granting of a basically condition-free inspection regime (what did happen to "anytime, anywhere" inspections?) and the removal of any linkage to improved Iranian behavior, including the release of four American hostages being held by the Iranian government. The bottom line: The Obama Administration's seminal foreign-policy achievement will be the formal elimination of the West's sacrosanct policy of ensuring a non-nuclear Iran—a bipartisan goal that has guided American foreign policy for the past 40 years. No wonder Israel and our moderate Sunni allies are so aggravated.

The president argues that he negotiated the best deal possible. After all, what other choice did he have? But this is a circular argument. The president's false choice that either we have war or we have this treaty ignores the alternative of a tighter, more comprehensive deal. Recall that Western sanctions (implemented in 2011 over Obama's objections) were crushing the Iranian economy, a state of affairs that not so long ago led tens of thousands of Iranian dissidents to embrace a pro-democracy "green" revolution.

Alas, that momentum toward freedom was short-lived and not supported by the always-acquiescent Obama Administration. Seven years into his presidency, Barack Obama's willpower and ego have not made the world's bad guys appreciate a newly dovish U.S. of A. No surprise here; bad guys traditionally take advantage of the weak—or at least the strong who (inexplicably) desire to be weak. They also love to fill power vacuums: Iran in Syria, Russia in Ukraine, and China in the South China Sea, to name a few. And so our most progressive president has cut a deal with one of the worst regimes in the world. It's all about legacy (and renting the Iranian army to kill ISIS fighters). Which takes us back to the one promise Barack Obama has (partially) kept: "…I will meet with not just our allies and our friends. I will initiate tough diplomacy with our enemies. That includes Syria, Iran, North Korea, and Venezuela. I would meet with them without preconditions although with preparation…." Of course, "tough" and "no preconditions" are oxymoronic; such an obvious contradiction is not lost on our newly aggressive enemies. How sad that this president has made the world a far more dangerous place than he found it upon arriving in the Oval Office.

PART 7

★ ★ ★

Cultural Divisions and Those Silly Lefties

EVERY SUCCESSFUL AUTHOR REQUIRES a talented editor. Fortunately, I have employed Ms. Stephanie Krikorian as mine for each of my three books. Among other duties, Stephanie's major task for this book was selecting columns for inclusion and choosing appropriate part titles for the sections. Alas, while most of these proved rather easy, the seventh, not so much. In Stephanie's words, the seventh would be "something along the lines of *The Wacky Left*." When I responded the *entire* book is devoted to that topic, she replied, "We need a bucket for the less-Obama-directed ones." So be it.

The following columns include anecdotes of politically correct, irrational thought—the kind of storylines that not so long ago would have been quickly dismissed from serious conversation. Of course, distressingly ludicrous reports from our colleges and universities tend to dominate this bucket. Where else would reports of *a room full of white people* (alleged micro-aggression to people of color) or a sign label depicting "Walk Zone" (alleged micro-aggression to disabled people) be treated as legitimate issues for discussion? And I will not let my alma mater off too easily. At my beloved Princeton, students launched a service ("Tiger micro-aggressions") to capture any and all campus offenses against political correctness on its Facebook page—in order that no one single student would be forced to "carry the burden alone." This, from our best and brightest.

The goal of an "offense-less society" would be funny if people were not paid to perpetuate these idiotic cultural guidelines. But there is some good news on the horizon. Comedians such as Jerry Seinfeld and Chris Rock have stepped forward to challenge the language police. *They* understand the importance of a sense of humor. Come to think of it, the more we laugh at such madness, the less likely this stuff has of ever becoming the subject of serious dialogue. In other words, (plenty of) chuckles welcome.

Road to Energy Independence Goes Through ANWR, Keystone

Robert Ehrlich says America needs local sources of cheap energy.

March 11, 2012, *The Baltimore Sun*

Sometimes it is worth our time to step back, to take the long view about seemingly intractable issues affecting our country. My long view begins with the gas-line days of 1973–74, when a recently minted owner of a 1966 Ford Falcon began the daily commute between his home in Arbutus and Gilman School in Roland Park (an hour away). Domestically, huge price hikes at the pump and draconian gas rationing (remember the "even-odd" license plate system?) nearly destroyed new automobile sales, a crushing burden for a father employed as a "commission only" car salesman. Fortunately, the Ehrlichs survived; we also took note as our elected leaders promised that "never again" would an **OPEC** cartel impose its will on a defenseless America; "never again" would hostile regimes be able to inflict such damage on the world's most vibrant economy.

Subsequent years have brought great turmoil to the oil-producing nations of the Middle East: periodic wars, the emergence of radical Islam, the Arab Spring (results still to be determined), and ever-increasing tensions with Israel, to name just a few.

What has not changed is America's continued reliance on sources of oil from increasingly unstable (and sometimes unfriendly) nations. This fact of energy policy life represents a monumental failure of political will. It also invites further instability in an unsettled region. Today, the world watches nervously as Iran again escalates its saber rattling ways in the Gulf of Hormuz.

A series of major domestic policy failures is to blame. And an inconvenient truth is at the center of the controversy: Our economy's ability to grow new jobs depends on available and inexpensive sources of energy. For the foreseeable future, those sources (primarily natural gas and oil) are fossil fuel driven. An additional inconvenient fact: The green jobs revolution so ardently promoted by progressives is not occurring anytime soon; wind, solar and biodiesel must be promoted and explored but will not produce the source supply required to sustain a growing economy over the next 10–20 years.

Reminders of our ongoing failure to secure energy independence are again in our daily news cycle.

The first concerns our continued unwillingness to explore an area estimated to produce greater than 1 million barrels of oil a day and 150 billion cubic feet of natural gas per year beneath the North Slope of the Arctic National Wildlife Refuge (ANWR). The land was purchased for oil and natural gas development by President Jimmy Carter and Congress. As a Member of Congress assigned to the Commerce Committee, I visited the proposed development site to learn firsthand about the issue. The proposed drilling footprint is small (less than 3 percent of ANWR's total acreage) under a House passed bill earlier this year. The area is predominantly dreary, barren wasteland. Indeed, the area is not designated as wilderness. Yet, the North Slope remains untouched to this day.

The Obama Administration's recent decision to deny approval of the extraordinarily important Keystone XL Pipeline project is equally egregious. The exhaustively researched project would run from Alberta, Canada, to the U.S. Gulf Coast. It would create thousands of new jobs. It represents a significant source of new supply from our friendly northern ally. Yet, the president decides to (again) placate the environmental left. Hence, another example of sound science and the national interest compromised by a small but vocal minority.

Politicians (as opposed to leaders) love to spout off about the need for energy security and environmental protection. The platitudes only proliferate during campaign season. Such pronouncements don't mean much when not backed up by action.

Some on the right contend the folks currently in charge of environmental policy are quietly pleased to see gas heading toward $4 per gallon. Such "anti-growthers" abhor consumption. They ask why America should be so different from Europe, where the price of gasoline in Germany recently topped $8 per gallon. A few, such as former "green czar" Van Jones, have been quite open in their dislike for cheaper oil. If this indeed represents the president's views, he should state and try to defend them.

Americans have had enough of the histrionics that accompany difficult environmental decisions. The country is weary of oil-related considerations that weigh on foreign policy decisions. "Blood for oil" debates are divisive. They weaken our national resolve.

We deserve energy independence. Our economic and strategic security depends on it. It's time to act.

Give Pols a Pass for Verbal Miscues

Everyone misspeaks in the heat of a campaign.
Issues are more important than gaffes.

March 19, 2012, *The Baltimore Sun*

My elementary school principal was fond of reminding his students that the last perfect person walked this Earth 2,000 years ago. (Note to the litigious types over at the ACLU: It was permissible to provide such insight in light of the school's affiliation with the Lutheran Church.) The reminder was typically offered whenever a misbehaving student admitted to a youthful indiscretion. Our wonderful Mr. Zielski simply wished to teach his kids that the human condition means mistakes will be made along the way, and owning up to them will earn forgiveness here and in the hereafter.

If only today's media pundits applied the same perspective to the sometimes inarticulate pronouncements and just plain mistakes made by national politicians.

My wish is narrowly drawn: It does not extend to statements meant for and delivered to their intended audience, but which I oppose. President Barack Obama's propensity for apologizing to the world for past U.S. policy decisions, for example.

Nor does my point extend to statements wherein the declarant was placed on the defensive due to his failure to communicate in an effective manner.

To wit, then-Gov. Michael Dukakis's un-empathetic debate response to the question of whether he would support the death penalty (despite his personal opposition) if his wife was raped and murdered.

Or Senator John Kerry explaining his position on a funding bill for U.S. troops in Iraq by declaring, "I actually did vote for the $87 billion before I voted against it." (As a former Member of Congress, I know what the senator meant to say but failed to articulate.)

More recently, former Gov. Mitt Romney's intended point that a social safety net exists for the very poor (but no other socioeconomic class) was cited by his opponents as an uncaring dismissal of the underclass from a wealthy man.

The foregoing incidents fall into the "didn't really mean how it was interpreted" category. Each resulted in substantive media scorn. Each had the respective presidential candidate scrambling to explain himself for weeks.

Statements intended to deceive are not pertinent, either. The infamous Clinton denial, "I did not have sex with that woman," comes to mind. Similarly, then-Senator Gary Hart's denial of an extramarital affair and doubling down dare to the press ("Follow me around . . . I'm serious . . . If anybody wants to put a tail on me, go ahead.") effectively ended his presidential campaign. The bottom line: These false declarations were received exactly as intended.

Rather, my point pertains to readily apparent misstatements made by serious, smart people in the intense glare of a high-stakes political campaign.

President Gerald Ford's assurance that Poland was not under Soviet domination (during a 1976 debate with Jimmy Carter) may be the most damaging example. The misguided observation became instant fodder for Chevy Chase and "Saturday Night Live"—not a good result for a politician intent on showing the country he could lead during the dark days of the Cold War.

Other examples race to mind: President Obama's reference to our "57 states"; Senator John McCain's recollection of attending a conference with "President Putin of Germany"; Vice President Joe Biden calling for wheelchair-bound Democratic state

Senator Chuck Graham to "stand up, let the people see you" during a campaign stop; Texas Governor Rick Perry's statement that the American Revolution was fought in the "16th Century"; and then-Governor Sarah Palin's reference to our North Korean "allies." I could go on, but you get the point.

These pronouncements were clearly incorrect. All were made by intelligent people. Each was corrected almost immediately. But each was used as alleged "proof" that the opposition may lack the necessary brains to do the job.

A thought for all of us sentenced to a 24/7 news cycle wherein every comment, statement or aside is endlessly vetted: Give 'em a break. Presidential campaigns are political pressure cookers. Politicians are human beings. They can get tired, cranky and careless. They remind us that nobody is perfect. As much as we might like to revel in the difficulties of our political opponents, obvious misstatements should not become prime campaign fodder. Our unsettled economy and numerous military engagements around the world provide us plenty of real issues to debate. Given the high stakes involved, we can do better than this.

Student-Athletes Need a Degree, Not a Paycheck

Robert L. Ehrlich Jr. says paying college athletes is asking for trouble.

May 6, 2012, *The Baltimore Sun*

Many of you know I was fortunate to play high school football at Gilman and college football at Princeton. What most of you do not know is that I worked as a graduate assistant on the Wake Forest football staff to pay for my room and board during law school. These experiences instilled in me a strong sense of the appropriate role of academics and athletics in our secondary schools and colleges. So it should come as no surprise that I have a strong opinion as to the increasingly aggressive calls to pay college athletes in revenue-producing sports.

The rationale is familiar: Big-time athletic programs (particularly football and basketball) produce in excess of $6 billion in annual income for our Division 1 colleges and universities. These institutions are constantly jumping at new revenue-producing opportunities. Indeed, the sports pages are full of reports about conference switching, new post-season tournaments, new media networks, and the extension of the regular season to unheard of lengths. (Remember when college football was played in the fall and basketball in the winter?) The money grab may have grown perverse, but the dollars keep coming in. And now advocates are asking the NCAA to cut the players in on the revenue pie.

On the common-sense side is a proposal to increase grant-in-aid scholarships to reflect the full annual cost of attending college. This is the one new proposal that makes sense to me. Some recent studies have concluded that the average scholarship package (including educational expenses) is approximately $3,500 below what it should be. So, just increase the package to reflect the actual cost of the educational and related expenses and be done with it.

Numerous other ideas floated to date are rife with problems. One would have college athletes contract out their marketing rights to sponsors, while another would have schools create a trust fund to be held in escrow until such time as a student athlete graduates. South Carolina Coach Steve Spurrier, a former Heisman Trophy winner, advocates a lump sum payment per season.

A brief review of recent pay-for-play proposals (mostly applicable to football and basketball) brings to light a multitude of potential issues: minimum salaries, Title IX, antitrust protection, unionization, workers' compensation, and endorsement revenue are but a sampling of the potential problems attendant to a college athlete wage scale.

Reportedly, some major college athletes are angry at what they perceive as unfair treatment. They feel as though they are being cheated out of their fair share of an ever-growing revenue stream. Leigh Steinberg, a top-drawer agent, shares this sense of disparate treatment: "The dominant attitude among players is that there is no moral or ethical reason not to take money, because the system is ripping them off."

Wow. I understand my athletic experience was not at the Division 1 level, but we're still talking about an expenses-paid college education—that ticket to success in post-industrial America. In this respect, it is appropriate that folks remember the consideration given in exchange for the athletic talent on display: a four-year free ride at many of America's leading universities. That brief sentence must sound pretty good indeed to the millions of American families presently struggling to pay for their non-athlete child to live the college dream.

It is not unusual for many scholarship athletes to drop out of school once their eligibility is complete. The resulting unacceptable graduation rates are more a reflection on the individual institutions than the student-athlete. And herein lies the real problem with revenue-driven college athletics: Too often, the young athlete fails to receive what he has been promised—a *real* education.

This is not a problem of dollars. It is a problem of moral responsibility too often forfeited in the glitter of big-time athletics. As the commercial says, most "D-1" kids will be going pro in a field other than professional athletics. Many gave their energy, talent and bodies to play in the big time. Their obligation is to attend class, learn and graduate. The university's obligation is to ensure that just such a result occurs, even if it takes five or six years to get it done. Anything less is simply immoral. That so many athletes fail to ever attain a degree means the immoral often wins in today's athletic arena.

Bloomberg vs. Freedom

NYC mayor and Hopkins benefactor has gone overboard in trying to control what people eat and drink.

June 24, 2012, *The Baltimore Sun*

The Ehrlich boys sure love their summer Slurpees. Even the fiftysomething Ehrlich kid is not averse to indulging on the way home from those hot summer football practices. (Mom does not share our male addiction but usually lets us slide in the interest of family unity.)

That the Ehrlich Slurpee bonding experience takes place in Annapolis and not New York City is a good thing, as the Big Apple now deals with the latest assault on individual freedom from Mayor Michael Bloomberg.

The successor to the wildly successful Rudy Giuliani is a billionaire Democrat-turned-Republican-turned-independent. He has flirted with a presidential run. In Maryland, he is widely recognized for his incredibly generous donations (about $800 million) to the Johns Hopkins University, where he paid his way through a combination of college loans and work as a parking lot attendant. Some may recall that he is the author of New York City's trans-fat ban of 2006. And today, he seems more intent than ever on limiting individual choice in ways that would make even the Obama Administration blush. (Oops, I spoke too soon. It now appears that First Lady Michelle Obama has blessed the mayor's latest dietary edict.)

The edict at issue concerns the mayor's campaign to ban that staple of summertime fun in the Big Apple: sugary drinks over 16 ounces. That's right—one's morning iced coffee, midday Big Gulp, after-workout Gatorade, and early evening venti frappuccino are slated for the chopping block within the confines of America's version of the "Forbidden City."

This aggressive desire to limit dietary choice throughout the city's restaurants, street vendors, and stadiums is not a new notion to Mr. Bloomberg. Some may recall a March order wherein perfectly good food donations meant for homeless shelters were outlawed because New York's "food police" would be unable to assess the salt, fat, and fiber content of the deliveries. This ban on charitable donations that do not meet NYC's dietary restrictions was proposed by an interagency task force and blessed by the Bloomberg Administration. Surprisingly, demands for a mayoral reversal of the "carbs edict" failed to appear on the Occupy protesters' list of demands. Seems dietary restrictions trump personal hygiene with that crowd. And, no, I did not make this story up.

In another instance, Mr. Bloomberg killed a bill that would have lifted the ban on cell phones in New York City public schools. This despite his latter statement that cell phones, (particularly smartphones), increase child safety and are the best way for parents to keep tabs on their teenage children.

There are limits to the mayor's sense of compassion for his people, however. Seems this command and control attitude about the health of New York City residents does not extend to the fiscal health of New York City taxpayers. The world's most famous sanctuary city is not only a safe haven for illegal aliens; the mayor has repeatedly assured his citizens that the presence of so many illegals does not drive up welfare costs imposed on the city's taxpayers. The rationale: Illegals do not fully understand the range of perks available in their sanctuary city, so they fail to avail themselves of public health services for fear of getting reported to immigration authorities. As for what to do about illegal aliens, the mayor simply wants to convert those already here to full citizenship, no penalties or sanctions involved.

Recent tax increases and egregious regulatory measures in Maryland have forced more than a few Free State residents to think long and hard about their family's future residency. Neighboring states such as Pennsylvania, Delaware, and Virginia lead the list of possible new homesteads for families inclined to reject our endless nanny-state indulgences. But one destination most assuredly not on the list of new venues is New York City. Here, the mayor-for-life (or at least the next two years) cannot seem to get enough of government intrusion into one's personal business.

New Yorkers may not have long to wait for the next set of regulatory initiatives. Reports have surfaced about an NYC health board plan to expand the latest ban to include large tubs of popcorn, milkshakes, and certain fruit juices. For this veteran political observer, the betting line is pretty clear: Chick-fil-A appears safe, Wendy's might be able to slide by, but if I were Baskin Robbins . . .

The "Green Jobs" Con Job

Robert Ehrlich says we're all for finding better energy sources,
but we shouldn't be suckered by empty promises.

July 15, 2012, *The Baltimore Sun*

There are a couple of serious problems with the so-called "green jobs revolution."

The first concerns the serial overpromising of new jobs from politicians of all stripes. And it's easy to understand why the overpromising is so rampant: All of us want to believe alternative sources of energy will free us of our overdependence on foreign (and often hostile) sources of energy. Throw in the possibility of thousands of new technology jobs and you have plenty of eager politicians ready to sell a green jobs platform. For context, check out the initial job-creation predictions that followed the Obama Administration's $535 million loan guarantee on behalf of Solyndra Corp.

This overpromising phenomenon is not new. Recall a few years ago when a social-justice narrative led to a "homeownership for all" campaign? A mortgage crisis ensued, followed by a housing-generated recession. Seems that income and creditworthiness remain fairly good barometers of one's ability to meet his financial obligations.

Similarly, it is now popular to market the promise of thousands of new green jobs on the stump. A tepid recovery and 41 straight months of unemployment over 8 percent (and underemployment at 15 percent) make such pronouncements attractive for a subset of snake oil salesmen—er, political leaders.

A prime example of this problem occurred a few weeks ago at a congressional oversight hearing regarding how the federal government goes about the business of counting green jobs. The main combatants were Bureau of Labor Statistics acting Commissioner John Galvin and Oversight Committee Chairman Darrell Issa. The testimony contained the following exchange:

> **Mr. Issa:** If you sweep the floor in a solar panel facility, is that a green job?

> **Mr. Galvin:** Yes.

> **Mr. Issa:** Thank you. If you drive a hybrid bus—public transportation—is that a green job?

> **Mr. Galvin:** According to our definition, yes.

> **Mr. Issa:** Thank you. What if you're a college professor teaching classes about environmental studies?

> **Mr. Galvin:** Yes.

> **Mr. Issa:** What about just any school bus driver?

> **Mr. Galvin:** Yes.

> **Mr. Issa:** What about the guy who puts gas in the school bus?

> **Mr. Galvin:** Yes.

> **Mr. Issa:** How about employees at a bicycle shop?

> **Mr. Galvin:** I guess I'm not sure about that.

> **Mr. Issa:** The answer is yes, according to your definition. And you've got a lot of them. What about a clerk at the bicycle repair shop?

> **Mr. Galvin:** Yes.

Mr. Issa: What about someone who works in an antique dealer?

Mr. Galvin: I'm not sure about that either.

Mr. Issa: The answer is yes. Those are—those are recycled goods. They're antiques; they're used. What about someone who works at the Salvation Army in their clothing recycling and furniture?

Mr. Galvin: Right. Because they're selling recycled goods.

Mr. Issa: OK. What about somebody who opened a store to sell rare manuscripts?

Mr. Galvin: What industry is that?

Mr. Issa: People sell rare books and manuscripts—but they're rare because they're old, so they're used.

Mr. Galvin: OK.

Mr. Issa: What about workers at a consignment shop?

Mr. Galvin: That's a green job.

Mr. Issa: Does the teenage kid who works full time at a used record shop count?

Mr. Galvin: Yes.

Such illuminating testimony is relatively rare on Capitol Hill. The abject silliness of the categorizations is a stark reminder about how far afield some will go in order to promote a politically popular agenda.

A related development: It appears the thousands of new green jobs promised by proponents of California's 2006 Climate Change law have failed to materialize. Two recent independent studies suggest that new environmental rules and cap-and-trade taxes on carbon emissions will actually contract California's GDP by between 3.5 percent and 8.9 percent by 2020. This, of course, means slower growth and fewer jobs. It also signals the (well reported) continued exodus of companies out of California.

All of us look forward to the day technological innovation ends our dangerous addiction to foreign fossil fuels. To the extent innovation produces new jobs, good for us. But such progress is not generated by press conferences or political wish lists. Real new jobs (green and otherwise) come about when technology allows the private market to turn a profit. Until then, we should be honest about our ability to produce the types of green jobs that will sustain a 21st century economy.

For Republicans, a Not So Happy New Year

Robert L. Ehrlich Jr. surveys the political landscape, from the fiscal cliff to immigration to Benghazi.

January 6, 2013, *The Baltimore Sun*

Author's disclaimer: Today's piece may cause my center/right readers severe irritability, sleeplessness, and a strong desire to limit your cable television options to Fox. The antidote may not arrive until the midterm elections of 2014.

Fiscal cliff negotiations: a real bummer. An empowered president intent on fulfilling his progressive inclination to raise taxes. An emboldened Harry Reid strangely silent about his inability to pass a budget through a Democratic Senate over the past three years. A weakened GOP reduced to limiting the damage from the anti-growth impacts of tax hikes and the onset of Obamacare.

Missing from the debate: any serious thought of cutting the Obama-era explosion ($2.9 trillion to $3.8 trillion) of federal spending. Indeed, the president's recent pronouncements reflect his desire to use the additional revenue from expiration of some of the Bush tax cuts for *new* spending. Also missing from the breathless 24/7 fiscal cliff coverage is a rational plan to spur economic growth at a time some economists believe we are teetering on the brink of another recession. Oh, and reform for entitlements (what really drives the debt) was last seen on the back of a milk carton. Maybe all this economic angst was the Armageddon scenario the Mayans foretold.

Earliest (and easiest) prediction of 2013: When the next fiscal cliff negotiations begin in March, the president will again target wealth and success. Small business owners beware: You remain a most inviting target for a president lacking in private sector experience and empathy. As my kids say, "It's just the way he rolls."

Illegal immigration: I know Mitt Romney's hard line is the popular explanation for the Hispanic and Asian tilt toward the president in November, but can't we have some degree of respectability when it comes to enforcing our immigration laws? Apparently not: The Mexican government has filed a brief in the Ninth Circuit Court of Appeals in support of the plaintiffs challenging the section of Arizona's new immigration law that allows the police to arrest those suspected of harboring illegal immigrants. The primary thrust of the foreign government's argument: The law "harms diplomatic relations [with] the United States, undermines the United States' ability to speak to a foreign country with one voice, and encourages the marginalization of Mexicans and people who appear to be from Latin America." I guess the specter of mass illegal border crossings does none of those things . . .

A further irony: The Mexican government enforces some of the toughest immigration laws in the world. What's that old adage? "Do as I say, not as I do."

Benghazi: I pray for Secretary of State Hillary Clinton's return to good health, but my good thoughts for her recovery are independent of my concern about her remarkable silence since an American ambassador and three diplomats were murdered at our consulate on September 11, 2012. For years, Hillary Clinton has been a case study in crisis management. So, how to interpret the great wall of silence surrounding the Benghazi fiasco? It seems as though most of the usual suspects have been trotted out (Susan Rice, Jay Carney, Joe Biden) with the exception of *the person in charge*.

It's been 117 days since the attack. The original company line about an anti-Muslim YouTube video has been discredited. A compliant mainstream media has naturally failed to press the case. And an election has been successfully delivered to the liberal media's chosen candidate. But an initially concerned and now suspicious America has a right to demand answers. Hillary must now step up prior to leaving office. Besides the general public, the families of four dead American heroes deserve to learn the unvarnished truth about that ill-fated day.

Secular culture: Rhode Island Gov. Lincoln Chafee proclaimed a "holiday tree" at his state's annual lighting event; the administration of a North Carolina community college rewrote an advertisement for a student Christmas tree sale (profits to be given to charity), replacing "Christmas" with "holiday"; the UC Berkeley (where else?) student senate wants to ban the Salvation Army's collection boxes from its campus due to the group's alleged anti-gay bias; and an Arkansas atheist group successfully blocked the scheduled field trip of a Little Rock elementary school to a production of "A Charlie Brown Christmas" (seems Linus' reading of Scripture sent the Arkansas Society of Freethinkers over the top).

Tidings of comfort (if not joy) to the relatively few of us conservatives/libertarians remaining in the Free State: "This too shall pass." Not soon enough.

Obama's Unpardonable Neglect
of Clemency

Robert Ehrlich, who knows something about the pardon process, questions President Obama's commitment to fairness.

January 13, 2013, *The Baltimore Sun*

One of the under-reported promises made by Congressman Ehrlich in the gubernatorial campaign of 2002 was to re-energize the pardon power in Maryland. My advisers thought it a bit loony to make the pledge, since the race promised to be close and there was little political advantage to be gained. After all, Gov. Parris Glendening had framed his clemency strategy with one brief line—"life means life"—to minimal criticism from his liberal base.

Still, I thought it an essential element of the job description to "do justice" through the exercise of this extraordinary power. Accordingly, my legal staff and I set about the business of reviewing clemency petitions from those Marylanders who had turned their lives around after a criminal conviction, a process that included input from victims, prosecutors, and defense counsel. Final scorecard:

- 444 requests for pardons received; 228 granted

- 72 commutation requests received; eight commutations (and six medical paroles) granted

- The Sentencing Project ranked Maryland as one of the "13 most active pardon states" in the country

This record has followed me in my post-public career, as I'm often asked to speak on the subject of post-conviction relief and clemency.

One fascinating aspect of the issue is the unpredictability surrounding its use. Partisan identification and philosophical predisposition are not accurate predictors of interest or activism. In fact, more Republican governors have shown an inclination to act than their Democratic colleagues.

Some cynics might dismiss this GOP activism with a "Nixon goes to China" indictment, as though more conservative Republican governors engage here to counterbalance more conservative inclinations on other criminal justice issues. Only one problem with the charge: There is very little to be gained (and an awful lot to be lost) by making clemency a priority issue. On the right, I found limited interest in and a sustained fear of a "Willie Horton" type scenario. On the left is a more inexplicable silence, since this type of activism goes to the heart of progressive social justice. Maybe it is simply an unwillingness to acknowledge Republican leadership on one of its issues, or maybe a similar sense of fear about charges of being "weak on crime."

In any event, my demonstrated credibility on the issue provides standing to critique the surprising lack of interest in clemency demonstrated by the former community organizer now occupying the White House.

The last week of 2012 saw the Office of the Inspector General torch the president's pardon attorney regarding the inappropriate withholding of information that could have led to the release of Clarence Aaron, an African American college student who was given a life sentence *for a first time, nonviolent drug offense* in 1993.

The dysfunction described in the Aaron case is not new, nor should it be surprising. After all, the office is located within the same agency (Department of Justice) that prosecutes cases in the first place. Further, critical views of the pardon office's bureaucracy have been around for years.

In his book *Decision Points*, former President George W. Bush recounts his frustration with the pardon process in the context of the Scooter Libby (Vice President Dick Cheney's chief of staff) obstruction of justice case. The president's advice to incoming President Barack Obama on Inauguration Day, 2009: "Announce a pardon policy early on, and stick to it." Alas, the Obama Administration has shown no such interest in fixing a broken system.

Although slow to the dance, President Bush was correct in bemoaning his lost opportunity. 1980s-era sentencing laws have led to historic incarceration rates in the U.S. The ugly facts speak for themselves:

- In 1980, the U.S. incarceration rate was 150 per 100,000 citizens; today, it's 753;

- this rate of incarceration compares to 153 in Great Britain, 96 in France, and 90 in Germany;

- the U.S. now imprisons a higher percentage of its population than any other country in the world .

Hopefully, a second term Obama Administration will do the right thing. Our federal system houses many thousands of nonviolent drug-related offenders. Each inmate costs the taxpayers in excess of $28,000 per year. I believe the vast majority are no threat to reoffend. Their cases should be reviewed within the context of a newly invigorated federal review process.

Only one man can effectuate this change. Mr. President, it's time to act.

The Vast Left-Wing Conspiracy

*Obama and his allies are trying to set America on a course
to European-style socialism.*

February 3, 2013, *The Baltimore Sun*

I'm not big into conspiracy theories. I never bought into the
grassy knoll in Dallas or the anti-Obama birther movement.
And it will take a lot of convincing for me to believe Oakland
Raiders coach Bill Callahan took a dive in Super Bowl XXXVII
to please his friend (and opposing coach) Jon Gruden.

But I do believe that America's political tilt toward progressivism is the product of a lot of grassroots work by very liberal groups
intent on remaking the American economy and culture.

One such example is the focus of an interesting piece in the
latest edition of the progressive magazine *Mother Jones*. The article chronicles a December 2012 mega-meeting of the left's most
powerful groups, including the National Education Association,
Sierra Club, Greenpeace, Communications Workers of America,
and the NAACP. The agreed upon coordinated agenda: get (right-
wing) money out of politics, fight voter photo identification laws,
and re-write Senate rules to limit the use of the filibuster to block
legislation.

Such initiatives are common in the Obama era, as the American left seeks to take advantage of a permissive, secular era in
America. One major goal: redefine the relationship between Americans and their government. And this time, the line will be favorably drawn toward a more intrusive state.

Other relevant players are familiar enough to followers of American politics. They range from special interest groups (Service Employees International Union; American Federation of Teachers; American Federation of State, County, and Municipal Employees; NARAL; People for the American Way) to super wealthy individuals stationed on Wall Street and in places like Hollywood. (George Soros, Warren Buffett, Bill Gates, and George Lucas).

That these and other left-leaning players were key to the election and re-election of President Barack Obama is irrefutable. Their members and money were in turn brilliantly utilized by a veteran Obama political team that now retires undefeated. (You might ask Hillary Clinton if you believe these folks don't play for keeps.)

But elections have consequences. And the hyper-progressive itinerary that Obama II and its associated interest groups bring to center stage now seeks to move American society and culture to the left: steadily, and permanently.

The evidence is there for all to see and extends to state as well as federal activism.

Read 'em and weep:

- a new federal entitlement (Obamacare)

- higher marginal tax rates

- abortion (and free birth control) on demand

- gun control

- gay marriage

- multiculturalism

- in-state tuition and drivers licenses for illegal aliens

- elimination of capital punishment

- compulsory unionism

- repeal of voter photo laws

- women in combat

- expansion of food stamps

- diminution of welfare work requirements

- "clean" energy subsidies

- same day voter registration

- limitless unemployment benefits

It's a play straight from the Democratic National Committee's platform, an agenda that values collectivism over individualism, regulation over markets, and entitlement over freedom. Traditional notions of individualism, entrepreneurism, and pulling oneself up by the bootstraps are given periodic lip service, if at all. And it makes sense—from the progressive's perspective. You see, this mindset covets limited economic horizons, energizes the redistribution of wealth, and generates the type of immense bureaucracy necessitated by the modern welfare state.

For context, watch (and listen to) the president. His rhetoric regularly celebrates big government, degrades individualism (recall the once popular "you didn't build that" narrative from Campaign 2012), and demands constant public sector growth, the more the better to spur economic activity.

The adherents do not pretend to advance balanced budgets or fiscal restraint. Rarely is their focus on private sector job growth or wealth creation. You see, their world is all about endless demands and the (tax) dollars required to feed them.

The good people who write the editorials on the facing page of this newspaper are wholly in tune with the foregoing agenda. They have opined as much over the last few decades. So, too, are the clear majority of voters in Blue State America, the formerly Free State of Maryland foremost among them.

But is America really on board? Is Reaganism now so 1980-ish? Has America truly become a center/left country on a comfortable glide path toward a European style social democracy?

I hope (and pray) this seismic shift can be stopped.

As Kids Head to College, Beware Liberal Groupthink

Robert Ehrlich denounces political correctness run amok on campus.

February 24, 2013, *The Baltimore Sun*

I've been thinking a lot about college lately. You see, one of my more time-consuming tasks is to write college recommendation letters. It's an occupational hazard from extended time in the state legislature, Congress, and the governorship. But it's one that I enjoy; there is nothing better than to receive notice that a hard-working kid has been accepted into the (often costly) school of his or her choice.

And herein lies the great dilemma for middle-class parents. The wealthy can afford to pay considerable tuition freight; the poor qualify for a wide variety of financial aid and scholarship assistance packages. But it is the wide swath of middle-income parents who continue to leverage themselves in order for their children to punch that four-year ticket to success called a college degree.

Our post-industrial economy demands that degree. The mantra is often repeated by our political and business leaders: Gotta have that sheepskin to compete in the technology economy. It's a cultural guilt trip that has proved to be quite profitable for our four-year institutions; tuitions always increase despite the presence of considerable endowments.

(The fact that some students are more appropriately situated in a technical school, community college, or other educational alternative can get lost in the fog of the guilt trip, but I digress.)

This column is directed to the aforementioned parents who sacrifice so much to send their children to college. Specifically, it is a reminder that your kids are often force-fed ludicrous, politically correct junk on your dime. And that the purveyors of this nonsense often hold those who pay the tab (aka "you") in contempt.

Some recent incidents:

- Palm Beach State College shut down the student recruiting booth for the conservative group Young Americans for Freedom for handing out anti-Obama Administration materials. The information criticizing the president was published by that hotbed of radicalism, the Heritage Foundation. This, after a college administrator had specifically given the club permission to recruit during "Club Rush Week." Seems the administrator in question changed her mind after reviewing the anti-Obama opinion pieces.

- Florida community college mathematics professor Sharon Sweet asked—and by some accounts, forced—her students to sign a card that stated "I pledge to vote for President Obama and Democrats up and down the ticket." The college has now rightfully concluded that such actions created a hostile environment for the students. Ms. Sweet has been placed on (paid) leave pending a board of trustees vote on her future.

- Vanderbilt University placed four Christian groups (including the Fellowship of Christian Athletes) on provisional status because the groups require their members to adhere to religious tenets. (In some cases, students are expected to sign a statement of faith.) According to school administrators, such religious orientation violates the school's wide-ranging nondiscrimination policy. Similar sanctions have been enacted at SUNY Buffalo, the University of Michigan, the University of North Carolina, Rutgers, Marquette, and numerous other schools. So there you have it: Christian groups that restrict their memberships to those who adhere to their beliefs are now viewed as discriminatory by many of our university administrators.

- Reports of military recruiters being kicked off campus or out of job fairs are too numerous to mention. The indictments include the usual charges: racism, sexism, classism, militarism. How easily these miscreants forget about who protects their fiery speech in the first place.

- Politically correct speech codes barring "offensive expression" continue unabated on many campuses. Such policies chill expression (protected by the First Amendment) that might be found offensive—to any and all. The codes are typically vague and contrary to the notion of a university as the facilitator of ideas and open debate. Fortunately, the language police almost always lose free-speech challenges in the courts.

- Last item: It's been six years since a group of 88 Duke University professors indicted, tried, convicted, and sentenced three innocent (not just "not guilty") varsity lacrosse players for a non-existent campus rape. No apology was ever issued. Academic life at one of our elite schools simply moved on . . . as do notions of fair-mindedness, balance, and open expression at so many of our leading colleges and universities.

The foregoing is most assuredly not meant to discourage the attainment of a college degree; nor do I wish to impeach all of academia. (I've even met a handful of conservative professors at Maryland schools.) It's just a reminder: Some of your kids may need to be deprogrammed after four years of expensive and progressive groupthink is shoved down their throats.

Fortunately, a glance at the flipside of a first paycheck often brings them back to reality. If only that same phenomenon worked on campus . . .

Did That Really Happen? In America?

It's hard for a conservative to read the news without setting the blood aboil.

April 28, 2013, *The Baltimore Sun*

My periodic "Did You Know" columns tend to raise the blood pressure of more conservative readers who are embarrassed/angry/frustrated by the increasingly aggressive counter-cultural policies of the hard left and their allies in Hollywood, on campus, and in Washington, D.C.

Yet, some of this stuff is so looney and/or outside what should be mainstream views and opinions that I can't help myself. So, with all due apologies to any irritated readers, did you know:

- The Defense Department continues to insist the deadly Fort Hood murders (which killed 13, including a pregnant soldier, and wounded 32 others) constitute "workplace violence" instead of "terrorism"—this despite extensive evidence that the shooter (Major Nidal Hasan) had direct communications with al-Qaida leader Anwar al-Awlaki in the days prior to the attack and that Major Hasan was heard to shout, "Allahu Akbar!" (God is great) prior to his murderous rampage.

- The local school system in Cranston, Rhode Island, has decided to ban father-daughter and mother-son activities for violation of the state's gender discrimination law after the American Civil Liberties Union filed a complaint on behalf of a single mother whose daughter (you guessed it) was unable to attend a father-daughter dance. (Guess those "Sadie Hawkins" dances of yesteryear would really heat up the gender police at the ACLU!)

- The Wisconsin Department of Public Instruction (the state agency in charge of public education) instructs its white VISTA volunteers who work with poor, minority students to thoughtfully examine the privilege their race confers on them; the DPI has devoted an entire web page to the "problem," including links to racial justice workshops where all those guilty white people can get in touch with their (presumably considerable) personal bias. FYI: Recent media coverage about the VISTA program materials has caused the Wisconsin DPI to remove the information from its website. Also FYI: I'm not making this stuff up.

- The Associated Press, the largest and most prestigious news outlet in the world, has decided to eliminate the phrase "illegal immigrant" from its news stories; it seems the phrase is now deemed too dehumanizing a term. This marks a major victory for immigration reform activists, many of whom have made linguistic redefinitions a major cause within the journalistic community.

- Progressive Insurance Company's wildly successful CEO Peter Lewis named his company to reflect his political views. The man who is number 366 on the Forbes list of the richest people in the world is a major contributor to far left wing groups such as MoveOn.org, The Democracy Alliance, America Coming Together, Media Matters for America, and many Democratic political candidates.

- The University of Maryland spent $15,000 of *your* tax money on an "inclusive language campaign" aimed at creating an "offenseless" dialogue on campus. How generations of Terps got along without this type of instruction I do not know, but one wonders how much longer before we see special "language courts" on college campuses.

- Full-time faculty members at America's four-year institutions have moved further left over the past three years, while those identifying as either moderate or conservative have continued to decline (according to the UCLA Higher Education Research Institute). Note: This finding, of course, falls under the category of "The sky is blue."

- The list of known Hollywood Republicans may be embarrassingly brief, but it is impressive: Matthew McConaughey, Kelsey Grammer, Drew Carey, 50 Cent, Britney Spears, Stephen Baldwin, Clint Eastwood, Bruce Willis, Adam Sandler, Vince Vaughn, Sylvester Stallone, Angie Harmon, Sarah Michelle Gellar, and Heather Locklear.

- The Maryland Canons of Judicial Conduct forbid Maryland judges from inquiring about a criminal defendant's immigration status at a sentencing or bail hearing; seems the Constitutional privilege against self-incrimination applies to a hearing (wherein a criminal sentence can be imposed) even where the defendant is not an American citizen.

- A group of Maryland legislators and the O'Malley Administration plan to introduce a carbon dioxide bill which would apply a graduated excise tax to the amount of carbon dioxide Marylanders breathe into the atmosphere, i.e., the heavier the individual—the more CO_2 expelled from one's lungs—the higher the tax; this new "breathing tax" would become a line item on Maryland state income tax returns and be computed using the taxpayer's height and weight (as recorded on the return) to ascertain how much excess CO_2 would be subject to the levy.

Every item reported above is factual, with the exception of the proposed carbon dioxide bill. But the fact that some (many?) of you believed a "breathing tax" could be introduced and passed in Maryland speaks volumes about how far we have fallen off the fiscal cliff of sensible tax and spending policy in the jurisdiction formerly known as "The Free State."

How Not to Run a Local Government

Robert Ehrlich says Stockton, California, reveals the perils of favoring public employee unions over taxpayers.

May 19, 2013, *The Baltimore Sun*

One of the more enjoyable aspects of my public career was an excellent relationship with public safety unions. Law enforcement, fire fighters, and EMT groups were supportive of my races for the state legislature, Congress, and governor.

Although not unheard of, such consistent support made for some uneasy moments when national labor organizations (almost exclusively associated with Democratic candidates) were informed about public safety union support for "that Republican Ehrlich." From a personal perspective, it was easy to separate the unique nature of public safety's job description (public protection being the No. 1 job of government) from other public-sector duties. My legislative support typically followed.

These memories are by way of background as we take a hard look at the (mis)fortunes of Stockton, California, the largest city to file for bankruptcy protection in the U.S. (Although Stockton is only the most well known of two dozen California municipalities that have mismanaged their finances in spectacular fashion.)

How, you might ask, did Stockton end up in such desperate straits? Well, it seems a bunch of local politicians took to promising a lot of goodies to a lot of people in exchange for a lot of votes. Primary beneficiaries were local public employee unions, who suckered the aforementioned politicians into a series of (beyond) sweetheart salary and pension deals.

How good? In some instances Stockton is paying 50-year old public safety retirees close to 100 percent of what they earned while on the job. Further perks included "Cadillac" health plans and the ability to bank unlimited vacation and sick time that could be cashed out at retirement time. With this gig, who needs a retirement party?

All this in addition to other negligent spending priorities, including the building of a new City Hall (at a cost of $48 million) during a historic economic downturn.

Stockton's cash crunch has resulted in dire consequences. Local police patrols are so reduced that they only respond to an emergency in progress. Result: The city's crime rate has skyrocketed. Many businesses (and people) are leaving, too—a widespread phenomenon in high-tax, high-cost, high-regulation California. And California's loss is Nevada's, Washington's, Oregon's, and Texas's gain; statistics reflect that 36,000 California corporations left the state between 1990 and 2010. Further, the state has lost 3.4 million citizens over the last 23 years, a loss rate faster than any other state. Sound familiar, Maryland?

Even emergency cost-saving measures such as employee layoffs and reducing health care benefits, library, and rec and parks services have failed to stem the flow of red ink. It's all a difficult reminder from your Economics 101 textbook: Over-promising, overspending, and over-taxing always lead to underperformance. In this case, the city's inability to pay its bills and make good on its debt.

All of which has led to an important decision with profound moral, legal and constitutional repercussions. To wit: Given limited cash, which creditors get paid—and how much?

The legal battle pits federal bankruptcy law against California state law. But in dollar (and political) terms, it is a showdown between public employee pension funds and other creditors. And on April 1, a federal bankruptcy judge ruled in favor of the union, which means that Stockton will continue to satisfy its gigantic pension obligations to the California Public Employees' Retirement System (present price tag: $900 million) before it pays other creditors. To date, the city has maintained its payouts while reneging on other debts. (FYI, as expected, outside creditor groups plan to appeal.)

One of the more delicious ironies to Stockton's fiscal plight pertains to the 10th Amendment. You know, the left's least favorite constitutional provision, usually invoked by conservatives in order to protect individuals and states from federal jurisdiction. But today it's the usually left-leaning unions screaming bloody murder about states' (and local) rights. Their view: Stockton's politicians freely signed contracts they could not afford—deal with it. And pay us.

Hard lessons abound. But one stands out: Everybody loses when government insists on spending beyond its means. Today, Stockton is located at the intersection of unacceptable politics and unsustainable spending. It is a national model for what not to do. It is going to be quite difficult to get the city's fiscal train back on track. And, as usual, it will be the taxpayers forced to foot the bill for gross political negligence.

But come to think of it, it was the taxpayer-voter who enabled negligent, free-spending politicians with their votes. In the sorry case of Stockton, there may be no innocent party. Elections *really do* have consequences.

Why the IRS Scandal Is Worse Than the Others

Bob Ehrlich says the targeting of conservative groups epitomizes what is wrong with an arrogant, overreaching government.

June 16, 2013, *The Baltimore Sun*

Happy Father's Day . . .

In over two decades in politics, my least favorite political type was the unabashed "hot dog," that media-seeking missile who would happily sell his grandmother for a 30-second hit on the evening news. The most dangerous place in the world is between such an animal and a television camera.

This personality type is plentiful on Capitol Hill, where the most outrageous statements of the day are sure to lead that evening's headlines. After all, 5,000 Capitol Hill reporters have to report something of interest every day.

All this is by way of background as the enormity of the IRS scandal continues to hit home with the American public. If there ever was an opportunity to hot dog a crisis, this is it. And although a handful of Members have sought to score political points in the short term, the ready availability for political showboating must not diminish the true gravity of *this* scandal.

Indeed, it's difficult to overstate all that is wrong about the targeting of American citizens for their political views. The following are five reasons why this one hits harder and digs deeper than the other Obama scandals of recent months:

Nobody likes the IRS. These are the public servants who conduct the audits that (can) lead to penalties, fines, or worse. Their examiners demand the supportive documents we too often disregard. (Where did I put that shoebox full of receipts?) Many of us get uptight just receiving correspondence from the IRS in the morning mail. Rarely is such correspondence of a congratulatory tone.

The IRS implements a tax code nobody really understands. It is a code that now extends to 73,954 pages of often arcane language. Fewer than half the population prepares their own taxes; it is estimated the private sector spends $193 billion annually on tax preparation. That's a huge amount of money going to compliance rather than productive, profitable pursuits.

The IRS is the primary agency charged with implementing Obamacare. Yes, the already unpopular agency must now regulate the increasingly unpopular "Affordable Care Act." And the last thing the American public needs to be reminded about is that Obamacare requires hiring of thousands of IRS agents to ensure that every individual, business, and nonprofit in America is Obamacare compliant. (Oh, one of the other things an already angry public does not want to see is a smug IRS commissioner telling Congress he made 157 trips to the White House and the only one he can remember is the Easter egg roll!)

Reports of lavish spending at IRS retreats. In the midst of all the bad press, now comes evidence of scandalous amounts of money ($50 million) spent on high-priced hotels, conferences, and homemade entertainment videos that confirm the worst fears of all those taxpayers suspicious about how their hard-earned tax dollars are (mis-)spent in Washington, D.C. (Note to present and future Cabinet secretaries of both parties: Fox News always seems to find the goofiest comedic videos made for agency retreats. And they always seem to come to light when the agency is in hot water for other alleged sins.)

IRS targeting of conservative-oriented groups. And the granddaddy of them all: irrefutable evidence the Obama IRS targeted conservative groups for special investigation smack dab in the middle of a tense presidential campaign. And at a time the president and his surrogates were running around the country complaining about the rise of the tea party and other similarly situated organizations.

This was an "in your face" operation: groups associated with the major conservative causes of the day (fiscal restraint, tax reform, marriage, pro-life) all came in for extraordinary (and highly questionable) scrutiny by certain alleged "rogue" personnel within the IRS in Cincinnati, Washington State, or both. Only time and future investigation will tell how far up the chain the miscreant trail will lead, but I'm betting this was not simply a basement operation confined to "The River City."

I will spare you the embarrassingly weak attempt at mitigation supplied by the reliably liberal Rep. Jim McDermott. Suffice to say the 12-term Democrat intimated that the ideological focus of the groups at issue was in and of itself enough to raise the interest level of the IRS. It took Rep. Paul Ryan about six seconds to take that high fastball over the fence. Sometimes, it's just better to sit there and take your medicine.

The irony of the IRS scandal is indeed thick: Groups that share a common distrust of the ways and means of the U.S. government were illegally targeted by . . . agents of the U.S. government.

Remember, just because you're paranoid does not mean that everybody is not out to get you. Unless, it appears, you are a liberal Democrat . . .

Concussions Won't Stop America's Love of Football

The NFL's popularity is due to its deep connections to the national culture.

September 29, 2013, *The Baltimore Sun*

The NFL's recent $765 million dollar settlement with its former players has taken one of the few negative storylines about our favorite pastime off the front pages.

Three quarters of a billion dollars sure sounds like a hefty settlement, but the $1 million per team annual contribution for 20 years represents a mere rounding error for a $10 billion industry that enjoys such influence over our culture. And many believe it was a cheap price to pay for eliminating a legal discovery process that may have revealed incriminating (early) knowledge of the long-term dangers associated with repeated concussions.

Nevertheless, it would take far more than a medical conspiracy to remove the NFL from our national fabric. Professional football has survived calls for its abolition, periodic betting and steroid scandals, intense competition from a number of aggressive start-up professional leagues, and so many off-the-field bad behavior incidents with its players that our eyes glaze over at each newly reported incident on ESPN.

A snapshot of the league's pervasive impact puts it all into perspective:

NFL television ratings remain extraordinarily strong; Monday Night Football is an American institution; fans willingly (if not happily) pay a fee for the privilege of buying season tickets; fantasy leagues dominate Internet and sports radio chatter; a 30-second Super Bowl commercial costs $3.5 million; off-season workouts generate major media coverage; the college draft has been transformed into a made-for-TV event; John Facenda (and his distinctive voice on "NFL Films") has evolved into cultural icon status; we (yes, I'm including the Ehrlichs) watch young guys in the latest Under Armour apparel run around the NFL Combine into the wee hours . . . in the dead of winter; and the president of the United States attempts to associate the league's popularity with the marketing of his decidedly unpopular health care reform. Oh, and don't forget the highly anticipated selection of Carrie Underwood (replacing Faith Hill) as the lead-in for the glitzy pyrotechnic opening to Sunday Night Football.

So, what is it about the NFL that makes it so immensely popular, and so prototypically American?

Four reasons come to mind.

First, we are typically attracted to aggressive sports. (Witness the increasing popularity of the brutal mixed martial arts). In fact, it was not so long ago that the NFL spent part of its advertising budget marketing "best hits" videos to its fans. And the toughest, hardest hitting players (Dick Butkus, Ronnie Lott, Jack Tatum) were used to market the league's tough guy image. (Fact: A Butkus poster hung on my bedroom wall as a young teenager.) Alas, such promotion will now go the way of the dinosaur in light of the new, litigious era of player protection and large fines for helmet-to-helmet hits.

Second, we tend to favor offense over defense. Major League Baseball understood this aspect of American culture when it lowered the pitcher's mound and juiced up its ball in response to an era of dominant pitching in the late 1960s and early 1970s. Similarly, the NFL transformed a running league into a wide-open passing league through rule changes that make it more difficult for defensive backs to cover receivers. And the NBA adopted the three-point shot and defensive three-second rule for similar reasons. (What, you thought the L.A. Lakers' highly marketed "Showtime" was about defense?)

Third, football is the direct beneficiary of another American passion—gambling. Seems as though every office has a weekly pool. And that pool's point spreads are established by the large Las Vegas sports books. Today, 41 percent of all Vegas sports betting is devoted to football. Thirty-three million Americans participate in fantasy football leagues, a participation rate that increases by 2 million per year. And it is estimated that up to $380 billion is wagered on illegal betting or offshore accounts during the season.

Parenthetically, but not surprisingly, my weekly football picks against WJFK's sports "Junkies" when I was governor produced more constituent feedback on the stump than did my positions on Maryland politics.

Last, professional football benefits from an extremely popular "minor league" known as "college football." Compare fandom's narrow interest in minor league baseball (where you probably only follow the progress of your team's minor league players, if that) to the huge network television ratings and revenues generated each Saturday during the fall.

In fact, some pundits say college football is America's second favorite sport. (It already is the second most popular gambling destination.) I once believed this opinion did a disservice to baseball, still commonly referred to as our national pastime. Then I read about ABC's placement of a "Johnny Cam" on the helmet of Texas A&M's quarterback Johnny Manziel for the big showdown with the Alabama Crimson Tide. As though the public hasn't been exposed to enough "Johnny Football" storylines over the past nine months. Which got me thinking about that second favorite sport thing again . . .

No Way to Run a Government: Reflections on the Latest D.C. Debacle

Republicans lost, Obama's victory was short, and we're about to do it all over again.

October 27, 2013, *The Baltimore Sun*

My conclusions about the latest mess in Washington, for your consumption:

The GOP lost: Yes, Obamacare is a predictably unruly mess. It consists of many bad ideas (and a few good ones) wrapped into an enormously expensive partisan missile supported by only one party and passed by means of an appropriations process ("reconciliation"), not regular order. But the Republican-led defunding effort was guaranteed to fail from the start. There was no way President Barack Obama and the hyper-partisan Senate Majority Leader Harry Reid would allow their "prized" legislative accomplishment to be starved of funds or amended in a substantive way. House Speaker John Boehner and Members of his leadership surely knew this fact but lacked the votes to overcome the defunding faction within the GOP caucus.

The lack of a solid endgame was further exemplified by the various fallback positions taken by the House. Once it became clear the Democrats were not going to negotiate over Obamacare or an increase in the debt limit, the House set about the business of offering a series of tasty à la carte policy votes in a failed attempt to entice the Democratic leadership to the negotiating table. In no particular order, the GOP served up the reopening of the national parks, payment of veterans benefits, repeal of Obamacare's odious medical-device tax, repeal of the health care subsidies under Obamacare for Members of Congress and their staffs, more serious income verification for those who apply for Obamacare subsidies, debt payment prioritization within the federal revenue stream, and tying the debt limit increase to broader budget reform and/or comprehensive tax reform.

But these worthy goals were unattainable in the short term. The president and Democratic leadership enjoyed the political high ground. They pressed their advantage and achieved a short-term political victory. All in all, a predictable result given the cards each party had to play.

One further political note: The GOP's actions gave rise to a fully expected onslaught of negative media reviews (not to mention a full-scale rhetorical assault by the president and various Democratic leaders) during a time the narrative should have been about the predictably sloppy (I'm being kind) start of Obamacare. Such is not exactly smart politics from those who wish to educate the public on the practical dangers of the "Affordable Care Act." Score a check-minus under the GOP's ledger.

President Obama did not cover himself in glory: Governors make better presidents than U.S. senators, Jimmy Carter notwithstanding. Governors must lead in difficult terrain; they do not have the option of voting "present" on significant legislation. In fact, a divided Congress requires the participation of the chief executive. Witness the active involvement of Presidents Ronald Reagan, George H.W. Bush, and Bill Clinton in the last three mega-budget deals.

Which brings us to the Obama leadership "style." The same guy who had few friends in the U.S. Senate has failed to make new friends while living at 1600 Pennsylvania Avenue. When the heat is on, he reverts to campaign mode. It is where he is most comfortable: saber rattling in front of large and enthusiastic supporters is what he does best. It is this (considerable) talent that propelled him to the White House.

But fire and brimstone do not a leader make. The fiercely ideological progressive does not sit down easily with the loyal opposition. Substantively, the president views Speaker Boehner and his band of right wingers as the last obstacles to his transformative goals; all the better to demonize them rather than engage in discussion and compromise.

The bottom line: Despite his short-term political victory, the president's approval numbers are in the mid-40s. He has many roads to travel if he intends to lead a midterm Democratic comeback in 2014.

The fiscal nightmare continues: The deal that ended the federal government shutdown and increased the debt limit (for the 54th time since 1978) will run out in about two months. All of which means you should brace yourself for another chapter of high stakes political poker this winter.

There is little reason for optimism. Republicans (tea party and other varieties) are serious about spending cuts and tax reform. Many ran on a fiscal reform platform. And they will not countenance another round of tax increases. But there are not enough Senate votes to leverage the president into a significant deal.

Across the aisle, a clear majority of liberal Democrats have neither the interest nor the inclination to change their big spending ways. Although many wish to relieve sequestration's impact on domestic spending, they do not wish to engage the GOP on permanent budget reforms. Serious entitlement reform is a non-starter, too. As for the president, he has repeatedly stated his position that any serious reform must be accompanied by major new taxes.

The respective political bases are dug-in. The vast majority of House Members enjoy "safe" seats. And there are few remaining conservative-leaning Democrats to act as honest brokers.

This is not a formula for progress.

The Nuclear Option: Then And Now

Politicians who favored the recent use of the nuclear option once opposed it.

December 1, 2013, *The Baltimore Sun*

Ehrlich: "It's time for all of us oppressed minorities to rise up!"

I'm usually not one to degrade my former profession. I still believe public service to be a noble career path. But this week I'm going to make an exception. Last month's events in the U.S. Senate provide the context.

The issue concerns the Senate filibuster, that ultimate legislative tool of the minority party. The, before now, sacrosanct parliamentary maneuver had been much discussed in the recent past, particularly the notion that a "nuclear option" (degrading the filibuster) would bring the end of times. Think I'm kidding? Check out these notable quotes from Democratic leaders:

"Mr. President, I rise today to urge my colleagues to think about the implications of what has been called the nuclear option and what effect that might have on this chamber and on this country. . . . I urge all of us to think not just about winning every debate but about protecting free and democratic debate."

—Senator Barack Obama

"Senators have used the filibuster to stand up to popular presidents, to block legislation, and, yes, even, as I've stated, to stall executive nominees. The roots of the filibuster are found in the Constitution and in our own rules."

—SENATOR HARRY REID

"I am very pleased that senators from both sides of the aisle have walked the Senate back from the brink and preserved the great tradition of the United States Senate. This is a victory for the American people. It is a defeat for the abuse of power known as the nuclear option."

—SENATOR BARBARA BOXER

"And I just had to hope that maybe between now and the time we have this vote there would be enough Senators who will say: Mr. President, no. We are sorry, we cannot go there. We are going to remember our Founders. We are going to remember what made this country great. We are going to maintain the integrity of the U.S. Senate."

—SENATOR HILLARY CLINTON

And then this one from the sitting vice president of the United States:

"We should make no mistake. This nuclear option is ultimately an example of the arrogance of power. It is a fundamental power grab by the majority party, propelled by its extreme right and designed to change the reading of the Constitution, particularly as it relates to individual rights and property rights. It is nothing more or nothing less."

—SENATOR JOE BIDEN

These high sounding quotes sought to warn of the repercussions should a GOP Senate lessen the traditional super majority (60 votes) needed to overcome a filibuster.

But this universally recognized tool of the minority is no more, at least when it comes to presidential appointees and most federal judges. Seems the need to "transform" America through the appointment of progressive federal judges intent on legislating from the bench takes precedence over minority voting rights.

Today's editorial pages are chock full of rationalizations from liberals of all stripes. What makes this reaction so interesting is the total acquiescence from pundits typically consumed with protecting minority rights. This "always on overdrive" group of progressives has created a cottage industry; they always recognize an oppressed minority when they see one. Until, that is, the targeted minority is a Republican. Here the angry mob draws a line and parks its selective indignation on the sideline.

All of which seems to fit an increasingly familiar pattern with the Obama Democrats. Consistency is not exactly the hallmark of this group, more like anything for the good of the cause.

Check it out:

"The most transparent administration in history" is anything but. All those stimulus generated "shovel ready" public works projects . . . weren't. ACORN and its progeny have set the community organizing industry back a generation. The "immoral" raising of the debt limit and accumulation of ever higher public debt is no longer such a big deal. And despite numerous promises to the contrary, millions of Americans have lost their doctors, their health insurance, and their trust in government.

And now Harry Reid's Senate has voted away its most valued rule—which means there are no rules—precisely what the framers warned against in building a more deliberative upper Chamber.

What to do?

The only plausible remedy to this progressive onslaught is a big fat midterm election victory—presently scheduled to be delivered to Harry Reid's doorstep by the "I'm mad as hell and I'm not going to take this anymore!" American public on November 4, 2014.

It's time for all of us oppressed minorities to rise up!

10 Wishes for the New Year

Maryland's former governor asks for an end to artificial turf in sports and a crack on the "Obama protection cocoon" worn by African Americans.

December 29, 2013, *The Baltimore Sun*

Writer's note: And they said it wouldn't last . . . Today's is column No. 100. Thanks to my readers (even the haters) for the tremendous response.

1. *Our Libertarian and tea party friends would stop nominating candidates who screw up winnable races.*

    Recall Nevada (Sen. Harry Reid in 2010), Delaware (Sen. Mike Castle in 2010), and last month's race in Virginia (more below). All probable GOP pick-ups. All lost opportunities due to primary challenge or third party candidacy.

    A factoid from Virginia: The petitions that helped the Libertarian gubernatorial candidate get on the ballot (and draw votes from Republican Ken Cuccinelli) were paid for by an Obama campaign bundler.

2. *"Merry Christmas" would make a holiday comeback.*

    Enough of "Happy Holidays." The founders never used the phrase "separation of church and state;" nor did they view their new government as hostile to religion. The "free exercise" clause means just that—the freedom to practice (or not) one's religious convictions. Religious observances cannot be removed from our culture. The bottom line: atheists/agnostics do not enjoy the "right" to be free from annoyance, whether it's Christmas decorations or carols on the radio.

3. *Republicans would crack the Obama protection cocoon maintained by (most) African Americans.*

An African American buddy of mine asked me *the question* last week: Why does the GOP hate President Barack Obama? A somewhat more diplomatic version would have inquired as to the *real* reason my lily white party opposes the president at every turn. My response cited Mr. Obama's political values, platform, agenda and record as antithetical to just about everything Republicans support—from fiscal restraint to educational choice to health care freedom. I'm far from convinced my answer advanced the ball, but one can hope . . .

4. *The merits of fracking would be decided by science—not politics.*

Hydraulic fracturing (extracting natural gas by injecting water and chemicals to fracture shale rock) is leading America to a place—energy independence—few thought possible only a few years ago. Yet some on the left can't accept the concept of fossil fuel energy independence. Why not let sound science drive sound political conclusions, even if they lead us in a surprising (and not so politically correct) direction?

5. *The voting public would contemplate the considerable difference between religious conscience and taxpayer-financed contraception.*

The difficulty stems from the Obama campaign's disingenuous (but ultimately successful) narrative that those who opposed Obamacare's contraception mandate (and free birth control) were somehow opposed to contraception. Now, I do not share the Catholic Church's position on artificial birth control, yet I support the church's right to honor its religious convictions in the provision of health insurance to its employees. It's called conscience clause protection. It had been well understood by those who value religious liberty for many years.

6. *Washington could conduct an honest debate about renewable energy.*

Conservatives want solar, wind, and bio-energy to work as much as liberals. But free markets use supply and demand in order to arrive at price. Mandatory renewable requirements have brought rapidly rising energy prices in Europe, making European manufacturers less competitive against their fossil fuel driven competitors in the U.S. Not exactly the way the green crowd envisioned it playing out.

7. *Schools and pro franchises would stop replacing grass with artificial turf.*

I understand the economics of artificial grass. More teams can practice in less space without beating up the playing field. But in this era of safety first, the fake stuff makes contact sports (particularly a collision sport such as football) faster and more dangerous. Less importantly, it's just a lot more fun to watch a game played on what God made—slips, slides, dirt, and mud notwithstanding.

8. *Dependency would not be so cool again.*

Fifty million people go on food stamps. Social Security Disability rolls quadruple. Medicaid rolls explode. Federal welfare work requirements fade. Twenty-six-year-olds get covered on their parents' insurance. And Congress debates federal unemployment benefits beyond two years. All signs of a sick economy . . . and a troubled culture.

9. *The "college" would get put back into "college football."*

OK, I know it's naïve. And most of this is not new. But things are spiraling out of control. A 12-game schedule. Intensive off-season conditioning. Extended practices for minor (and poorly attended) bowl games. Conference switching. Seven-million-dollar coaches. Joke academic courses. Poor graduation rates. It will be near impossible to turn it around. Makes me appreciate the FCS. Go Towson Tigers!!!!

10. *A federal sentencing review panel would be appointed.*

Thousands of Americans face long prison sentences for relatively minor offenses. These low-risk prisoners are expensive (approximately $25,000/inmate) and take up space better used for violent offenders. Yet, this most progressive of administrations sits on its hands. This bipartisan issue demands action . . . now!

The Media Beast Targets
N.J. Gov. Chris Christie

*Former Md. Gov. Robert L. Ehrlich has deep empathy for
N.J. Gov. Chris Christie in recent bridge scandal.*

January 26, 2014, *The Baltimore Sun*

I know and like New Jersey Gov. Chris Christie, the man who has accomplished so much while leading a blue-leaning, labor-dominated Northeastern state.

And so it was with much angst that I watched the media circus (dressed up as a press conference) in the immediate aftermath of "Bridgegate"—the revenge play wherein two senior Christie staffers ordered lane closures on the congested George Washington Bridge—allegedly to punish the Democratic mayor of Fort Lee, N.J., who failed to support the governor's re-election campaign.

It was all high drama, at great length. Actually, two hours worth of media interrogation and plenty of mea culpas broadcast to a curious world. In the end, it was quintessential Chris Christie, albeit with a bit more remorsefulness than usual.

My only criticism was the extended time frame; 25 minutes would have sufficed. Alas, Mr. Christie truly believed a no holds barred, answer 'til they drop performance would "feed the (media) beast" for a bit. He was wrong.

Once upon a time (during my tenure in Congress), I also believed that feeding (and defeating) the beast was possible. Fortunately for me, several early negative experiences with Annapolis beat reporters convinced me that my "easy access" Congressional modus operandi had to change. A lesson was learned: Every day brings new queries, rumors, and deadlines to those who get paid to write about you on a daily basis and who buy ink by the barrel. And so began a journey to more brief encounters wherein I at least gained some control over the daily grind.

Not so much for my friend Mr. Christie in the bridge story, however. A day had not yet passed before a new series of questions and storylines emerged. And every newly unearthed fact brought the story back to the seminal question behind all modern day scandals: "What did he know, and when did he know it?"

In the short term, Mr. Christie and his staff have much daily unpleasantness to look forward to, including unrelenting partisan piling on, hostile media inquiries, grand jury subpoenas, and a likely (significant) drop in poll ratings. Throw in daily media coverage of *The Scandal That Could Derail a Presidential Nominee* and there you have it: a pretty lousy winter for a guy grown accustomed to generally positive press over the past four years.

For my part, empathy runs deep. Recall the multi-year, seven-figure "investigation" into the hiring practices of my Administration, replete with independent counsel and daily bad headlines, during a re-election campaign no less. An ultimate conclusion of no nefarious activity did little to mitigate months of negative coverage. The damage had been accomplished by the mere existence of the story, not the ultimate outcome.

Back to Mr. Christie's press event. He was humble, transparent, and adamant about his innocence in the bridge shenanigans. Basically, he pulled a Gary Hart ("follow me if you want") but with one critical difference: We have every reason to believe the former U.S. Attorney known for his brutal honesty was telling the absolute truth.

All of which leads to two possible conclusions:

In the first, new evidence is uncovered that implicates Mr. Christie in the plan to exact political retribution on an entire city. Such a result would surely spell the end of Mr. Christie's presidential ambitions and guarantee four miserable years in Trenton.

Alternatively, and far more likely, months of investigation bolster Mr. Christie's original assurances about his non-involvement in the bridge debacle. Such an outcome has more than the obvious advantage, as Governor Christie can then contrast his "let it all hang out" leadership style against the imperial and never blameworthy President Barack Obama and former Secretary of State Hillary Clinton (she of "What does it matter?" Benghazi fame).

In scandal politics, it's always the cover-up rather than the original sin that is most damning and lasting. For context, check out Richard Millhouse Nixon, William Jefferson Clinton, and Sen. John Edwards. These and other ugly cover-ups make an already cynical public justifiably suspicious of adamant denials from high profile politicians.

But maybe, just maybe, one governor's handling of a third rate dirty trick will show that "up front" and "brutally honest" can make a comeback—even provide a leg up in digging out of a mess that you did not create, but took place on your watch.

Now that would be a nice moral to an otherwise messy story.

Liberals, Too, Get Foot-In-Mouth Disease

But slips from progressives are rarely harped upon by the mainstream media.

February 2, 2014, *The Baltimore Sun*

Chew on these for a minute:

"Who are they? Are they these extreme conservatives, who are right-to-life, pro-assault-weapon, anti-gay, is that who they are? Because if that is who they are, and if they are the extreme conservatives, they have no place in the state of New York. Because that is not who New Yorkers are."

> —NEW YORK GOVERNOR ANDREW CUOMO,
> with a directive for New York's GOP candidates, Janurary, 2013

"It's not surprising then they get bitter. They cling to guns or religion or antipathy to people who aren't like them."

> —PRESIDENT BARACK OBAMA,
> at a private campaign fundraiser in April 2008

"She doesn't understand why any Jew who really understands the issues could support" Robert Ehrlich.

> —Baltimore *Jewish Times* on a conversation with
> Lt. Gov. Kathleen Kennedy Townsend, who has denied the statement,
> circa Maryland's 2002 gubernatorial campaign

"A ventriloquist can always find a good dummy [for tea party Republicans]."

—Rev. William Barber

President of North Carolina's NAACP describing South Carolina's
Republican, African American U.S. Senator Tim Scott in January

"One of these things is not like the others, one of these things just isn't the same."

—MSNBC panelist Pia Glenn in December 2013
on an adopted black grandson in Mitt Romney's family photo

"He is a community organizer like Jesus was, and now we're a community and he can organize us."

—Susan Sarandon

Hollywood actress and activist on Barack Obama in 2009

Rants of this progressive genre are no longer newsworthy. Indeed, they have become regular admonitions directed to those who do not fit the progressive stereotype.

Take Lt. Governor Michael Steele, just a "token" and "Uncle Tom," according to two of Maryland's leading Democrats. Worse, Mr. Steele's personal triple whammy (Catholic, pro-life, and pro-gun) once led a Maryland state senator to exclaim that "party trumps race" when dealing with the counter-intuitive likes of Mr. Steele.

The same tunnel vision is applied to independent Jewish voters. I'm sure it was stunning for Ms. Townsend to see my support in the Jewish community. After all, weren't all Jews supposed to fall in line behind the liberal Democrat? Alas, I guess only those who "really" understood the issues.

It's the same deal with gay issues. Per Harry Reid, Nancy Pelosi, and many prominent Democrats, opposition to gay marriage carries a mandatory charge of homophobia. And no amount of evidence to the contrary can mitigate the cultural indictment.

There is a common theme running through these quotes: a staggering intolerance (on regular display) as practiced by the country's culturally progressive police.

Not so long ago, it was (far) right miscreants who could be counted on for an inflammatory sound bite every now and then. Recall David Duke's racial rants and these aberrations from Missouri and Indiana GOP Senate candidates that served the Democrats' "war on women" narrative perfectly: "If it's a legitimate rape, the female body has ways to try to shut that whole thing down" (Rep. Todd Akin, Missouri); "Even when life begins in that horrible situation of rape, that it is something that God intended to happen." (Richard Mourdock, Indiana).

But there is a profound difference between the two extremes. Overheated right-wing rhetoric or malapropisms tend to lead the evening news and are followed by high-profile apologies, but nevertheless remain fodder for opposition attack ads.

Not so much today's progressive indictments. The new millennium has brought left-wing intolerance to the mainstream, its divisive messaging is now a regular critique in our political discourse, and only subject to mea culpa when the target is deemed just too innocent for even the sensibilities of MSNBC (witness the tearful apology of Melissa Harris-Perry for laughing about Mitt Romney's adopted black grandchild).

Certainly the most encompassing of the recent rants comes from the good governor of New York. Here, it's all so clear: Citizens of New York must demonstrate the requisite support for abortion-on-demand, gun control, illegal immigration, gay marriage, and multiculturalism or . . . you are not welcome in . . . New York.

Breathtakingly arrogant? Yes.

Incredibly intolerant? Yeah.

Stunningly anti-intellectual? You bet.

Mainstream progressive thinking? Increasingly so, to the detriment (and coarsening) of our culture—and country.

If you think I'm overreacting, check out a sampling of the ridiculous "speech codes" now proliferating on our college campuses. Or, just watch the next Democratic National Convention where sanitized language is manufactured and delivered to every real or invented interest group imaginable—and please don't take offense if they forgot yours.

This new breed of intolerance should be taken down, now. Nothing more than our grand traditions of pluralism, free association, and respectful dissent are at stake.

Chris Christie Is Not a "Small Ball" Politician

Maryland's former governor offers thoughts on unionizing college athletes and Chris Christie's innocence.

April 13, 2014, *The Baltimore Sun*

Perhaps you missed . . . a regional National Labor Relations Board decision that ruled Northwestern University's football players are "employees" subject to union representation. And before you dismiss this decision as the ravings of some bureaucrat laborite, remember that the appeal goes to the full Barack Obama-controlled board, now simply a satellite operation for the AFL-CIO.

My readers can figure out the myriad problems with this concept on their own, but allow me one simple illustration of the awkwardness involved. Let's say your (fullback) son is recruited to Northwestern because the school uses the "I formation," a set that requires a fullback. But (as so often occurs in big-time athletics), there is a coaching change during your son's sophomore year. The new coach brings a "spread" formation, which does not require a fullback. Your son is now out of a job. Query: Can your 19-year-old bring an unfair labor practices complaint against the offensive coordinator and/or the head coach and/or the school? And, if yes, what is the appropriate remedy? Please feel free to add your horrific scenario to this poorly thought out proposal.

There *is* a need for reform within big time college athletics. Sharing the wealth is a good idea. (For example, a higher stipend for revenue producing athletes makes sense.) So do proposals that require schools to fulfill their end of the scholarship bargain—you know, the "scholar" end. Requiring schools to pay tuition and fees for the full four years has merit as well.

But the idea of a "linebacker/shop steward" should be a non-starter.

Perhaps you missed . . . the report issued by a group of former prosecutors that concluded New Jersey Gov. Chris Christie had no knowledge of the September lane closures on the George Washington Bridge—the so-called "bridgegate scandal." No surprise here; Mr. Christie was adamant about his lack of culpability in the politically motivated bridge caper. As a former U.S. Attorney, he knew that any credible evidence to the contrary would mean the end of his national political ambitions. On a personal note, I predicted in this column a few months back that Mr. Christie would be exonerated. I know Chris Christie to be a straightforward, no nonsense guy unlikely to get himself mixed up in this type of "small ball" politics.

Whether the story will continue to haunt Mr. Christie's emerging presidential campaign is anyone's guess. But the way in which the unfolding scandal was handled should serve as a model for anyone caught up in a media whirlwind. Up front and transparent will usually ensure you live another day—at least, that is, unless your last name is "Clinton."

Perhaps you missed . . . the appointment of Sen. Mary Landrieu, a Democrat from Louisiana, as the new chairman of the Senate Energy and National Resources Panel.

Possibly the most vulnerable of the Senate Democrats up for re-election in November, Ms. Landrieu is using her new position to push a pro energy industry agenda popular at home but anathema to the vast majority of her liberal Democratic colleagues.

All of which represents an interesting challenge to the more conservative voters of Louisiana: Do they support their hometown senator now that she runs the most important committee for an oil and gas state, or do they replace her with a Republican who will more closely reflect their views on a wider range of economic and social issues?

Recent polls have Ms. Landrieu trailing her top GOP challenger, Rep. Bill Cassidy, within the margin of error. And the incumbent's numerous votes in support of Obamacare will be front and center this November.

Some southern "Blue Dog" Democrats have it both ways— talking business at home but voting labor in Washington. In this respect, Louisiana voters now must decide if Senator Landrieu put up one too many Obamacare votes on the scoreboard. A word to the wise: Voting with Harry Reid can be a dangerous habit in a red state.

Speaking of Majority Leader Reid, perhaps you missed . . . recent announcements by Members of the Senate Democratic Leadership that they back Mr. Reid's return as leader regardless of whether Democrats retain the Senate in November.

Such pronouncements serve to remind political observers that leadership positions (in both parties) are not necessarily awarded to the most telegenic or effective communicators. Rather, it is those who best handle internecine conflict and possess strong fundraising prowess who tend to ascend. This Capitol Hill fact of life may be distressing to some, but it will not change in the foreseeable future.

A Barrage of Wedgies

The Democratic Party is relying on social "wedge issues" to mask poor political policies.

April 20, 2014, *The Baltimore Sun*

Social issues are labeled "wedge issues" for a reason. They appeal to emotion. They are easily communicated. They count when ballots are cast. Throw in poll-tested rhetoric and effective manipulation of facts, and there you have it: the capture of an important voting bloc.

I do not know the genesis of the term. It may have been hatched in a Nixon-era appeal to southern white conservative Democrats none too happy with court ordered school desegregation and a sharp left-hand turn by a McGovern-ite Democratic Party in 1972. Whether by nefarious design or more benign factors, the tactic worked. Today, the once "solid (Democratic) south" is safe GOP territory.

In more recent years, it is the Democrats who have perfected the art of wedge politics. And Democratic candidates are enjoying the fruits of the party's tactical successes.

One thing to keep in mind, however. Repeated reliance on wedge issues usually means the utilizing party's political fortunes have begun to sag. Today, that whimpering you hear is an administration in trouble. A feckless foreign policy has our opportunistic adversaries anything but scared. A tepid economic recovery continues to keep the middle class on edge. Obamacare is an ad hoc mess. The president's public approval is dipping into the high 30s. Time for a barrage of wedgies.

To wit:

"Income Inequality." A strategy straight from the "Occupy Wall Street" playbook. It is the sentimental favorite of class warriors through the ages. The logic is transparent: The wealthy attained their status at the expense of the poor. So the preferred remedy is the "Robin Hood" variety—take from the rich and give to the poor, and don't let up, there will always be plenty of poor people. In this way, an "even playing field" will be forever in sight—if not attainable under a capitalist economy.

"Minimum Wage." This beauty is playing out before our eyes. Whether a boost in the minimum wage or the labor union invented "living wage," the mantra is "fairness." And never mind that most minimum wage earners are typically at that level for less than a year, or that fewer still are the family's chief wage earner, or that hundreds of thousands of people will lose their jobs (according to the bipartisan Congressional Budget Office) as a result of the proposed federal increase. The bottom line: Raising the minimum wage does not reduce poverty, it simply provides a raise for some marginal workers, while others (the most marginal) lose their jobs. And all in the name of that feel good intangible: "compassion."

"Gender Inequality." The latest and greatest scam from the Obama Administration. But what was supposed to be a gender-gap-widening thunderbolt turned ugly when reports surfaced that a sizable salary gap exists within the White House itself. When questioned about this apparent contradiction, presidential Press Secretary Jay Carney asserted that 88 cents on the dollar for female White House workers "is not 100, but it is better than the national average." That's a pitiful response and inaccurate to boot: Recent economic studies reflect a far more narrow income gap between the sexes—not the 23 cents so often quoted by the president. And with regard to that shortfall, there are equal pay laws on the books ("The Equal Pay Act of 1963" remains the law of the land) to ensure against gender discrimination for similarly situated employees of equal skills not subject to seniority or merit systems: the true definition of gender discrimination.

"The Politics of Personal Destruction." The casual political observer may be surprised to watch the Harry Reid-led rhetorical onslaught against two men most Americans have never heard of—David and Charles Koch. The target of the Senate majority leader's demonization campaign are successful, wealthy businessmen who had the temerity to start a non-profit (Americans for Prosperity) that runs around the country touting the advantages of competition and free markets. They also run television commercials highlighting controversial votes cast by vulnerable Democrats in marginal seats—most especially votes in support of Obamacare. Unsurprisingly, their equally wealthy counterparts on the left (George Soros, Ted Turner, Michael Bloomberg) are never brought into the discussions about the dangers of money in politics. Selective indignation indeed!

Whether the GOP can effectively counter this "lowest common denominator" strategy will determine whether it will re-emerge as a viable national party. Failure means a continued role as a diminished homogeneous player only able to muster majorities in off-year elections. High stakes for the party of Lincoln.

Musings on Intolerant Lefties and Wars on Women

Liberals can be the most narrow-minded and hypocritical.

May 18, 2014, *The Baltimore Sun*

Random observations for your reading pleasure:

- When have you ever heard about a group of conservative students shouting down a campus speaker, invading and occupying a campus building or pressuring a school to withdraw a candidate for an honorary degree? Well . . . never. Yet today's headlines are full of left wing faculty and student demands for ideological purity within the ivory tower. All of which raises a question: Why do college lefties feel so free to engage in such activities? Aren't these young activists supposed to be the last true defenders of academic freedom?

Not really. Today's academic left is the most intolerant group you never hope to meet. Their message: only progressives allowed around here. Not exactly what a liberal arts education is supposed to be!

- I, like many of you, remain agitated about the wholesale success of the Democrats' "war on women" narrative. Hence, I just can't see how my sincere opposition to the desire by Sandra Fluke (remember the "heroic" Georgetown Law student who became a campaign fixture for the president?) for free birth control pills translates into a nefarious campaign to keep women down. (The fact that such ludicrous campaign tactics work is an indictment of every major Republican consultant in Washington.) Yet a brutal war on women unfolds daily right before our eyes. It's brought to you by radical Islam. It propagates honor killings of women. It forbids young girls to be educated. It makes a mockery of rape. And it recently kidnapped nearly 300 young girls with the intent to market them as slaves. Yet I don't see the same outrage as that generated by Ms. Fluke's desire to enjoy tax-payer-financed sex, just a bunch of hash tags and excuses for our previous failure to label the perpetrators of this hideous crime (Boko Haram) a terrorist organization.

- Speaking of which, did you see where ultra-left Brandeis University rescinded a commencement invitation and honorary degree intended for women's rights advocate Aysan Hirsi? You may recognize Ms. Hirsi. She has garnered worldwide acclaim for her one-woman crusade against honor killings and other dreadful acts committed against women by Muslim extremists. The lady is not exactly a Republican mole, either. She is a secularist feminist and leading advocate for gay rights. So, why would this bastion of collegiate progressivism (formed in the wake of the Holocaust) seek to humiliate her?

Well, it seems the "Politically Correct Police, Radical Islam Sensitivity Division" has pronounced Ms. Hirsi's critique of women and Islam a bit too harsh—and in violation of Brandeis' "core values." An astonishing moral emerges: Even beloved crusaders against rape, torture, and murder need to toe the PC line these days. If only Ms. Hirsi would redirect her vitriol toward Christianity. If so moved, betcha the Harvards, Browns, and Brandeises of the world would be lining up to give her a degree.

- More war—this time on chaste, religious women—is being conducted by the Obama Administration. You will recall my previous column railing against Obamacare's preemption of long established conscience clause protections for religious institutions. Now, along come the Little Sisters of the Poor with a lawsuit claiming that Obamacare mandates they (or their insurer) provide contraceptives and abortifacients to remain Affordable Care Act compliant, a requirement that violates their religious convictions.

Early skirmishes do not bode well for the Administration. The Supreme Court granted a rare New Year's Eve emergency injunction to the Sisters. The order was signed by the very liberal Judge Sonia Sotomayor. Then a permanent stay pending appeal (with no dissenters) was granted in late January. Still, the Justice Department continues its war against the Catholic nuns and all others similarly situated. (A decision on this and related ACA religious liberty cases will be issued later this year.) I don't know about you, but my money is on the nuns. They might have the "X factor" on their side, if you know what I mean . . .

- If you truly wonder how Obama apologists rationalize even deadly serious events, so do I. Nevertheless, there are few better illustrations of "reality denial" than Daily Beast columnist Eleanor Clift's comments concerning the death of Ambassador Christopher Stevens at our Consulate in Benghazi. Seems that Ms. Clift does not view the ambassador's passing as a "murder" since the actual cause of death was "smoke inhalation." Of course, the smoke was a product of exploding ordnance fired by terrorists intent on ravaging our consulate on the anniversary of 9/11. Your expressions of disbelief may be directed to Ms. Clift's attention at The Daily Beast. Your expressions of outrage regarding our lack of preparedness and serial lies about the cause of the attack may be directed to President Barack Obama, 1600 Pennsylvania Avenue, Washington, D.C., and former Secretary of State Hillary Clinton in Chappaqua, New York.

College: Where Kids Become Leftists

Today's campuses are increasingly, and disturbingly, progressive.

May 25, 2014, *The Baltimore Sun*

I've been thinking a lot about college lately. It's not as though it's staring me in the face, either. The oldest is finishing his freshman year in high school. The youngest is still in elementary school.

Still, what's occurring on America's college campuses is on my front burner.

First and foremost is the ever-escalating cost of a four-year degree, the cause of many a sleepless night for moms and dads. Tuition, fees, and room and board for many private colleges has now hit $60,000 a year. Middle-income parents usually qualify for some aid, but how much? And will they be able to set aside enough for their other kids? The same challenge applies to public colleges, where the price tag is lower but nevertheless represents a huge commitment from everyone other than wealthy families.

Another concern is the value of a liberal arts degree in today's society. What was once the gold standard is under increasing scrutiny. Our technology economy is the primary culprit. Post-industrial American employers value science and economics over English and history. Accordingly, business and engineering schools continue to do a brisk business, while many law schools are cutting back on class size and telling their students that the days of relatively easy job placements are gone.

The statistics tell the real story. Over the next six years, America's 300,000 additional law graduates will be competing for approximately 73,000 law-related jobs. Top of the class grads from elite schools will continue to find fertile ground and attractive starting salaries. Not so much for everyone else. The bottom line is that the days of smart kids going to law school because they are unsure of their career path is over. Just not enough jobs and too much debt.

A third issue is familiar to my readers, yet seems to be getting worse over time. I refer to uber-left academic indoctrination that dominates our university environment.

Many of you are familiar with a famous maxim often (albeit falsely) attributed to Winston Churchill regarding political maturation: "If you're not a liberal when you're 25, you have no heart. If you're not a conservative by the time you're 35, you have no brain."

But there is something different about today's campus-based progressivism. This brand proceeds far beyond a familiar anti-war, pro-choice, and affirmative action agenda. It is decidedly more far reaching—radical redistribution of wealth, a preoccupation with "white privilege," government sponsored medicine, open borders, retrenchment abroad, and an aggressively intrusive federal government. These and other à la carte causes are accompanied by an arrogant intolerance of dissenting views and a longing for an "offense-less" society.

Don't believe me? Check out this year's list of disinvited commencement speakers, the proliferation of campus-based "speech codes," the newly minted offense of "micro aggressions" (tiny offenses that could lead to major offenses), and my new personal favorite "trigger warnings"—academic materials that could trigger symptoms of post-traumatic stress disorder in those who have experienced racism, sexism, classism, chauvinism, homophobia, colonialism, imperialism, nativism, and presumably the heartbreak of psoriasis.

All of which creates an interesting dilemma for parents. Every parent wants his or her child to be successful. A proven avenue to success is a college degree: the more competitive the school, the better. And so, despite financial hardship, most parents are happy to sacrifice to ensure their child's future.

This wonderful moral arrives with a caveat, however. At most schools, America's young adults are exposed to a steady dose of advanced leftist theology directly at odds with the values (many if not most) parents have attempted to instill in them.

This theology includes a rather value-less approach to "values." Women in combat—same as men. Illegal immigration—same as legal immigration. Same sex marriage—same as traditional marriage. Social Security disability—same as work. It's "Occupy Wall Street" in a syllabus, at great expense to you and yours. And know that public opposition will label you with whatever "ic" or "ism" the P.C. police decide to bestow. (See list above.)

Of course, our institutions of higher learning have long been bastions of secular progressivism. What distinguishes today's brand is an insidious intolerance toward dissenting views—this is a doctrinal approach heretofore alien to open dialogue and "liberal" education.

Maybe post-Obama millennials will become reacquainted with freedom. It used to have quite a cachet. Students even led mass protests to support it. Here, one can really "hope" for "change."

On Cantor's Defeat, Obama's Foreign Policy Debacle, and Old-School Basketball

Ehrlich says the upset of the House majority leader follows an old storyline.

June 22, 2014, *The Baltimore Sun*

Item: Washington is abuzz with the shocking defeat of House majority Leader Eric Cantor in a Republican primary. David Brat, a tea party-inspired college professor with little money but plenty of energy, pulled off the historic upset.

Most of the mainstream media coverage focused on Mr. Cantor's support (albeit tepid) for a set of immigration reform principles that some on the right interpreted as "amnesty"—and that such support was the primary cause of his loss at the hands of an unknown, underfunded candidate.

Yet every other incumbent Republican who has signaled an openness toward reform legislation has won his primary this cycle. And if Mr. Cantor was seen as *so* soft on immigration, why did *Politico* (a popular Capitol Hill political daily) write a story on the day of the primary about an aggressive White House-sponsored campaign to educate and punish Mr. Cantor due to his alleged opposition to comprehensive reform?

My numerous discussions with former colleagues reflect another (under the radar) reason for the majority leader's demise: the familiar and always effective "he's gone Washington on us" indictment. It is a charge easily made against leadership types in both parties. Recall House Speaker Tom Foley and Senate Majority Leader

Tom Daschle losing re-election bids on identical grounds while Senate leaders Bob Dole and Bill Frist faced similar obstacles in their respective presidential bids.

The dilemma is easy to understand. Speakers and majority leaders must keep the legislative trains running on time, negotiate a variety of thorny issues with opposing leaders, travel and raise money on behalf of their fellow colleagues (and viable challengers), and fulfill their legislative obligations as Members of Congress. Notice this demanding schedule offers little time to attend local Little League parades, road openings, and volunteer fire department dinners—places where elected officials are able to be seen while interacting with voters. And it is here where too many missed public opportunities "back home" can result in an embarrassing loss. The bottom line: Even in the age of social media and instant electronic communication, spending time tending to the home flock counts.

Item: Remember when President Barack Obama assured a concerned electorate that "al-Qaida was on the run" during a hotly contested re-election campaign? Such rhetoric represented welcome assurance for a war weary people. And, after all, Osama Bin Laden had been taken down by SEAL Team Six, and an aggressive drone campaign was killing high ranking terrorists at an impressive rate.

Fast forward 18 months. Extremists in Nigeria have kidnapped and held hostage 300 young school girls, a third of Iraq has fallen to the Islamic State of Iraq and Syria (an army of killers too violent for al-Qaida), the Taliban and related jihadist groups are resurgent in Afghanistan, drone strikes are down but the number of jihadist fighters worldwide has more than doubled, and now the U.S. looks to the number one state sponsor of terrorism in the world, Iran, for support in stopping ISIS's murderous campaign against Shiite Iraqis and the further destabilization of Iraq.

Mr. Obama's campaign statement was untrue when originally uttered. Today, it's merely further evidence of seriously flawed foreign policy assumptions from a White House far better at the art of campaigning than governing.

Item: My new favorite NBA player is San Antonio Spurs forward Kawhi Leonard. And it's not for the 22-year-old's leaping ability, his feathery jump shot, his defense against Lebron James during the playoffs, his excellent ball handling skills, or his remarkable dedication to improving his game. It's not even due to the resiliency he developed following the still unsolved murder of his dad at the Compton, California car wash he owned.

These attributes are compelling, of course. But my admiration stems from the way he conducts himself on and off the court. The kid is all old school. You never see an "it's all about me" chest thump or a crowd glare, or even much of a smile after a big play. In fact, the man is downright dull. A terrible interview; mostly clichés about all 13 guys working together toward a common goal. Oh, and plenty of respect for the opponent. Mostly, he reflects the handling of success and failure with the exact same quotient of personal class.

Flashback question: What did Johnny Unitas do immediately after Alan Ameche scored the most famous touchdown in pro football history—the winning score in "The Greatest Game Ever Played"? Answer: He just turned and walked away. Betcha Kawhi Leonard would have done the same . . .

Why No Outrage Over the IRS's Tea Party Targeting?

They are citizen victims, yet there has been little outcry.

June 29, 2014, *The Baltimore Sun*

In Citizens United vs. FEC, the U.S. Supreme Court held in January 2012 that the federal government is prohibited from restricting independent political expenditures by businesses, associations, and labor unions. The opinion allows such groups to spend unlimited sums of money on advocacy ads, but not direct contributions to candidate committees. It also set the American left off its rocker. What follows is a chronology of events that has set the American right off its rocker, too.

The immediate aftermath of Citizens United saw a worried president engage in a series of hard hitting speeches concerning the corrupting influence of money in politics and warning about a proliferation of newly formed, conservative groups seeking to take advantage of their expanded free speech rights. It was at some point shortly thereafter that the good folks at the Tax Exempt Division of the IRS began to slow-walk new non-profit applications from conservative organizations, according to a 2013 Inspector General's report.

This "additional scrutiny" phase delayed the approval of said applications until after the 2012 election. In fact, not a single "tea party" affiliated group received tax exempt approval over the course of 27 months. Of special interest to the IRS examiners were tea party-associated groups opposed to the federal government's fiscal practices. IRS staff also flagged those groups dedicated to "mak[ing] America a better place to live."

Intentional delay was only part of the plan, however. Conservative activists were also singled out for audits and had their confidential information disclosed to left wing interest groups. One such example of the latter was the treatment afforded to the "National Organization for Marriage"—proponents of traditional marriage. The organization's application included a sampling of its major financial supporters, which is not an unusual request to fulfill, though the information is typically redacted by the IRS for privacy reasons. But the redaction failed to occur, and the names of all of NOFM's financial supporters suddenly appeared on the website of the pro-gay marriage group "Human Rights Campaign." Can you spell INTIMIDATION? Note: It is a federal offense (punishable by up to five years in prison) for anyone to publish private tax information. Cynical note: Raise your hand if you think even one IRS employee will serve time for this crime.

Now, fast-forward to the past few weeks wherein we have seen the IRS admit that it "lost" the emails of retired IRS official Lois Lerner and at least six of her colleagues from 2009 to mid-2011. Seems the hard drives of the "chosen seven" crashed in 2011, then were recycled. IRS leadership knew about, but sat on, the critical information for nearly a year. And so two years of critical emails are (presumably) lost forever. This is the same Ms. Lerner who told Congress in sworn testimony that she did "nothing wrong," before invoking her Fifth Amendment right against self-incrimination.

An equally disturbing aspect of IRS arrogance is the agency's recent admission that it had selectively produced Ms. Lerner's surviving emails—despite *two* House Committee requests to produce all Lerner emails "regardless of subject matter." A private attorney exhibiting the same disregard for the law would face significant court imposed sanctions.

To be sure, President Obama has repeatedly sought to assure the American public that nothing of a nefarious nature was (is) at work here. Recall the president's initial explanation that the improper targeting was caused by a couple of "rogue" employees in the Cincinnati office. But the old Cincinnati narrative was instantly discredited when "River City" staff pointed the finger right back at IRS staff in Washington D.C. Nevertheless, the president really wants you to know that this illegal stunt had no direction or encouragement from his White House.

We may never get the truth as to how this embarrassing episode of government incompetence came about. But the foregoing facts are not in dispute: American citizens were targeted by a powerful government agency on account of their political opinions—an unforgivable sin in a democracy where freedom of speech is protected and valued.

Democratic party reaction has been muted, even defensive. The old "there's nothing there" mantra has been trotted out every time another new and relevant revelation comes to light. Come to think of it, this would be the type of scenario a young, community activist, Harvard Law professor would typically get excited about. After all, these citizens are victims.

Alas, these particular victims are tea party folks—an exception to the rule. Such is the way of selective progressive indignation circa 2014. Can you imagine the outrage if the shoe were on the other foot?

Supreme Court Divide Riles Political Parties

July 6, 2014, *The Baltimore Sun*

"If the Supreme Court will not protect women's access to health care, then Democrats will. . . It's time that five men on the Supreme Court stop deciding what happens to women."

—SENATE MAJORITY LEADER HARRY REID

Such over-the-top rhetoric will be coming your way over the next four months, as Democrats desperately seek to hold on to their majority in the U.S. Senate. But it's worth stepping back from generally ludicrous sound bites regarding a spate of recent Supreme Court decisions that have so vexed the president and Democratic leaders.

I say this because partisans are typically more interested in raising money than explaining the intricacies of high court decisions. Here, it makes sense to divide the recent holdings into two categories.

The first (and larger one) reflects a series of 9-0 decisions (13 in all) regarding instances of constitutional over-reaching. These "shutouts" mean that the reliably liberal wing of the court (Justices Ruth Bader Ginsburg, Elena Kagan, Stephen Breyer and Sonia Sotomayor) saw the outcome (if not the reasoning) in the same light as their five conservative colleagues (Chief Justice John Roberts and Justices Samuel Alito, Anthony Kennedy, Clarence Thomas and Antonin Scalia).

In two of the more high-profile cases, the court ruled that the president had exceeded his constitutional powers by making recess appointments when the Senate was not in recess, but rather in pro forma session. And in a win for civil libertarians, the court held that police must obtain a search warrant prior to searching a seized cell phone.

The second category reflects the deep philosophical divide within the court. These divisions are seen in 5-4 rulings decided along predictable ideological lines:

- In Illinois, eight Medicaid-reimbursed home health aides caring for disabled family members sued because they were required to pay "agency fee" dues to a union they did not wish to join. Such fees are the lifeblood of public-sector unions. The court ruled that the workers were not state employees since they could be fired by the individuals who employed them, and so were not required to pay dues. Chalk one up for freedom of choice in the workplace. In response, the union will likely allege a "war" on public-sector unions.

- In a highly anticipated Environmental Protection Agency case, the court struck down a regulation wherein the agency had asserted unilateral power to "tailor" (i.e., expand) exact statutory emissions thresholds for a given pollutant set by the Clean Air Act. The majority opinion reminded the Obama Administration that Congress still writes laws while the executive branch enforces them. In response, the environmental lobby will no doubt allege a "war" on the environment.

- In yet another defeat for campaign finance reform, the court struck down limits on the total amount of money individual donors can give to political candidates. Note this is the fifth campaign finance reform initiative to be rejected in recent years. This court is really serious about protecting free speech. And, yes, good-government types alleged a "war" on the poor and under-represented.

- The fourth noteworthy case emanates from our favorite man-made disaster: Obamacare. In this case, the owners of Hobby Lobby craft stores claimed the health law's mandate to provide certain contraception coverage for it's employees violated the owners' religious freedom. The court agreed and suggested that the government make the same accommodation for religious practices followed by those within closely held companies as it does for employees of religiously affiliated nonprofits. A barrage of "war on women" statements followed, including the beauty that leads this column.

The media will continue to focus on 5-4 rather than 9-0. This one-vote margin will be a front-burner issue in the presidential sweepstakes of 2016. As for the president, he has certainly done his part for the left. Both Justices Kagan and Sotomayor are young and unabashedly liberal. They will champion progressive causes for decades.

Conversely, reliably conservative Justices Antonin Scalia (78), Anthony Kennedy (78 on July 23), and Clarence Thomas (66), are not getting any younger. You can bet Republicans will expend plenty of energy reminding their base of this fact in the run-up to 2016.

Whether left or right, the fight over who gets to name the next court justice will generate plenty of fire as the presidential election season begins in earnest.

Liberals Continue to Mess Up the Country

A former governor's "facts and opinions" on Hamas, fracking, baseball, and pot

August 3, 2014, *The Baltimore Sun*

Fact: Captured Hamas fighters confirm that their maze of secret tunnels into Israel was to be the entry point for a series of coordinated terror attacks during the Jewish High Holidays—all in order to massacre Israeli citizens at lightly guarded border settlements.

Opinion: Americans should keep this scenario in mind as Secretary of State John Kerry readily adopts Hamas talking points and positions in his attempts to secure a "humanitarian" cease-fire. Hamas views such cessations of hostilities as mere opportunities to re-load in their ongoing campaign to reign terror (and ultimately destroy) the Jewish state.

Second Opinion: Unfortunately, the Obama Administration's determined anti-Israel tilt will not cost Jewish Democratic votes in the next presidential election.

Fact: The IRS had a legal duty to retain the allegedly lost emails of former Tax-Exempt Division Chief Lois Lerner. It had a further duty to immediately inform Congress once it learned that potentially relevant emails in its targeting scandal had been "lost."

Opinion: Regardless of one's political persuasion, the Federal Rules of Civil Procedure require such protection of important documents. We now know the IRS failed to follow the law when it recycled the tapes used to back up its emails and then sat on this information for months. Today, Ms. Lerner takes the 5th. We also know that the "rogue employees in Cincinnati" story has been disproved, as well as the claim that "not even a smidgen" of damaging evidence exists. But the FBI investigation is reportedly going nowhere. This mess gets worse by the hour.

Fact: The shale gas/fracking revolution has made America more energy independent and created tens of thousands of high paying jobs.

Opinion: Predictably, it's been difficult for the environmental community to wrap its arms around a fossil fuel alternative to coal. Most simply do not trust state government to regulate an industry that is producing so much wealth for its coffers. They prefer more "sustainable" solutions such as biofuels, wind and solar. Yet, such alternatives have not proven to be economically viable to date.

Fact: Scoring in Major League Baseball has decreased to an average of 8.25 runs per game, continuing a steady decrease from a high of 10.28 runs per game in 2000.

Opinion: Less scoring is always a danger sign in American sports. Recall how the NFL, NBA and NHL changed their rules to allow for higher scoring when defense became too dominant in their respective sports. I must admit to a certain longing for the days of 10-8 games, yet we know cheating (steroids) drove that offensive era. Here's hoping MLB will either "juice" its ball (along the lines of college baseball) or find another way to generate more run production.

Fact: Bill Ayers was a member of the "Weather Underground" and participated in a series of terrorist bombings as a part of the group's "Days of Rage" protests—including the 1971 bombing of the U.S. Capitol building and the 1972 bombing of the Pentagon. Today, Mr. Ayers is a professor at the University of Illinois at Chicago.

Opinion: If you missed Mr. Ayers' recent interview with Megyn Kelly on Fox, please review it. If you are a mental health professional, please feel free to render a diagnosis. This was one of the creepiest television appearances I've ever witnessed—just a continual series of rationalizations for serial, random acts of terror. This guy now teaches our children. What a travesty.

Fact: New York Mayor Bill de Blasio's hyper-liberalism has made him a budding superstar in progressive Democratic Party circles.

Opinion: The mayor's policy agenda is straight out of the European Social Democrat playbook. Initiatives are equal parts major tax increases (the good ole "income inequality" narrative), a major offensive against charter schools, universal pre-K, welfare expansion and rampant unionism. Mayor de Blasio is the anti-Giuliani, intent on steering NYC into the far left lane of American cities. If you loved NYC's David Dinkins era, welcome back. And good luck—you'll need it.

Fact: The mind altering ingredient tetrahydrocannabinol (THC) in today's marijuana is far more potent than the 1970s brand.

Opinion: The legalization of marijuana in Washington State and Colorado and the drug's increased potency are raising red flags in the public health community, particularly regarding potential adverse cardiovascular impact. Other areas of concern include lung problems, memory impairment, and poor cognitive performance—particularly among young people. But don't expect THC content to decrease any time soon. Market savvy producers know the more concentrated product can be marketed in smaller volumes at higher prices. Just another thought for your consideration as states continue to scramble aboard the legalization (and revenue) bandwagon.

World Comments That Elicit a "Yep" or "Nope"

Some statements leave you shaking or nodding your head.

August 30, 2014, *The Baltimore Sun*

Sometimes, you come across a quote or phrase that jolts your sensibilities. The words can be as deep and thought provoking as those supplied by Golda Meir below, or as mind numbingly ludicrous as those uttered by the Dartmouth College protesters of last spring, also below. Regarding the former, your response might be an immediate "Yep." On the latter, it could easily be a simple "Nope!"

Herewith, a sampling of yeps and nopes from recent research:

We can forgive the Arabs for killing our children. We cannot forgive them for forcing us to kill their children. . . . We will only have peace with the Arabs when they love their children more than they hate us.

—GOLDA MEIR, Former Israeli Prime Minister

Yep. Think about these moving words the next time you read about Hamas hiding weapons and command centers in homes, schools, and hospitals. Their disdain for innocents reveals the soullessness of their cause. And it's the average Palestinian who pays the price for such immoral antics.

Al Qaida is on the run.—PRESIDENT BARACK OBAMA

Al Qaida is 'a shadow of its former self.'

    —JOHN BRENNAN, White House counterterrorism advisor

Nope and nope. The purveyors of 9/11 and their affiliates are more numerous than ever; well over 100,000 active fighters worldwide. Affiliated groups in the Middle East and Africa pose a frightening threat to third world stability. And then there is that new terrorist caliphate in Iraq.

He served the United States with honor and distinction.

    —National Security Advisor SUSAN RICE on
    U.S. Army Sgt. Bowe Bergdahl

Almost certainly nope. Without exception, every soldier who served with Bergdahl in Afghanistan believes he willingly went AWOL from his post before being captured by the Taliban. Desertion is bad enough, but placing brothers in arms in harm's way during rescue missions is worse. Ms. Rice was previously the Administration's "fall guy" during the Benghazi Muslim video fiasco. Why bring more dishonor through a transparently false description of the man swapped for five high ranking terrorists?

The Department of Veterans Affairs is a triumph of socialized medicine . . . an integrated system, which provides health care as well as paying for it. So it's free from the pervasive incentives created when doctors and hospitals profit from expensive tests and procedures, whether or not those procedures actually make medical sense.

    —PAUL KRUGMAN, Nobel Prize recipient, Professor of Economics
    (at Princeton) and *New York Times* columnist

Nope. As many commentators have noted, we now have a glimpse into the "perverse incentives" that accompany government health care, especially the rationing of care that characterizes government run systems around the world. Mr. Krugman is a smart guy, but elementary economics dictate that unlimited demand and limited resources equal rationing.

> *Further physical and emotional violence enacted against us by the racist, classist, sexist, heterosexist, transphobic, xenophobic, and ableist structures at Dartmouth . . . our bodies are already on the line, in danger and under attack.*
> —STUDENT OCCUPIERS OF DARTMOUTH COLLEGE talking to
> Dartmouth President Phil Hanlon about what a conversation
> about their demands will lead to

Nope—or should I say "dope," as in dopey, entitled college brats who should be arrested and thrown in jail upon their next "occupation" (actually it's called "criminal trespass") of the president's office. A bit of jail time might actually make their concluding words more accurate.

> *Simply collecting agreements will not buy peace. Agreements generally reinforce peace only when they are kept. Otherwise, we are building a paper castle that will be blown away by the winds of war.*
> —PRESIDENT RONALD REAGAN on arms control agreements
> with the Soviet Union

Yep. The "gipper" was simple, direct, and correct. Consistent cheating by the Russians has made a mockery of arms control treaties with the U.S. Obama's fecklessness in response to Vladimir Putin's saber rattling in Syria and Ukraine will surely strengthen Russian resolve to violate its treaty commitments.

> *The border is secure.*—SENATE MAJORITY LEADER HARRY REID

Nope. Not even close (Hey—did that one make coffee come out of your nose?). Per the Department of Homeland Security, 11.4 million undocumented people live illegally in the U.S. Many thousands more cross our southern border each year. And the number of unaccompanied children entering the country is expected to reach 90,000 this year alone.

> *The Hobby Lobby decision 'was arrived at by five white men.'*
> —SENATE MAJORITY LEADER HARRY REID

Nope. Justice Thomas assures us he is still black—unless, of course, Sen. Reid wanted to imply that Justice Thomas's political affiliation makes him "un-black"—an all too familiar mindset to conservative black intellectuals, politicians, and media personalities. Ask Mike Steele about such racial caricatures.

Kitzhaber and How the Left
Cooks the Books

*How we feel about economic development is no substitute
for honest analysis.*

February 17, 2015, *National Review*

The resignation last week of Oregon's Governor John Kitzhaber was big news.

Big, but not terribly surprising. The Oregon attorney general's office had previously opened an investigation into allegations that the state's first lady, Cylvia Hayes, had improperly utilized state employees in the implementation of a new state metrics policy while she was being paid by an outside group. In the end, Kitzhaber could not stem mounting criticism of his fiancée's dual roles as a gubernatorial adviser and a paid consultant with business before the state—both roles being well known to the four-term governor.

Alas, today's social-media-driven news cycle will move on to the "next big story" in short order. But there is another aspect to this story worth our attention.

You see, the genesis of Governor Kitzhaber's problems lies in Oregon's decision to adopt the so-called Genuine Progress Indicator (GPI), an alternative economic and social-welfare metric that is in various stages of review or implementation in five of America's most liberal states (Vermont, Washington, Hawaii, and Maryland are the others), and which was the project Ms. Hayes had been paid to help manage in Oregon.

GPI's alternative analysis uses 26 indicators (divided into economic, environmental, and social) to measure a jurisdiction's overall "health." The individual metrics used will come as no surprise to those who study the progressive playbook: Income inequality, carbon footprint, resource depletion, and CO_2 emissions are prominent economic/environmental indicators. On the social side, costs that are impossible to measure—including positive or negative values of housework, volunteer work, leisure time, and automobile dependency—are included in the index. Such "soft measures" are indeed convenient to those who wish to distance themselves from objective, value-neutral methodologies (such as Gross Domestic Product) that have long been the mainstay of economic-development science.

GPI is classic liberal snake oil for what ails anti-business states. Such knock-off indexes cannot change the objective facts of high tax rates and wealth flight, but they are designed to delegitimize them through a new and politically correct set of criteria more attuned to how one feels about economic development. The GPI mindset is especially useful in explaining away the effects of ill-conceived public policies on hiring and employment. If you are reminded of the famous White House attempt to explain away Obamacare's destructive impact on job creation by pointing out the advantages of increased leisure time . . . well, so am I.

In reality, GPI represents nothing other than a convenient instrument for progressives to use in obfuscating poor economic performance. In other words, taxpayer beware whenever liberal politicians tell you they're going to measure what really should matter to you—and why you shouldn't worry that so many of your neighbors have retired to more tax-friendly states. One of the five GPI states, Maryland, is Exhibit A.

Eight years of unrelenting tax increases (40 in all) and a labor-controlled, oppressive regulatory environment saw jobs, wealth, and corporate headquarters fleeing my state. Maryland's Gross Domestic Product showed zero growth in 2013, ranking 49th in the country. All of which was a bridge too far for even this deepest blue of jurisdictions: Larry Hogan became only the sixth Republican governor of Maryland in 2014 on a transparently clear promise to "stop the [progressive] bleeding."

Now, I'm just as interested in recycling programs, avoiding traffic congestion, and leisure time as the next guy. (Indeed, I would put my environmental record up against any one of my Democratic predecessors.) But I just don't see how soft, non-objective criteria help policy-makers understand what ails job creation. Phrased another way: Hard data are much more valuable than soft in attempting to figure out why your 26-year-old is living in your basement and not on a private-sector payroll.

It is ironic that a government program meant to instill progressive values in Oregon amounts to crony capitalism. If you find yourself living in one of the above-mentioned states and have come to the same conclusion, you might send an e-mail to your governor with the news that you have found a new way to save tax dollars: Try ending feel-good programs that tell us nothing and paper over real problems. Maybe, just maybe, we can return old-fashioned common sense to state government—our feelings notwithstanding.

Giuliani's New York, Shattered

August 27, 2015, *The Weekly Standard*

As New York City suffers through yet another challenging era of ineffective political leadership, it is worthwhile to recall what one leader can accomplish under the most difficult circumstances.

Context here is New York, New York, circa the bad old days of the 1980s. Many of that era's pundits had decided to write off The Big Apple. The David Dinkins era was the nadir—rampant crime, dangerous schools, a declining real estate market, and a depressed (and fleeing) small business community—a scene reminiscent of the bleeding, burning New York of the 1960s.

Then there came along a tough-talking, crime fighting former federal prosecutor with a can-do attitude and willingness to mix it up with the most strident progressives of the time. His name was Rudy Giuliani—and he was a Republican in a town where Democrats enjoyed an overwhelming registration advantage.

But he knew how to lead. Specifically, he understood the need to identify what was broken and then fix it in a quantifiable way. And so the Giuliani Administration instituted a "broken windows" crime fighting strategy whereby law enforcement was empowered to draw a line in the sand at the commission of minor offenses. In the process, a newfound sense of security was delivered to a worn down populous more than fed up with the great City's obvious decline.

New York's monumental turnaround has been well documented by observers right and left. As they say, statistics don't lie, and in the case of Giuliani's New York, the statistics were dramatic. How dramatic? A $2 billion deficit turned into a multi-billion dollar sur-plus, a 58 percent decline in welfare rolls, a 56 percent decrease in violent crime between 1993 and 2001 (the number of street cops increased from 28,000 to 40,000), a public-private partner-ship cleaned up Times Square, high-performing charter schools exploded, small businesses returned, and tourism made dramatic gains. The Big Apple was back.

Of course, many people contributed along the way, not the least of which was a police force newly re-engaged in restoring a great city's pride. But it was the unrelenting drive of one indispensable man that turned it around.

History records that a "Giuliani-Light" Administration fol-lowed under the leadership of Michael Bloomberg. "Giuliani" because many of Rudy's crime and economic policies were kept in place; "Light" because the billionaire-turned-politician also dis-played an un-Giuliani-like proclivity for government interference into individual liberty—the popularity of Big Gulps and sugary desserts notwithstanding.

Fast forward to Gotham 2015 and the delusory Administra-tion of Mayor Bill de Blasio. You have to give it to the new anti-Gi-uliani—he never sought to hide the uber-progressivism of his program. Indeed, year one of the de Blasio Administration has borne witness to the worst inclinations of the progressive agenda.

The only problem is that progressivism *does not work* outside of certain college campuses and Washington, D.C. In the real world of markets and wealth mobility, calls for massive tax increases (a pro-posed "mansion tax") have started calls for another exodus of the wealthy. (If you recall the great State of Maryland losing one third of its millionaires in the year after passage of Martin O'Malley's millionaire's tax in 2009, please go to the head of the class.)

But the damage is not confined to the economic realm. The attempted redirection of funds intended for the city's spectacularly successful charter schools was fully in line with the teachers' union agenda. Sanctuary City status prohibits the police from inquiring into legal status *and* guarantees access to taxpayer-financed welfare benefits. And de Blasio's deeply grounded disregard for law enforcement was again on prominent display in the days and weeks following Ferguson and its progeny (yet not without remarkable displays of anti-de Blasio sentiment from the rank and file in the aftermath of the cold-blooded murders of two of New York's finest).

If you thought that de Blasio would take a break after the unrelenting negative coverage of his police problems . . . think again. Only within the past few weeks did a federal judge save NYC's banks from catastrophe by finding the city's attempt to impose "socially responsible" lending practices on them unconstitutional. For those of you who lived through our recent mortgage crisis and recession, this attempted shakedown of local banks to benefit progressive causes brings back bad memories of ACORN and its activist progeny. The former community organizer in the White House was no doubt disappointed.

Your local Barnes & Noble is chock full of "how to" leadership manuals. Indeed, how to prod massive bureaucracies to work more efficiently is always going to be a hot topic in think-tank world. Most of these books analyze the power of one individual to effectuate change. But citizens beware: this well-detailed power cuts *both ways* when voters screw it up.

The "City that never sleeps" is again in steady, serious decline.

Our old friend "Frankie" would not be happy.

Neither should you.

PART 8

★ ★ ★

Humor Made Oh-So-Easy by the Obama Era

Jack Kennedy had it in abundance and used it to great effect. Ditto for Ron Reagan and Bill Clinton. "W" and Barack Obama were not so practiced. Jimmy Carter and Richard Nixon not so gifted.

The "it" I refer to is an appropriate sense of humor. Particularly, a sense of irony. Politicians possessed with the gift typically use it to great benefit in the public realm. And why not? Humor is the great tension cutter of public life. It is equally valuable as either a shield or a sword. Its effectiveness is irrefutable, as it's difficult to dislike someone (even a politician) who makes you laugh.

This considerable weapon is a bit more difficult to pull off from the written page. Here, satire provides a useful assist—especially where the subject matter is fairly ridiculous in its own right.

A sampling of today's headlines (and storylines) provides obvious fodder. "Micro-aggressions" as the bane for the most vulnerable of hypersensitive college students. Politically correct "speech codes" in order to ensure the most offense-less campus environment possible. Al Gore flying private jets around the planet . . . while preaching against the evils of private jets. Lefty politicians extolling the benefits of public education while sending their offspring to the most expensive private schools. Wealthy liberals bemoaning the specter of income inequality while charging six-figure fees for one-hour speeches.

Yes, Obama-era examples are plentiful; some might say irresistible for some politician-authors. Which is simply another way of asking what could possibly have possessed the Obama White House to deliver crooner James Taylor to France in the immediate aftermath of a terror attack on a Jewish deli? I mean, we all love "You've Got A Friend" and "Sweet Baby James," but the president, vice president, attorney general, or *someone* from the U.S. government would have been a far better option to join *other world leaders* at a major unity rally—don't you think?

Hence, a sampling of satirical views of what could be . . . made evermore humorous (and embarrassing) by what is.

What Might Have Been: Life Under President Romney

Robert L. Ehrlich Jr. imagines an administration reducing taxes, ending Obamacare, and slashing spending.

January 27, 2013, *The Baltimore Sun*

N***ews flash:*** President Romney and congressional leaders met today to review the terms of the recently concluded fiscal cliff deal wherein the Bush tax cuts were extended by four years, the corporate income tax rate was reduced from 35 percent to 25 percent, and the capital gains tax rate for middle class taxpayers was lowered to 10 percent.

The leaders returned to Washington to encouraging news from Wall Street, where the Dow Jones Industrial Average is up 800 points since the fiscal deal was announced. More good news: Consumer confidence reached a five-year high, and employers reacted to the aggressive, pro-growth agenda from Washington by creating 200,000 new jobs last month.

On the health care front, the Romney Administration announced it had convinced enough Democratic senators to support the full repeal of Obamacare. Myriad private sector and religious groups praised the forthcoming repeal while promising to revisit plans to eliminate thousands of jobs and reclassify full-time employees to part-time status. A bipartisan group of Members pledged to submit a health care reform measure that would target the escalating cost of health care delivery, including provisions allowing insurance policies to be written across state lines, expand popular Health

Savings Accounts, increase federal support for community health care centers in poor neighborhoods, and encourage state-based tort reform to help high-risk specialists maintain their practices.

Another bipartisan group of legislators announced the outline of a fiscal plan to cut $4 trillion of federal spending over the next four years. To the astonishment of the Washington press corps, a number of hard-core liberals in the House signed onto the plan to cut 1 percent from every federal agency's budget over the next fiscal year. A joint statement read in part: "[We] simply can no longer stand trillion-dollar annual deficits; our children and grandchildren deserve so much better . . ."

But history was truly made when that same group announced an agreement in principle to raise the eligibility thresholds for Social Security and Medicare to 68 (for those 50 years old or younger). Other agreed-to Medicare reform measures include means-testing of benefits for wealthier seniors and requiring drug companies to pay higher Medicare rebates for older, poor senior citizens.

From the diplomatic front, former Bush Administration Secretary of State Colin Powell criticized the Obama Administration for its failure to negotiate a long-term security partnership with the Iraqi government. The man once widely touted as a Republican presidential nominee blamed the Administration for the resulting Iraqi tilt toward the ayatollahs in Iran and the Assad dictatorship in Syria. The Administration's misreading of the Arab Spring and bungling of the Benghazi consulate attack were also condemned by the clearly irritated former four-star general.

In other news, the Romney Administration did not issue any executive orders today, but called upon guidance counselors, school administrators, PTAs and teachers unions in every school district to generate guidelines for the carrying of firearms by security/supervisory personnel on school grounds. The president has further asked groups on both sides of the gun debate to formulate bipartisan recommendations to strengthen background checks in order to keep firearms out of the hands of felons and those suffering from mental illness.

In sports, the Baltimore Ravens' run to the Super Bowl hit a bump in the road as the American Civil Liberties Union, in a desperate bid for relevance, sued Ravens linebacker Ray Lewis for his constant invocation of God during post-game interviews. An ACLU spokesman also confirmed the group's intent to rid all athletic competitions of pre- and post-game prayer. Regarding the Lewis litigation, the group insisted its action did not signal a preference for San Francisco, the most progressive city in America. In a related matter, the ACLU's Louisiana affiliate confirmed a preliminary investigation into the New Orleans "Saints," on similar grounds.

Final item: The Associated Press and a consortium of news organizations confirmed that the election of Mitt Romney signals the return of weekly news stories devoted to homelessness. In a remarkably forthright insight into the ways and means of the mainstream press, the media outlets admitted that while homelessness existed under Democratic administrations, the plight of the homeless was so much more newsworthy with a Republican in the White House. Occupy Wall Street immediately issued a press release adding homelessness to a laundry list of 164 social ills caused by "the rich"—but mostly wealthy Republicans.

In a similar vein, *The Baltimore Sun* reiterated its position that increases in tuition at Maryland's public institutions are likewise "not news" during Democratic administrations.

(That last one ended my dream of "What-Might-Have-Been-Ville" with a shudder. Guess I gotta stop those late night chili burgers . . .)

Unsure of Your Affiliation? Take This Test

Help for the confused few who haven't yet taken party sides

December 22, 2013, *The Baltimore Sun*

One of the interesting aspects of public life (even for those of us retired from public life) is the frequency with which total strangers engage me in political conversation.

Most of these unscheduled encounters are pleasant. They can break out anywhere. But it is the variety of self-descriptions (and disclaimers) that make these conversations so entertaining.

Not every discussion includes a qualifier; about a third of folks self-identify as core partisans. Unsurprisingly, most of the core Democrats love the president; their counterparts on the right possess a profound dislike of Mr. Obama. On the flip side, President Reagan remains a conservative hero but receives little love from liberals.

A smaller but more complex group appears in need of a psychotherapist. These are the "soft conservatives"—their conservative credentials come with strings attached. Their oft-heard disclaimer, "I'm a fiscal conservative, but a social liberal" sends warning alarms to pro-lifers and tea partiers alike. Many are nostalgic for the "good ole days" when a far more moderate (pretty liberal in fact) northeastern contingent exerted significant influence over the GOP's candidates and campaigns. Locally, this wing was represented by the well-respected but progressive Sen. Mac Mathias.

Some of my friends and a number of my supporters fall here. They lean Republican because of business and budgets but can swing to the Democrats when the GOP's candidate is deemed too socially conservative. More than a few swung to Barack Obama in 2008.

A similarly predictable group on the other side of the aisle are the troubled "Democrats from birth." These disconsolate folks assure me their mom, dad, or other close relative would roll over in their respective graves if they dared change party registration. These are the ethnic Catholics (mostly Italian, Irish, Polish) whose forbearers settled in large cities when there were *no* Republicans within the city limits. Indeed, they were the foundation of FDR's "New Deal" coalition, until upward mobility into the middle class, a creeping Democratic march toward progressivism, and a president by the name of Reagan made it acceptable to vote Republican "up ticket." A clear majority of these voters broke for Mitt Romney in 2012.

A personal aside: A subset of this group includes Marylanders who assure me I was the first Republican they ever voted for—a wonderful compliment. Yet, a majority continue to vote Democratic in local elections (old habits *are* difficult to break). For context, compare precinct results for state legislative seats in Dundalk and Arbutus in Maryland to gubernatorial and presidential results from the same precincts. There are many split tickets to be found.

Many of you will identify with the foregoing (albeit) generalized descriptions. A few of you, however, remain unsure about your political identity. Well, your search is over. The purpose of this column is to inform my readers. And so, as a public service for the "confused few," I offer the following political identity test. Take it at your leisure, but answer honestly. Only truthful responses will lead you to your comfort zone.

Harvard or Liberty University

MSNBC or Fox

Bon Jovi or Kid Rock

FDR or Reagan

1st or 2nd Amendment

(Federal) Dept. of Education or PTA

Jane Fonda or Bo Derek

Air America or Rush Limbaugh

Multi-culturalism or American-exceptionalism

AFL-CIO or NFIB

"Happy Holidays" or "Merry Christmas"

Obamacare or the insurance you wanted to keep

The Baltimore Sun or *Wall Street Journal*

Two-tiered drivers licenses or border security

Sean Penn or Charlton Heston

Moveon.org or Americans For Prosperity

Rolling Stone or *National Review*

Nancy Pelosi or Newt Gingrich

Project Labor Agreements or Right-to-work

Windmills or Keystone Pipeline

For those who chose the left-hand more than half the time, you may safely identify as a Democrat. Those of you who leaned right more times than not will feel at home with the GOP.

For the few of you who ended up exactly half and half, you are that rare breed known as the true moderate. Without doubt, the pollsters will flock to your door next election cycle; you are the holy grail of "swing voters" ripe for participation in an endless stream of cable television focus groups.

But Buyer Beware: "they" say the only things found in the middle of the road are straight white lines and dead animals. In today's hyper-partisan Washington, you might add a smattering of dead politicians of a certain moderate bent.

News of the Future

Maryland's former governor predicts what the country will be up to in 20 years, given current political—and politically correct—leanings.

February 22, 2014, *The Baltimore Sun*

A 36-inch blizzard in the Mid-Atlantic was cited by Harvard Professor and former Vice President Al Gore as yet further proof of global warming. "The colder it gets, the more we should worry," commented Professor Gore, shortly before leaving on his private jet for the annual "Environmentalists Against Private Jets" convention held in Honolulu, Hawaii.

The 118th Congress kicked off its one-day session this morning. The Congress came to a close shortly after noon due to lack of work. Historians noted that sustained congressional inactivity began during the latter stages of the Obama Administration, wherein thousands of executive orders began reducing the congressional workload. Speaker Nancy Pelosi commented that Congress adjourned early in order for her Members to "find out what was in the bills" passed that day.

The town of Shrewsbury, Pa., officially changed its name to "Northern Maryland" today. Two hours later, Baltimore election officials noted that GOP registration in Baltimore had been reduced to "zero." Maryland State Senate "President for Life" Mike Miller noted that despite the new registration numbers, Democrats in Annapolis would continue to blame Republicans for the city's countless ills.

The new federal crime of "income inequity" was signed into law today by President Bill de Blasio. Progressives rejoiced as the "Allowable Legal Income Earnings Number" (ALIEN) was set by the federal government at $51,621 per year. Per the new law, any earned income over the ALIEN will result in confiscation by the Internal Revenue Service. President de Blasio also announced an ALIEN waiver program whereby selected labor unions and Hollywood actors would be allowed to keep whatever they make.

Republican opposition to a proposed extension of federal unemployment benefits was decried by Senate Majority Leader Al Franken. With chants of "10 years or nothing" echoing in the background, Franken lashed out at "coldhearted" Republicans who had sought to maintain the present benefit level at 468 weeks, or nine years. ACORN spokesman Anthony Weiner assured concerned taxpayers that "10 years is no entitlement," just a reminder of how difficult it's been since "shovel ready" jobs dried up in 2009.

With much fanfare, a coalition of activist groups announced that "homelessness" would no longer be a part of the progressive agenda. Sponsors cautioned that the issue would resurface once a Republican was returned to the White House. The newly constituted "ACORN II" said it would forego public demonstrations for four years, preferring instead to "assist" people in qualifying for Obamacare subsidies.

High school football was officially outlawed in every state today. Leaders of "Concerned Parents Against Violence and Keeping Score" (CPAVAKS) praised the move, pointing out that football's militarist jargon and emphasis on winning was not the way forward for a more sensitive, egalitarian culture. A spokesman for the group noted that "bigger, faster, stronger" was more an '80s throwback than a mantra for an accepting culture no longer preoccupied with winning and losing. Interestingly, the campaign to do away with keeping score appears to have originated in Montgomery County, Md., where outdoor scoreboards were first eliminated in 2020.

The 25th extension of Obamacare's employer mandate was granted today, ensuring that most American small businesses would not be forced to comply with the law's draconian mandates until "hell freezes over." (Al Gore could not be reached for comment in Honolulu.) The postponement makes the 2,488th unilateral amendment to the Affordable Care Act and means the original 2,300-page bill has now been reduced to about half a page, title included.

In a related story, a small Indian tribe in southwest North Dakota became the latest beneficiary of an Obamacare waiver. Seems the tribe's compelling legal argument ("Hasn't the government done enough to us?") carried the day. Fully 98 percent of the country is now exempted from the Affordable Care Act.

MSNBC offered its weekly apology for insulting remarks directed to black, Asian, Jewish, Muslim or gay Republicans by its hosts. NBC President the Rev. Al Sharpton admitted that while most of his hosts just don't buy into the notion of anything other than a white, straight Republican, it would be advisable to keep their thoughts private, before ratings on his network dip below reruns of *Gilligan's Island*.

The American Civil Liberties Union today sued Major League Baseball for allowing players to cross themselves prior to entering the batter's box. The civil liberties group pointed out that such religious practice has no place in a secular sport—and besides, such demonstrations do not in fact help a weak hitter reach a slider in the dirt. The group further promised to investigate the Wake Forest Demon Deacons, New Orleans Saints, New Jersey Devils and Holy Cross Crusaders.

The News of the Future

Maryland's former governor imagines the news of tomorrow.

July 27, 2014, *The Baltimore Sun*

News from the future:

- President Elizabeth Warren welcomed the 10 millionth under-age child to illegally immigrate to the U.S. and immediately offered each of them and their children free tuition at the university of their choosing. The president explained that such tuition "assistance" represented reparations for America's racist, imperialist past. Interestingly, the Warren Administration exempted the children from Obamacare coverage, explaining that new arrivals had a right to higher quality health care than where they came from.

- An innovative Republican direct mail campaign came under fire by a number of prominent civil rights organizations. The plan, entitled "You've Got Mail: Dead or Alive" will deliver campaign brochures to the last known address of deceased voters nationwide. GOP leaders responded unapologetically, noting there was no good reason why the deceased should be forced to vote the straight Democratic ticket. A second report surfaced that the Republican National Committee is preparing a similar mail campaign targeted to illegal aliens.

- Russian President Edward Snowden today announced support for the Russian-speaking citizens of northern France. In a provocative move, Vladimir Putin's successor cited longstanding support for socialist policies in certain French provinces and the likelihood that some French citizens had taken Russian as a second language in high school as the primary reasons behind his "outreach" campaign. In a related news item, Snowden indicated further support for the cities of Cambridge, Mass.; Berkeley, Calif.; and parts of Montgomery County, Maryland.

- The AFL-CIO Ohio State Buckeyes today filed an unfair labor practice complaint against the AFSCME University of Michigan Wolverines. Seems last year's Michigan team utilized a "no huddle" offense, which in turn required the Buckeye defense to engage in more plays from scrimmage than originally agreed upon in the NCAA's collective bargaining agreement. The Teamsters-affiliated Collegiate Officials Association was rumored to be contemplating similar action, as the extra plays required more running—which made the officials "tired"—in violation of new "referee work rules."

- Brown University rescinded its honorary degree to actress Jane Fonda. While applauding Ms. Fonda's open and notorious support for the North Vietnamese during the Vietnam War, the Ivy League school's faculty nevertheless found Ms. Fonda's actions "did not go far enough in helping the enemy." Ms. Fonda took the bad news in good cheer. "If I had it to do over again, I'd go out on patrol with the Viet Cong," stated the Hollywood diva, on tour in North Korea with her new exercise video, "Stay Fit on 750 Calories a Day."

- A Dartmouth faculty panel voted to eliminate grade point averages from student transcripts to avoid so-called "trigger warnings." The newest craze in academic psychology, trigger warnings are contained in academic materials that could lead to the onset of post-traumatic stress disorder. "The ridiculous chase for good grades triggers all kinds of stress-related ailments, including anxiety, depression, and feelings of inadequacy—especially in lazy, under-performing students," commented Dean Oprah Winfrey. "No grades means everyone at Dartmouth can feel good about themselves—the real purpose of a liberal arts education."

- The NFL owners and Players Association announced support for the construction of 32 new strip clubs adjacent to each NFL stadium. Jim Irsay, spokesman for the owners, noted that 97.8 percent of player-involved criminal offenses occur at the clubs. "Our goal is to furnish a comfortable locale where the players can relax—and we can keep an eye on them," commented Mr. Irsay. NFL players' rep "Pac Man" Jones called the move a welcome step forward in player safety but sounded a cautionary note: "Who's going to keep an eye on owners like Irsay?"

- The last private sector business departed Maryland today. "Joe's Car Wash," a five employee operation in Bel Air, took down the Maryland flag on its way to Shrewsbury, Pa.—a so-called "sanctuary city" for small businesses that have escaped from Maryland. Maryland Democrats immediately declared victory. "Good riddance," responded Maryland Senate "President-for-Life" Mike Miller. "All these business people do is complain about high taxes anyway. Geez, there were even a few who believed their BG&E bills were going to be cut if they voted Democratic—don't know where *that* came from."

Obama's "Diary" Revelations

Maryland's former governor takes a satirical look at what the president might enter into his personal journal regarding Benghazi.

September 14, 2014, *The Baltimore Sun*

Dear Diary,

Looks as though our folks must finally come clean on Benghazi.

In my defense, the attack on our consulate occurred in the middle of my re-election campaign. Mitt Romney and the Republicans were banging me pretty good about foreign policy failures—particularly our new "leading from behind" strategy in dealing with the world's trouble spots. They seemed to forget I was elected on a platform to bring the boys and girls home, regardless of consequences!

To make matters worse, Mr. Romney and his cowboy allies were alleging a retreat in the war on terror . . . er, our "overseas contingency operations." This was so unfair. After all, I was the one who ordered the hit on Bin Laden when it was anything but clear that the operation would be a success. There was no way I was going to let Romney operatives "swift boat" me on the terror theme—even if my "al-Qaida is now on the run" mantra was quite a stretch.

You must admit the original cover story was pretty good. Americans are accustomed to watching video of angry Islamists protesting just about anything America did around the world. You know the scene: shouting protesters raising their fists in anti-American rants while burning "Old Glory" outside American embassies.

Of course, it all came together when the CIA found the anti-Muslim video. And did we run with it! Just blame the video for a spur-of-the-moment attack on our consulate and protests at other American embassies around the world. It all fit into a neat narrative—too good to pass up even after subsequent intelligence discredited the storyline. After all, nobody had actually seen the video. Yet, Americans know a mere rumor about an alleged insult directed toward Mohammed would generate major protests throughout the Muslim world.

The believable storyline and a compliant press kept this story off the front pages for a couple of years. And it would have stayed that way but for the pesky lawsuit brought by "Judicial Watch." These right-wing kooks have now forced us to produce embarrassing emails that show our communications advisers orchestrated the entire Internet video charade. Worse, the emails were reported in the mainstream press. Seems even our cronies at MSNBC and CNN don't appreciate being lied to.

Nevertheless, our go-to option for "all things that go wrong" continues to produce for us. Of course, I refer to the "angry, racist, right-wing zealots will do anything to bring me down" narrative. Although now six years old, this oldie but goodie continues to register in the opinion polls. Even today, despite a weak recovery and continuing bad reviews on Obamacare, congressional Democrats remain on message. Just check out media reports wherein Democratic leaders repeat the "nothing more can be learned from the Benghazi witch hunt" mantra in answer to every revelation about our botched cover up. "Speaker in Waiting" Nancy Pelosi even had the media repeating her "equal representation" demand for the Benghazi select committee—for a while. Alas, we had to give on that one. It's always better to be in the room than standing outside.

Our good timing may not extend to my former secretary of state, however.

From the jump, Hillary Clinton played it straight up with our White House "Talking Points." Recall her incredible performance wherein she assured the world that no member of the U.S. government played a part in the dissemination of the "disgusting" video.

Man, she can really pretend to be mad—and on cue. Better still was her promise to track down the perpetrators of the evil tape and make them pay—sorta like OJ promising to track down the "real killers."

It was a terrific performance, but all for nought in the aftermath of her unfortunate testimony before the U.S. Senate. You can bet the ". . . at this point, what does it matter?" clip will show up in every Republican attack ad come the fall of 2016.

At the end of the day, it does matter. A sitting ambassador and three other American heroes were murdered by a coordinated terrorist attack. We just couldn't level with the voters because it was far more important that I win than get sidetracked by Republican attack dogs intent on ending my presidency.

Once the country gets over all the bad news from the Middle East, I'm going back to my "can't we all just get along" mantra. I know the "leading from behind" thing hasn't worked too well, but maybe, just maybe, Vladimir will fall for it before western Ukraine "rejoins" Mother Russia, too!

Now . . . off to another night of fundraising!

Love,
President Obama

More News of the Future

I Just Can't Stop Imagining the Consequences of the Obama Era.

Previously unpublished

- President Hillary Clinton today expressed her fierce opposition to private tuition vouchers and public school choice. The president made her remarks while visiting her grandchildren at the prestigious St. Albans School in Washington, D.C. When questioned about the apparent inconsistency, Mrs. Clinton explained that "We liberals have always sent our children to elite private schools rather than the public schools we so often praise . . . the teachers' union bosses don't really care . . . and, at this point, what does it matter?"

- The University of Maryland's "Speech Code Enforcement Team" officially labeled the nouns "Republican" and "tea party" as "hate speech" in their new "Campus Guide to Offense-less Living." Members of the GOP will henceforth be called "W.A.S.P.E.R.S." (White-Anglo-Saxon-Protestant-Evil-Rich-Stiffs) and confined to campus "Insensitivity Living Zones" wherein hateful language ("tax cut," "success," "American Sniper," "American exceptionalism," "Duck Dynasty," "Fox News," "private equity," "Ronald Reagan") would be permitted without "trigger warning" disclaimers. In response, the group formerly known as the "Young Republicans" announced plans for a campus debate on "freedom of speech." The proposed event was canceled when no faculty member recognized the phrase. College Park "President for Life" Mike Miller welcomed the move. "It's about time our Speech Code Police cracked down on those greedy, intolerant troublemakers," commented Miller. Women's Studies Department Chair Debbie Wasserman Schultz added that no WASPERS would be admitted into her program since "no 'real' women could be a Republican anyway."

• The prison facility formerly known as "Guantanamo Bay" officially changed its name to "Club Med-Gitmo" during changeover ceremonies today. Former terrorist inmates praised the move, saying that while Bush era interrogations were pretty rough, conditions improved markedly during the tenure of President Barack Obama. "We thought the new state-of-the-art athletic turf soccer field and the availability of basic cable was nice," commented a former enemy combatant, "but the addition of ESPNU and the Olympic-size forever pool gave it a 'Vegas feel,' if you know what I mean." One terrorist interviewed for this article reserved special praise for former Attorney General Eric Holder. "Mr. Holder's decision to treat us like street criminals gave us all kinds of due process rights (and free lawyers) regular old terror soldiers could never afford," added the man. Another added, "I'd recommend the remodeled Gitmo to any jihadist getting ready for a return to the battlefield!"

• A coalition of ethnic pride groups sued the University of Notre Dame "Fighting Irish" for the school's "callous, insensitive depiction of Irishman as short, inebriated, skinny leprechauns with bad attitudes." After brief conversations with Attorney General Nancy Pelosi, the school changed its nickname to the "Notre Dame Feckless Apologists" in honor of our 44th President's foreign policy.

• A cash-strapped Maryland General Assembly today passed a first-in-the-nation Ebola Tax. "Speaker for Life" Mike Busch was the first to defend the new levy, reaffirming the Democratic majority's intent to tax "every possible thing, living or deceased, on God's green earth." The Speaker added, "We'll *never* miss an opportunity to impose a tax . . . even where the target is suffering from a painful, deadly disease." The new legislation follows passage of Maryland's historic "rain tax" in 2012, "snow tax" in 2025, "sleet tax" in 2028, "hail tax" in 2030, and "partly cloudy tax" in 2033.

• A jubilant Democratic Congress today passed a new federal minimum wage of $44 per hour. "This was *SO* easy," stated Senate Majority Leader Elizabeth Warren. "Just pull any big number out of the air and BAM! . . . no more poverty. We should have done this years ago!" Leader Warren also blasted the GOP for their "cold-hearted, mean spirited" opposition to the higher wage. In a related story, fast food giants McDonald's, Wendy's, Burger King, Chick-Fil-A, and Chipotle announced their "average employees per store" had dropped to . . . three workers. "Basically, a cook, cashier, and janitor is all we need," remarked McDonald's CEO Michael Blumberg. Analysts cited the demise of "large sugary drinks" and exorbitant labor costs for the dramatic reduction in jobs.

• The last of the original Occupy Wall Street organizers left the group today, citing his need to "get a job" now that his Obamacare coverage was scheduled to run out on his 27th birthday. "Truth be told, my job search was not going over well with my former colleagues," stated the novice job seeker. "Our movement is so not about waking up, taking a shower, and going to work. What kind of life is that anyway?" On a brighter note, the former community organizer expressed optimism that the street protest business will pick up volunteers once a Republican returns to the White House.

Conclusion

★ ★ ★

I TYPICALLY END MY PUBLIC APPEARANCES WITH a question and answer session. On campuses, the most asked question is how the student can "give back" to our country. My first response is to ask them to consider public service, despite public life's considerable downside. (A partial list of such negatives would include loss of privacy, career path interruptions, loss of income, public criticism, the perpetual chase for campaign dollars, and missed family obligations.) Yet, the upside is equally considerable and can be condensed into a single irrefutable statement: public life allows for engagement in the task of "making things better." And there are few higher callings than making things better for your fellow citizens.

That I was given the opportunity to make Maryland and America better for two decades is a source of great pride. My experiences in the Maryland General Assembly, U.S. Congress, and as Maryland's 60th Governor included passionate work on behalf of school choice, the Chesapeake Bay, race relations, job creation, people with disabilities, and criminal justice reform. Some of this work resulted in wins, while others were losses. But all were important because real people were impacted in very real terms. And it is public service that provides a unique forum to do this work.

Alas, politics is similar to a professional sports career: typically brief and anything but guaranteed. So, how to give back and make things better once the power of public office is gone? It is here where writing has played a critical part in continuing my efforts. I do not equate writing opinion pieces and books to service in public office. The former can be cathartic, even profitable; the latter carries profound consequences for the governed. But informed writing does count, especially where it serves to influence public opinion and impact the status quo. And this is the very reason I chose to write so much over the last decade. The power may be gone, but the desire to make things better is not—not by a long shot.

About the Author

GOVERNOR ROBERT L. EHRLICH JR. is a graduate of Princeton University and Wake Forest University School of Law, and is a former Governor of Maryland as well as a former United States Congressman and Maryland state legislator.

He is the author of *Turn This Car Around* (2011) and *America: Hope for Change* (2013) in addition to columns and opinion pieces that have appeared in America's leading newspapers and periodicals, including *The Washington Post, The Baltimore Sun, The Washington Times, The Weekly Standard*, and *National Review*.

Governor Ehrlich is a partner at the firm of King & Spalding in Washington, D.C., and lives with his wife, Kendel, and his children, Drew and Josh, in Annapolis, Maryland.